PROFILING THE CRIMINAL MIND

PROFILING THE CRIMINAL MIND

BEHAVIORAL SCIENCE AND CRIMINAL INVESTIGATIVE ANALYSIS

Dr. Robert J. Girod, Sr.

iUniverse, Inc.
New York Lincoln Shanghai

Profiling The Criminal Mind
Behavioral Science and Criminal Investigative Analysis

iUniverse, Inc.

For information address:
iUniverse, Inc.
2021 Pine Lake Road, Suite 100
Lincoln, NE 68512
www.iuniverse.com

ISBN: 0-595-33277-3 (Pbk)
ISBN: 0-595-66811-9 (Cloth)

Printed in the United States of America

CONTENTS

PREFACE

This book is about the criminology of the criminal mind and "criminal profiling and behavioral analysis," now referred to as "criminal investigative analysis." This work is intended to provide practical criminologists (practitioners from law enforcement, prosecution, and forensics) a comprehensive overview of this field. It is also intended to provide a scholars and academic criminologists with a conduit to link theoretical and applied criminology.

In the Introduction I not only introduce the organization of the text's chapters, but also provide some personal anecdotes to help explain why this work was written and to clarify the context of my research. Hopefully, the introduction will also help the practitioner to relate to the topics and the academic to appreciate the practical aspects of this field of study.

The first three chapters review relevant social science theories on *criminology*, the *sociology of deviance*, and *abnormal psychology*, followed by the fundamentals of *forensic psychology* and *forensic science*.

Other chapters address *Criminal Profiling and Behavioral Analysis*; *Mass, Serial, and Spree Crimes*; and *Ritualistic and Cult crimes*, as well as the relatively contemporary phenomena of *School, Workplace, and Domestic Violence*.

Research into the Criminal Mind uses personal experiences and case studies, surveys, and crime statistics patterns to yield some useful information on violent encounters involving armed robberies. While criminal profiling and behavioral analysis has been innovative in profiling and predicting behavior about murderers, rapists, and arsonists, little attention has been given to the increasingly violent nature of armed robbers.

In my "applied research," I attempt to understand this type of criminal mind and make a small contribution to the war on crime. While other texts explore the behavioral theories of criminology, the forensic sciences of crimes scenes, and even the art and science of criminal profiling, this work binds these subjects together and provides a nearly comprehensive overview of these interrelated, interdisciplinary fields of study.

Ideally, city and county homicide detectives and state and federal crime analysts, correctional diagnostic and classification professionals, forensic psychologists and psychiatrists from the mental health community, and sociologists and criminologists from the academic field should work in multi-task work groups to continue this study.

INTRODUCTION

CRIMINOLOGY OF THE CRIMINAL MIND

I have a T-shirt that my wife does not permit me to wear in public. It depicts a murder scene. The caption, which also hangs over my "office" in the Robbery-Homicide Squad, reads:

> *Our day begins*
> *when your day ends.*
> *Homicide Squad*

While a bit off-color, this caption illustrates that when one deals with violence and the criminal mind on a daily basis, it is often necessary to make *light* of an ordinarily *dark* subject. This "tombstone humor" is usually recognized as a psychological defense mechanism for those who deal with the most vicious and depressing part of societies' problems.

This book is the study of the criminal mind. Criminal profiling and behavioral analysis or criminal investigative analysis, often referred to as "psychological profiling," is the study of the criminal mind and criminal behavior from a multidisciplinary view. This text was written for upper-level undergraduate courses on the criminology of the criminal mind and behavior and for practitioners of practical criminology. Such practitioners include detectives, crime scene technicians, police administrators, prosecutors, coroners, and criminologists.

This work is a compilation of research on the physical and behavioral sciences required for a multidisciplinary study of criminal behavioral. Criminal Investigative Analysis, also known as criminal profiling and behavioral analysis, is the fascinating art and science of deductive and inductive reasoning about the characteristics of criminal offenders based upon physical and behavioral evidence.

Such evidence not only gives an accurate portrayal of the perpetrator, but can also be used to predict behavior in some cases. Because this is a multidisciplinary study, an understanding of the fundamental principles of these interrelated disciplines is necessary.

Therefore, this research is a study of not only crime, but also the criminal mind and criminal behavior. This study begins with the traditional review of the literature and follows with an attempt to apply this research to new areas or applied research.

I LAUGHED SO HARD, I ALMOST DIED

As "grave" as murder investigations are (pun intended), the police who are homicide detectives and crime scene technicians and the medical doctors who are coroners and forensic pathologists mean no disrespect to the deceased in the humor that helps to shield them from the stark reality of investigating felonious fatalities.

In my den is a copy of an old cartoon depicting a crime scene with crime scene technicians, detectives, and the usual "thundering herd attendant at crime scenes. Below it is the caption:

First Snap, then Crackle, now Pop.
*It's obviously a **Cereal Murder**.*

This is not only another macabre example of "police humor," but is also a humorous example of "deductive reasoning." I thought it was worth sharing as a prelude to the very serious and disturbing subject of "the criminal mind."

Each time I have attended a post-mortem examination, or autopsy, I am reminded of gravity of what I do for a profession and what has happened. While the weight of such circumstances is felt by all who are involved in follow-up investigations, it makes the task at hand nearly impossible if the professionals assigned to such cases personalize these investigations.

When law enforcement officers take the visions of their daily tasks home with them each night, it is no laughing matter. While these practicing criminologists use humor for psychological defense, they can never forget the images of carnage that goes with a twenty or thirty year career of fighting the war on crime.

LINE ITEM ACCOUNT

The first nine chapters of this work build the prerequisite knowledge for the research conducted in final chapter. The first three chapters review relevant social science theories that may be useful in profiling the criminal mind. This consists of chapters on *criminology, the sociology of deviance*, and *abnormal psychology*.

Chapter four moves directly into *forensic psychology* and is followed by a chapter on *forensic science*, which outlines the physical sciences that help understand what crime scenes mean.

Chapter six becomes more specific, directly addressing *criminal profiling and behavioral analysis*. The three chapters that follow become even more specific and specialized. Chapter seven is concerned with *Mass, Serial, and Spree Crimes*. Chapter eight looks into the dark subject of *Ritualistic and Cult crimes*. Finally, chapter nine addresses the relatively contemporary phenomena of *School, Workplace, and Domestic Violence*.

The concluding chapter, *Research into the Criminal Mind*, uses personal experiences and case studies, a series of surveys and crime statistics patterns to yield some useful information on violent encounters involving armed robberies. I hope to have made a small contribution to the efforts made in the war on crime.

STANDING GUARD ON THE WALLS OF FREEDOM

While to some "freedom," "justice," "honor," and "integrity" are mere words, to others they are way of life and concepts worth defending and preserving for society and those we love. The concepts and theories in this scholarly endeavor are aimed at making a contribution to the body of criminological knowledge that can be applied in the war on crime.

Law enforcement is a fascinating career to anyone who seeks to practice it as a profession and a career rather than merely a job or occupation. The bulk of books, movies, television shows, and "reality TV" deal with the police and the courts and what they do. In my career and profession I am fortunate to be attendant of "the greatest show on earth"–life and sometimes, unfortunately, death.

It has also been my great good fortune to have known or worked with some of the greatest lawmen and women, peace officers, and jurists in the world. I have met or associated with the best of my profession from New York to Los Angeles, from Texas to Canada, and from the halls of the Justice Department to the walls of Scotland Yard.

I would be remiss in a scholarly work on criminology if I did not recognize the contributions of the great scholars, jurists, and super sleuths who have carved out a body of knowledge for those of us who have followed them. I must acknowledge the mentoring that I have been fortunate enough to receive from the great law enforcers, investigators, and forensic scientists of my time.

Finally, I am compelled to show some reverence for those who have mortally fallen from the thin blue while standing guard on the wall of freedom. While these heroes made the ultimate sacrifice, even to defend the rights of their critics to criticize them, they also gave us an example to live by and a code that says "freedom," "justice," "honor," and "integrity" are *more* than mere words.

A MULTIDISCIPLINARY STUDY OF CRIMINAL BEHAVIOR

While other texts explore the behavioral theories of criminology, the forensic sciences of crimes scenes, and even the art and science of criminal profiling, this work binds these subjects together and provides a nearly comprehensive overview of these interrelated, interdisciplinary fields of study.

A great deal of behavioral and diagnostic data is available from correctional and penal sources, yet their confidentiality seems to be valued more than their usefulness to the criminal justice system they are designed to serve. The mental health community appears to be even more reluctant to contribute to this body of knowledge.

In order to continue the successes in the research of this field, it is evident that this study should continue from a multi-disciplinary, mutli-vocational, multi-systems approach. That is, this study would be most effective if continued through the teamwork of city, county, sate, and federal law enforcement and corrections professionals, mental health experts, and the academic community.

The case studies, data, and diagnoses required for the methodology must be from multi-source resources and exploit interdisciplinary expertise. Ideally, city and county homicide detectives and state and federal crime analysts, correctional diagnostic and classification professionals, forensic psychologists and psychiatrists from the mental health community, and sociologists and criminologists from the academic field should work in multi-task work groups to continue this study.

PERSONAL REFLECTIONS

As my doctoral Committee reviewed my research in this field, they encouraged me to include my personal experiences and reflections. As they commented on some of my "war stories" about shoot-outs I had been in or narrowly averted, I quipped, "Maybe I could arrange to be shot again so I could add another chapter." (Again that dark sense of police humor).

Yet it was just a few days earlier that I had had my most recent "narrowly averted" encounter. While I was en route (that's police talk for "on my way to") an armed robbery some of my detectives were responding to, I was passing a fast food restaurant next to a truck stop when a "shots fired" call was dispatched.

I attempted to notify the dispatcher that I was on the scene of the shots, but radio traffic was hectic due to the robbery scene being so fresh. (Another officer had also happened upon that scene as it was being dispatched).

As I continued attempting to notify the dispatcher of my arrival, someone who matched the description that was aired of the "complaining party" waived me down. It turned out that he thought my unmarked police car was the taxicab he had called for. As I turned away the man next to him announced that he had witnessed the fight and shots.

As this "new" witness began telling his tale, I asked him which way the man with the gun ran. He told me that he ran inside of the service station we standing next to. I asked rather urgently, "He's not still in there, is he?" The unconcerned witness replied, "Yeah, I think so."

The "suspect" exited at about that time. I asked, "Is that him?" "Yup," the witness confirmed. Faster than Barney Fifes' fast draw I cleared leather and put the armed man on his knees in the parking lot until backup could arrive to help disarm him.

As I "reflected" upon this to my Committee, my peer and fellow peace officer, James Oddo, a twenty plus years veteran of the Chicago Police Department, moved one chair away from me as we sat in our dining room. Again, that warped sense of "police humor" let him know that I was known as a "bullet magnet" among my colleagues. (In the final chapter of this work I reflect upon two of my most serious gunfights).

As I continued to reflect and share war stories I recalled several incidents when I had investigated violent crimes, shootings of and by police officers, and had been involved in or nearly involved in shootings myself.

Most police officers, whether they are in large urban departments or small rural departments, never are involved in lethal gun battles, despite what television and the movies portray. Yet nearly all law enforcement officers have direct experience with the violence that afflicts our society.

As I reflect upon my own experiences there is a bonding that takes place when I realize that I am sharing the reflections of thousands of police officers and generations of law enforcers. It is this fraternal legion that takes on the covenant to protect society from the violence that is the subject of this text.

CONCLUSION

I can sit around all night swapping war stories. Like the one when I was detective with a university police department and I investigated the theft of a cadaver head from the medical school.

Yes, I headed up that investigation. I headed over to see the head man at the medical school. He, of course, had a good head on his shoulders. You would have to in order to get *a head* at the university. (And so on and so on). Well, you know where I'm heading with this. (That sick "police humor" again).

But more war stories and elaboration on my research would not make my point any more clear or my thesis any more valid than to succinctly state that this research is the study of criminal behavior. It is a multi-disciplinary study of the psychology, criminology, sociology, forensic sciences, and related disciplines that help detectives and criminologists profile behavioral patterns and characteristics of criminals. These profiles help predict criminal behavior and make analytical deductions about criminal behavior.

ACKNOWLEDGEMENTS

First, I want to acknowledge my grandmother, Lydia K. Girod, and my grandfather, Robert Girod; long gone, but never forgotten. I also want to acknowledge my mother, Carolyn M. Neely. What I feel at this moment cannot be expressed in words.

I want to acknowledge those who have contributed to my academic, professional, and personal development throughout my life. It has been my great fortune to have had some of the most nurturing teachers and professors one could find. I have also been trained by some of the best and legendary instructors available in their respective fields. And I have been mentored by some of the greatest professionals that my field has been fortunate enough to produce.

I want to thank my Doctoral Committee for their patience, guidance, editing, and "nit-picking," as they tried to forge my metal into a product of excellence. They include:

Dr. William McKelvie, The Union Institute,
Dr. David May, Indiana University, School of Public and Environmental Affairs,
Dr. Joseph Jones, Taylor University, Department of Criminal Justice,
F. Nelson Peters IV, Allen County Council and Adjunct Professor, Indiana University and Concordia University,
Thomas Cronin, Commander, Chicago Police Department and Adjunct Professor, Northwestern University,
Raymond M. Pierce, Detective (Retired), New York Police Department and Adjunct Professor, John Jay College of Criminal Justice (CUNY),
David Hough, Ohio Department of Corrections (Office of Investigations) and former Professor of Criminal Justice, University of Findlay, and James Oddo, Chicago Police Department and Adjunct Professor of Criminal Justice.

I want to acknowledge my supportive family and my friends. And I would be remise if I did not acknowledge my fraternal comrades–the men and women of law enforcement–who serve with pride, integrity, and devotion each day to keep our country and our communities a little safer.

I want to thank my wife, Marian Elizabeth (Mimi) Girod. She is not only an extraordinary wife of great patience, she is a helpmate and my partner in every endeavor. She is the sunshine of my life and my best friend.

Of course, I want to acknowledge my son and my other best friend, Robert J David (Bobby) Girod. He has been very understanding, for a three-year-old, while Daddy does his homework and goes to work. He is my pride and the "moonlight" of my life, because he is a reflection of his mother.

Finally, I want to thank God for all of His many blessings in my life. They are too many to count, but I have just acknowledged a few.

Thank you all for helping me reach my goals. I love you all.

Chapter One

CRIMINOLOGY

INTRODUCTION

Criminology is a field encompassing three areas of study: forensic science (physical criminology), behavioral science (sociology and psychology of crime and criminals), and the criminal justice system (law enforcement, probation, corrections, parole, etc.). Criminology as a field of study developed from sociology and continues as a specialty or sub-field of sociology. Other areas of study, such as anthropology, pathology, and forensic medicine, have also contributed to the study of criminology.

Physical criminology or forensic science evolved from early research in criminal identification. Other sciences, such as chemistry and toxicology, evolved and fingerprints and photography became crime scene staples. Criminalistics and other sciences continue to emerge and develop.

Behavioral criminology attempts to understand crime, delinquency, and criminal behavior. The fields of sociology, psychology, psychiatry, anthropology, etc. all contribute to this study and theory development.

Criminal justice studies or the criminology of the criminal justice system deals with law enforcement, prosecution, pre-trial release, the courts, probation, corrections and penology, and parole and clemency, etc. as systems and processes. The organization and operations of the criminal justice system is the primary focus of this study.

PHYSICAL CRIMINOLOGY—FORENSIC SCIENCE
HISTORY OF CRIMINOLOGY AND FORENSIC SCIENCE

The history of criminology and forensic science begins with early research in criminal identification. Photographs and physical descriptions were relied upon for some time, but were not that reliable. As new methods were sought, Alphonse Bertillon (1853-1914) became the head of the identification service in the office of the Prefect of Police in Paris, France.

Identification

Bertillon developed a system of identification that involved the measurement of body parts (anthropometry). Though this was an improvement, it was expensive to apply, took a great deal of time to learn, could not be used for children (adults only), and was subject to error and duplication. Yet Bertillon was opposed to a later identification technique called fingerprinting.

Anthropologist Arthur Kollmann first suggested the use of fingerprinting, as we know it today, in 1883. Even before this William Herschel used handprints to prevent impersonations in Bengal, India.

Christian J. Hintze (1751), Bernard S. Albinus (1764), and J. C. A. Mayer (1788) each observed that the ridges on the fingers were never duplicated in two or more individuals. Anthropologist Herman Welcker (1856) published a study on this and Prof. Johannes E. Purkinje (1823) wrote a thesis on the subject. It was not until 1880, however, that Dr. Henry Faulds suggested the use of fingerprints for the detection of criminals.

In 1882 biologist Francis Galton (1822-1911) wrote a text on fingerprinting. Edward Richard Henry (1850-1931), however, developed a classification system that is the basis for today's system of identification.

Science and Crime

In 1901 Scotland Yard established the first fingerprint file in Europe. Forensic medicine and chemistry were collaborating in the study of poisons, sperm, body substances, and bloodstains, etc. (Thorwald, p. 5) as science became an ally in the fight with crime.

In 1904 Berlin detectives enlisted the aid of forensic physicians in the identification of bloodstains which marked the development of the science of forensic serology (Thorwald, p. 5).

In 1887, while Alphonse Bertillon was developing scientific criminology, Sir Arthur Conan Doyle, a physician, introduced readers to Sherlock Holmes (Thorwald, p. 233). The research of Bertillon and others, along with the imagination of Doyle, sparked research in forensic chemistry, biology and other forensic sciences (Thorwald, p. 234-5).

FINGERPRINT SCIENCE

While Sir Francis Galton wrote the first text on fingerprinting, published in 1892, French policeman Alphonse Bertillon developed "anthropometry," the measurement of body parts for identification. As previously noted, it was not until 1901 that Scotland Yard adopted the Henry fingerprint system, named after its developer, Edward Richard Henry.

Latent Prints

The fingers, palms, soles of the feet, and toes all have friction ridges, which are used to grip surfaces. These friction ridges are covered with a series of pores which deposit sweat containing salt, amino acids, and other substances, including oils from oil-secreting areas of the skin. These deposits produce the friction-ridge pattern known as fingerprints (Goddard, p. 186).

Because the sweat pore deposits and oils often have a different refractive index (ability to bend light) than the surface, latent prints are often visible to the eye (Goddard, p. 187). Technicians search for potential prints and develop them with fingerprint powders, vapors (such as iodine fumes), or chemical solutions (such as silver nitrate or ninhydrin) (Inbau, et.al., p. 36). A technique known as "superglue fuming" is also used when an object can be placed in a fuming tank.

Items that are dusted or developed are photographed, labeled, and packed in protective containers. (Inbau, et.al., p. 36). Items too large to collect are dusted, photographed, and the prints are "lifted" with clear fingerprint tape (Goddard, p. 191). Latent prints may then be compared with known suspects' standards.

Classification

The "classification" of fingerprints and "identification" of fingerprints are two distinct concepts. The classification of fingerprints is derived from a mathematical formula based on the types of patterns occurring on the ten digits (fingers and thumbs) and the subclassifications and divisions given to patterns on the basis of their location, fixed reference points (deltas and cores), etc. (Inbau, et.al., 28-30).

Identification is concerned with the comparison of individual ridge characteristics (rather than pattern types), such as bifurcations, ridge endings, enclosures, and ridge dots. To establish an identification a sufficient number of ridge characteristics must be found in the same position and relative frequency (quantitatively and qualitatively) in both fingerprint impressions (known exemplars and latents, etc.) (Inbau, et.al., p. 30).

The three main patterns of fingerprints are *arches* (approximately 5%), *loops* (approximately 60%), and *whorls* (approximately 35%). Arches are subdivided into plain arches and tented arches. Loops are subdivided into ulnar and radial loops and further subdivided by "ridge counting." Whorls are subdivided into plain whorls, central pocket loops, doubled loops, and accidental whorls. These are also further subdivided by "ridge tracing" (Inbau, et.al., p. 31).

Technical rules exist to determine under which classification patterns fall. Loop and whorl patterns, for instance, are classified using fixed reference points known as *deltas*. Loops also have fixed reference points known as the *core*.

Specified rules determine the location of deltas and cores. Ridge counting and ridge tracing are used to classify fingerprints (Inbau, et.al., p. 31-33).

The process of interpreting and "blocking out" a set of fingerprints involves recording the symbols for each pattern, ridge counts and traces, etc., on fingerprint cards (Inbau, et.al., p. 34).

PHOTOGRAPHY

While fingerprinting is the science of identification most commonly associated with criminology and forensic science, photography is also a staple of the criminalistics sciences. Photography is used to record crime scenes, fingerprints, and other evidence, document details, identify criminals (mug shots), and enhance surveillance. Photography and, relatedly, video recording, have a variety of uses in forensic science.

Kenneth W. Goddard writes, "The primary purposes of crime scene photography is to provide the investigator and the court with visual records of a crime scene, of the related evidence, and of the victims or suspects who were involved in the crime scene activity" (Goddard, p. 171).

Inbau, Moenssens, and Vitullo observe that, "Photography provides probably the most potent tool in conveying facts to a jury." They also note that photography plays an important role in nearly every phase of police work because it provides the most accurate method for recording a maximum of information in the shortest time possible (Inbau, et.al., p. 2-3).

The subject of photography, like fingerprinting, fills entire texts. It involves a knowledge of both equipment and techniques. Special equipment and techniques may also require a knowledge of infrared, ultraviolet, x-ray, photomicrography, photomacrography, and other types of photography.

Photographic and video documentation is usually supported and supplemented by notes, diagrams, maps, casts, and models (Inbau, et.al., p. 1). Accurately recording a crime scene and its related evidence is one of the most important functions of an investigation.

Notes should include the date and time, location, description of processed or collected evidence, the names of victims and suspects, and other relevant details. These should explain: *who, what, when, where, why,* and *how* (Goddard, p. 140).

CRIMINALISTICS

Criminalistics is the science of collecting, analyzing, interpreting, reporting, and testifying about physical evidence (Goddard, p. 2). One specialty within criminalistics is questioned document examination or handwriting and typewriting analysis.

A document is "questioned" when there is any doubt about its authenticity or of any of its parts (Inbau, et.al., p. 43). The comparison of handwriting (known exemplars or samples with the questioned document), analysis of typewriting, and the examination of inks, papers, and other materials are involved. For example, identification of inks may involve the use of reagents, spectrographic methods, thin-layer chromatography, and specialized photographic techniques (Inbau, et al., p. 67).

Another specialty involves toolmark and impression analysis (Comparative Micrography). Tools used in crimes may leave impressions of their individual characteristics, such as nicks and burrs. Such tools should be submitted to the laboratory where a standard impression can be made (Goddard, p. 208).

Do not attempt to fit the tool into the suspected tool mark. The resulting fresh striations will probably destroy or alter the original striations and "taint" or obliterate the evidence (Goddard, p. 208).

"Comparative micrography" may only reveal not only that obvious gross impressions were made by a type of tool or instrument, but it may also identify minute impressions that help determine if a particular tool was used (Inbau, et.al., p. 87).

Impression evidence also includes footprints, tire tracks, fingerprints in soil, clay, or other materials, etc. Collection may be accomplished by collecting the impression, photography, or a cast of the impression (Goddard, p. 195).

Related to toolmark and impression analysis is firearms and ballistic analysis. Commonly known to the public as "ballistics experts," these criminalists are often firearms and toolmarks examiners. "Ballistics" properly refers to the study of trajectory, rather than guns and bullets themselves.

"Firearms evidence centers around bullets and shells," say Inbau, Moenssens, and Vitullo. They go on to write that these are "examined for the purpose of determining the type or make of guns from which they were fired, or for determining whether or not they were fired from a particular weapon" (Inbau, et.al., p. 70).

Firearms examiners also study powder and shot patterns (e.g. on clothing or bodies), restore obliterated serial numbers on guns, and perform other firearms-related tests (Inbau, et.al., p. 70).

Recovered firearms should be photographed where they are located and the position of safety devices and the hammer noted. Firearms should be rendered safe before marking and packaging.

The collection of firearms residue usually involves testing for primer components, such as barium and antimony. Paraffin tests have been replaced by G.S.R.

tests (gunshot residue) using cotton swabs and 5% solution of nitric acid (Goddard, pp. 223-225). Many agencies, however, do not consider such tests reliable and no longer use them.

Trace evidence (Microanalysis) includes paint, glass, soil, hair, fiber, and other small objects and particle comparison.

The microanalysis of *hair* at a crime scene, on the body of a victim, or on the body or in the vehicle of a suspect can be helpful (Inbau, et al., p. 97). Hairs and *fibers* are rarely matched to a specific person, but do provide leads. Lab analysis can determine if the hair is of human origin or a species of animal, the color and length of the hair, and the race, in some cases (Goddard, p 213).

Fibers may be of various origins: cotton, hemp, asbestos, fiberglass, nylon, orlon, etc. These may be recovered from the hands and fingernails of victims, from other body parts, clothing, vehicles, weapons, other artifacts, or the crime scene itself (Inbau, et al., p. 100). A vacuum with a collection trap should be used to collect both hair and fiber. Using tape as a collection method should be avoided (Goddard, p. 214).

Glass fragments may be compared for matching physical and chemical properties, the refractive index and dispersion (by dispersion staining) (Inbau, et al., pp. 103-104). Other characteristics include thickness, color, density (weight per volume), and elemental composition (Goddard, p. 218).

Paint chips and smears removed from or transferred to objects are examined through microscopic examinations, chemical solubility tests and instrumentation to determine the pigment, pigment distribution, number of layers and sequences of layers (Inbau, et al., p. 106). The types of paint involved (e.g. primer, latex, or enamel) and the elemental composition (e.g. lead, zinc, or titanium) can also be ascertained through analysis (Goddard, p. 215).

Soil evidence consists of minerals, vegetable materials, bacteria, insect parts, and debris. Characteristics of soil analysis involves the density distribution of soil components, the type of minerals present, the distribution of mineral fragments, the percentage distribution of minerals and organic material, the types of bacteria present, the enzyme activity, and the insect parts and parasites present (Goddard, pp. 221-222).

Biological evidence may be examined by a serologist/hematologist or other specialist. Inbau, Moenssens, and Vitullo have noted that, "Among the most frequently encountered traces of biological evidence are blood, semen, saliva, fecal matter and perspiration" (Inbau, et.al., p. 114). Biological evidence also includes urinalysis (Inbau, et al., p. 128) and the analysis of other body fluids and biochemical examinations.

Serological testing determines species, blood grouping (Inbau, et al., pp. 114-119), and the DNA pattern. Human blood consists of blood cells (red and white corpuscles) and serum (mostly water containing dissolved salts, enzymes, proteins, sugars, etc.) (Goddard, p. 177). *Toxicological testing* test for poisons, blood-alcohol content, drugs, etc. not only in the blood, but other body fluids, organs, and tissue.

These are just some of the techniques and specialty areas in the continually growing field of criminalistics and forensic science. These are the physical sciences of criminology.

BEHAVIORAL CRIMINOLOGY
THE STUDY OF CRIME

Criminal acts may be perpetrated by strangers who are predators upon people they have never met or by friends and family members committing acts of intimate violence (Siegel, p. 3). Crimes may be sensational, involving mass or serial violence, celebrities, or ritualistic acts, or be unreported or even unknown acts.

Criminology is the scientific approach to the study of criminal behavior (Siegel, p. 6) and the causes of crime. It includes inquiries into the process of making laws, breaking laws, and reacting to the breaking of laws. Criminology is sometimes the label used to describe scientific crime detection techniques. Sociologists who specialize in crime as a topic are referred to as *criminologists* (Gibbons, p. 3).

That part of criminology that deals with the analysis of physical evidence is known as *criminalistics* and is a subarea of criminology. Criminology also studies the etiological (causal) variables of criminal behavior (Mannle and Hirschel, p. 8).

The *methodologies* in the study of crime are: 1) statistics on the characteristics of crime, 2) statistics on traits and conditions of criminals, 3) case studies of criminals, 4) studies of criminals in their natural settings, and 5) the experimental method (Quinney, p. 12).

CRIMINOLOGICAL THEORIES

The broad theories of criminology that have developed historically include:
1. **The Classical Theory**—based on the rational decision making of motivated criminals and the concept that:
   a) people choose their behavior, including criminal behavior,
   b) people's choices can be controlled by the fear of punishment, and
   c) the more severe, certain, and swift the punishment, the greater its ability to control criminal behavior (Siegel, p. 101).

2. **Marxist/Conflict Theory**—Marx's writings were applied by social thinkers, including Ralf Dahrendorf, George Vold, and Willem Bonger, to describe a *conflict theory* of criminology (Siegel, p.11) that views crime as a function or result of class struggle in a capitalistic socio-economic environment.

3. **Biological Positivism**—a merging of biology, psychology, and sociology with both genetic and environmental variables (Monk, p. 20). The *positivism* theory believes that human behavior is based on uncontrollable external forces and the scientific method can be used to solve problems (Siegel, p. 9). *Biological positivism* asserts that inherited biological and physical traits are the cause of crime.

4. **Sociological Theories**—studies the influence of social changes (Siegel, p. 10). These theories asserts that a person's place in the social structure determines behavior and socialization controls behavior.

Current theories of criminology have emerged from these theories. These contemporary theories include: a) the *biolsocial theory*, b) the *psychological theory*, c) the *choice theory*, d) *social conflict theories*, e) *social structure theories*, f) social *process theories*, and g) *integrated theories*.

BIOSOCIAL THEORY

Criminologists have suggested that biological and psychological traits may influence behavior. This includes the **biological trait theory** and the **psychological trait theory**. The *biological theory* or *biosocial theory* will be discussed first.

Criminologists interested in identifying a physical basis of antisocial behavior refer to themselves as trait theorists, biocriminologists, biosocial criminologists, or biologically oriented criminologists. These terms are often used interchangeably (Siegel, p. 133).

Richard C. Monk writes, "The new criminology must represent a merging of biology, psychology, and sociology." He notes that *biosocial criminology* deals with behavior reflected by both genetic and environmental variables (Monk, p. 20). Sociobiologists view biology, environment, and learning as mutually interdependent factors (Siegel, p. 132).

Some trait theorists believe that biochemical conditions such as genetics, diet, environment, etc., control and influence antisocial behavior (Siegel, p. 133). Biological explanations for crime involve theories based on body types, glandular dysfunctions, chromosome irregularities, and brain or nervous system activity (Mannle and Hirschel, p. 78).

Research supports theories that crime and aggression are influenced by nutritional deficiencies, sugar and carbohydrates, hypoglycemia, hormonal influences (androgens and testosterone), premenstrual syndrome (PMS), cerebral allergies, and environmental contaminants (Siegel, pp. 134-136).

Other research has dealt with **neurophysiology** (brain activity) and theorizes that neurological and physical abnormalities acquired as early as the fetal or pre-natal stage affect behavior throughout life. Charles Whitman, for example, the infamous University of Texas "Tower Killer", had gone to a psychiatrist seeking help for uncontrollable urges to kill. He kept notes documenting his feelings and inability to control his homicidal urges. An autopsy revealed a malignant brain tumor (Siegel, p. 136).

Neurological impairment has been measured using memorization and visual awareness tests, short-term auditory memory tests, verbal IQ tests, and electroen-cephalograph (EEG) tests. The normal EEG range is usually 0.5 to 30 Hz. Research has indicated that habitually aggressive subjects showed a 57% abnor-mality rate on the EEG (Siegel, pp. 136-137).

Other neurophysiological theories involve **Minimal Brain Dysfunction** (MBD) (dyslexia, visual perception problems, hyperactivity, poor attention span, temper tantrums, and aggressiveness), **Attention Deficit/Hyperactivity Disorder,** other brain dysfunctions, tumors, injuries, and disease, brain chemistry abnor-malities, and arousal theory. *Arousal theory* asserts that too much stimulation causes stress and anxiety and too little causes boredom and fatigue (Siegel, pp. 136-139).

Finally, biosocialists believe genetics may be a cause of crime and antisocial behavior. One example is Richard Speck who reportedly inherited an abnormal XYY chromosomal structure (XY is the normal pattern). Genetic studies have compared monozygotic (MZ) twins with fraternal, dizygotic (DZ) twins of the same sex. Such studies indicate a significant relationship between the criminal activities of MZ twins and a lower correlation between DZ twins (Siegel, p. 139-140).

Adoption studies indicate a strong relationship between biological parent's and children's behavior. When both the biological and adoptive fathers were criminal, the probability increased. The **R/K Selection Theory** holds that the "R" end reproduce rapidly and invest little in their offspring, while the "K" end repro-duce slowly but devote more care to offspring. R-males seem to be more prevalent and are also associated with character flaws, such as crime (Siegel, p. 141).

Relatedly, the "Cheater Theory" asserts that those more likely to be sexually aggressive and apt to use devious means to reproduce are also likely to be aggres-sive and devious criminals (Siegel, p. 141). Neuroscientists have mapped brain abnormalities in both lab animals and human murderers that indicate such abnormalities may be associated with crime and aggression (Roberson and Wallace, p. 70).

PYSCHOLOGICAL TRAIT THEORIES

The second branch of *trait theory* is the **psychological trait theory**, which focuses on the mental aspects of crime. This theory deals with the relationships between intelligence, personality, learning, and criminal behavior (Siegel, p. 142). Psychiatry studies *organic disorders* (physical problems) and *functional disorders* (strange behavior without known organic problems) (Roberson and Wallace, 126).

Psychological and psychiatric theories may be grouped by studies of mental capabilities, personality structures, or personality development (Mannle and Hirschel, p. 81). The term *personality* refers to the complex set of emotions and behavioral attributes that remain relatively constant (Vold and Bernard, p. 108).

Gibbons refers to the etiological or causal analysis in criminology from a socialization standpoint as the social psychology of criminal acts and careers. In this case social psychology is used to analyze the attitudes and behavior patterns of socialization through which individuals learn certain behaviors (Gibbons, p. 11).

The social psychology of conventional criminals involves an analysis of the patterns of action that provide individuals with a personal identity, which is the basis for their social behavior (Quinney, p. 228). Psychological and psychiatric theories are typically grouped by mental capabilities, personality structures, or personality development in an attempt to explain crime and delinquency (Mannle and Hirschel, p. 81).

The psychological perspective of criminality has five major theories (Siegel, p. 143):

1. **Psychodynamic Theory** (psychoanalytic) is based upon intrapsychic processes such as unconscious conflicts, defenses, tendencies, anger, and sexuality. According to this theory the human mind performs *conscious, preconscious* (memories and experiences), and *unconscious* functions. Repression is the part of the unconscious that keeps feelings about sex and hostility below the surface (Siegel, p. 143).

In the human personality structure, the **id** is the primitive part that follows the *pleasure principle* and seeks instant gratification without regard for others. The **ego** develops early when one learns that desires cannot be instantly gratified. The ego helps compensate for the id's demands by guiding one's actions within the boundaries of social conventions (the *reality principle*). The **superego** develops within the personality the moral standards and values of parents, community, and significant others and passes judgments on one's behavior (Siegel, p. 143). (This will be an important concept to understand in the discussion of *Personality* in Chapter Three).

As humans develop, they pass through the *oral stage* (sucking and biting), the *anal stage* (elimination of bodily wastes), the *phallic stage* (age 4-5 when children focus attention on their genitals), the *latency stage* (around age 6 when feelings of sexuality are repressed), and the *genital stage* (puberty marks the beginning of adult sexuality). If conflicts occur during any of these psychosexual stages of development, a person may become fixated at that point (Siegel, p. 143).

In the psychodynamic perspective of abnormal behavior, people who experience mental anguish or fear of losing control of their personalities are believed to be experiencing a form of neurosis and are referred to as *neurotics*. People who have lost total control and are dominated by their *id* are believed to be experiencing psychosis and are referred to as *psychotics*, characterized by bizarre episodes, hallucinations, and inappropriate responses. Neurotics tend to commit less serious "delinquent acts and status offenses" while psychotics may commit more serious antisocial acts and crimes, often taking the form of schizophrenia (Siegel, p. 144).

2. **Behavioral Theories** maintain that human actions are developed through learning experiences. This involves *social learning* which suggests people are not born with the ability to act violently, but learn to through life experiences or *behavior modeling* (family members, environmental experiences, and mass media) (Siegel, pp. 144-145).

3. **Cognitive Theory** focuses on mental processes and how people perceive and mentally represent the world around them and solve problems. This theory reflects on the *moral and intellectual development* of individuals to make decisions and judgments about issues of right and wrong. It also deals with *information processing* as a sequence of thought processes involved in violent or antisocial behavior (Siegel, pp. 148-149).

4. **Personality Theory** attempts to identify criminal personality traits, including thoughts, emotions, and behavior. Personality traits associated with antisocial behavior include extroversion-introversion and stability-instability deficits (Siegel, p. 150).

5. **Intelligence Theory** asserts a relationship between below-average intelligence and low IQ and criminal behavior. The *nature theory* argues that low intelligence is predominately determined genetically and low IQ scores are linked to behavior, including criminal behavior. The *nurture theory* views intelligence as partly biological, but predominantly sociological and that environmental stimulation affects both IQ levels and criminal behavior (Siegel, pp. 151-152).

CHOICE THEORY

The next major criminological theory is the *Choice Theory* or *Classical Perspective*. This theory asserts that people choose to commit crime after weighing the benefits and costs of their actions and that crime can be deterred by the certainty of swift and severe punishment.

The classical theory consists of the *rational choice theory* and the *deterrence theory*. Siegel says that choice theorists argue that "criminals are rational and use available information to decide whether crime is a worthwhile undertaking" and that deterrence involves choice "structured by the fear of punishment" (Siegel, p. 12).

This is a pretty simple and straightforward theory but has recently seen a revival of interest based on dissatisfaction with the effectiveness of other theories (Vold and Bernard, p. 33). The choice theory or *classical criminology*, succinctly, describes criminal behavior as freely chosen (Vold and Bernard, p. 359). The term "classical" refers to the fact that this was one of the first organized perspectives on the criminal nature (Roberson and Wallace, p. 52).

SOCIAL CONFLICT THEORY

Social conflict theorists attempt to explain crime "within economic and social contexts and to express the connections among social class, crime, and social control" (Siegel, p. 227). This Marxist theory asserts that the organized state creates conflict when it does not represent the values and interests of society at large, rather, it represents only powerful groups (Vold and Bernard, p. 269).

Marx argued that capitalistic societies represent the interests of the people who own the means of production (Vold and Bernard, p. 269) and the legal system is designed to protect them from the "have-not" masses. In this view, crime is merely a concept of behavior that threatens the ruling class (Roberson and Wallace, p. 148).

Conflict theorists, therefore, view crime as the outcome of class struggle and conflict promotes crime by creating a society in which the legal system controls the lower classes and maintains the position of the powerful (Siegel, pp. 227-228). This perspective holds that laws emerge from the special interests of powerful groups and criminal norms are a consequence of conflicts of interest between groups (Gibbons, p. 28).

SOCIAL STRUCTURE THEORIES

Sociology has dominated the field of criminology in the United States and attempts to identify patterns of crime in geographic areas. Sociologists emphasize "intergroup and interpersonal transactions" and an understanding of the "dynamics of interactions between individuals and important social institutions" as a means to study criminology (Siegel, p. 163).

Robert K. Merton, elaborating on Emile Durkheim's theory, presented his theory of "Social Structure and Anomie," seeking to explain crime through the "kinds and amounts of deviation in society." The explanation for crime was held to be found in "society's social and cultural structure," rather than in individuals (Quinney, p. 11).

Social structure theories are based upon the belief that "forces operating in deteriorated lower-class areas push many of their residents into criminal behavior patterns." This theory is aimed at the disadvantaged economic class and emphasizes unsupervised teen gangs, high crime rate areas, and the social disorder of slum areas (Siegel, p. 167).

The three overlapping branches of the **social structure theory** perspective are:

1. *Social disorganization theory*—the focus is on urban environmental conditions that affect crime rates, such as:
>   a) deteriorated neighborhoods,
>   b) inadequate social controls,
>   c) lawless groups and gangs, and
>   d) conflicting social values (Siegel, p. 168)

2. *Strain Theory*—suggests crime is caused by conflict between the goals people have and the means by which they can legally achieve their goals (Vold and Bernard, pp. 186-187).

3. *Cultural Deviance Theory*—a combination of the social disorganization and strain theories that suggests:
>   a) a development of subcultures as a result of disorganization and stress and
>   b) subcultural values developed in opposition to conventional values (Siegel, p. 168)

SOCIAL PROCESS THEORIES

Social process theories suggest that criminal behavior is a result of individual socialization which results from the interactions people have with various organizations, institutions, and processes in society. These theories assert that all people, regardless of race, class, or gender, have the potential to become delinquents or criminals (Siegel, p. 196).

The branches of social process theories include:

1. *Social Learning Theory*—emphasizes the point that behavior may be reinforced not only through rewards and punishments, but also through learned

expectations (Vold and Bernard, p. 207); crime is learned behavior from criminal peers (Siegel, p. 199).

2. *Control Theory*—delinquency and criminal conduct result when an individual's bonds to society are weak or severed; the socialization process, if effective, is the control mechanism that prevents one from committing crimes (Roberson and Wallace, p. 107).

3. *Labeling Theory*—society's reaction to some forms of behavior may encourage the development of criminal or delinquent careers (Mannle and Hirschel, p. 93); often significant institutions, even those charged with rehabilitation, produce labels that aggravate the problems of deviance (Gibbons, p. 216).

INTEGRATED THEORIES

Integrated theories focus on the "chronic or persistent offender" where single-factor theories have failed to explain why relatively few of the many individuals exposed to "criminogenic influences" become chronic offenders (Siegel, p. 253).

The three divisions of *integrated theories* include:

1. *Multifactor Theories*—the view that social, personal, and economic factors influence criminal behavior; these theories combine the influences of variables that have been used in *structural, socialization, conflict, choice,* and *trait theories* (Siegel, p. 253).

2. *Latent Trait Theories*—attempts to explain the "flow of crime over the life cycle;" the assumption is that a number of people in the population have personal attributes or characteristics that control their inclination or propensity to commit crimes (Siegel, p. 254).

3. *Life-Course Theory*—the view that the propensity to commit crimes is not stable and may change over time; it is a developmental process. Some criminals may terminate their criminal activity for a time, only to resume them again later. Some commit offenses at a steady pace, others escalate; some offenders specialize while others become criminal "generalists." This theory recognizes that people mature and change their behavior (Siegel, p. 254).

CRIME AND CRIMINAL ACTS

While social and behavioral theories attempt to explain the causes of crime and criminal behavior, it is important to understand the nature and legal classifications of crime.

The majority of crime can be categorized legally and sociologically as either a) violent crimes, b) property crimes, c) white-collar and organized crime (including vice and narcotics), and d) crimes against public order and administration. Vice and narcotics may be a category of it's own, often referred to as "public morals" and "controlled substances," or included with organized crime.

Crimes against persons or *violent crimes* include murder and manslaughter offenses, robbery (theft by force or fear of force), rape and other sex crimes, and a variety of assault and battery offenses. Assault is an attempted or threatened battery while battery is an unjustified offensive touching of another person (Roberson and Wallace, pp. 200-201).

Crimes against property include auto-theft, forgery, (Gibbons, pp. 273 and 319), but predominantly involve larceny (theft) and burglary related offenses (Quinney, p. 240). Property crimes are the most prevalent of all criminal acts and the methods of committing such offenses vary greatly (Quinney, p. 241). (Note: forgery is sometimes classified with "white-collar" or economic crimes).

Property offenses, such as burglary, larceny, auto theft (vehicle theft), and arson (sometimes considered a violent crime) make up approximately 90 percent of all known Index crimes. Larceny (theft) is the most common of these. Theft differs from burglary in that it does not involve an illegal entry and differs from robbery, which is a violent or potentially violent crime against persons (victims) (Mannle and Hirschel, pp. 128-129).

White-Collar and *Organized Crime* refer to economic and racketeering offenses, respectively. In the late 1930s criminologist Edwin Sutherland coined the phrase "white-collar crime" to describe the criminal activities of the rich and powerful, committed by persons of respectable and high social class in the course of their occupation (Siegel, p. 337). Organized crime refers to any ongoing criminal enterprise group with the purpose of economic gain through illegitimate means (Siegel, p. 360).

White-collar crime, sometimes known as *economic crime* or *corporate crime*, involves a diverse array of schemes and offenses against workers, crimes committed by "businessmen and professionals against the public," crimes committed by corporations, price-fixing, misrepresentation in advertising, fraudulent financial manipulations, pollution, etc. (Quinney, p. 191).

Organized crime involves a secret society, which is tightly controlled, opposed to the public's values and interests, and resembles a corporate structure and behavior (Mannle and Hirschel, p. 150). The key feature of organized crime is its organizational structure geared toward illegal profits (Quinney, p. 203).

This broad definition can encompass syndicated crime groups, such as "the Mafia," outlaw motorcycle gangs, street gangs, terrorist organizations, etc. Organized crime and economic crime are often interrelated.

Organized crime and racketeering often involve public morals offenses for profit. Controlled substance offenses (narcotics, dangerous drugs, and alcohol) and vice offenses (gambling, prostitution, pornography, etc.) are often involved in organized criminal enterprises. These are sometimes studied as separate classifications of crimes because of their prevalence.

Crimes against public order and administration include acts that "interfere with the operations of society and the ability of people to function efficiently." Offenses against public morals (discussed above), sometimes referred to as "victimless crimes," are sometimes included in this category (Siegel, p. 376).

Vold and Bernard list "victimless crimes" as those involving drunkenness, vagrancy and begging, gambling, prostitution and related offenses, drug and narcotics violations, and juvenile status offenses (curfew, truancy, runaway, etc.) (Vold and Bernard, p. 318). Quinney writes that most officially defined crimes are violations against public order, yet much of the behavior is consistent with dominant societal patterns (Quinney, p. 248).

In some states crimes against public order and administration more correctly refers to offenses such as resisting law enforcement, obstructing justice, perjury, and related offenses. Mannle and Hirschel identify "political crime" as offenses such as hijacking aircraft, terrorism, political corruption, violations of the public trust, treason, espionage, and perversion of due process (Mannle and Hirschel, pp. 175, 177, 178, and 180). Political offenses are committed as attacks against the government or offenses by the government (Mannle and Hirschel, pp. 176-180).

VICTIMS AND VICTIMOLOGY

A discussion of *criminology* would not be complete without mentioning victims and the specialty field of *victimology*. Victimology is the scientific study of the victim and their relationship to the criminal process (Siegel, p. 77). Though this does not involve the detection or treatment of crime or the behavior of criminals, victimology studies the sociological problems of victims' loss and suffering caused by antisocial behavior.

Victimology deals with the nature of victimization, care given to victims by the police, courts, crisis intervention programs, etc., and victims' rights and compensation. Theories of victimization explore routine activities, lifestyles, and precipitation of victims. These were once referred to as "victims studies" (Gibbons, p. 107).

CONCLUSIONS FOR THE FUTURE

Crime is a complex problem. Its roots are in the center of collective social life. Theories attempt to understand, describe, and explain crime and criminal behavior, but there is no one theory that encompasses the whole of individual and collective criminal behavior. Such theories, however, give us a better opportunity to analyze crime as a social phenomenon.

CRIMINOLOGY AND THE CRIMINAL JUSTICE SYSTEM
CORRECTIONS AND PENOLOGY

Corrections is a term used to describe the use of pre-trial services, probation, incarceration, parole, and clemency to correct behavior. Prisons or penitentiaries are penal institutions for confinement. Penology, therefore, implies a punitive measure, where correctional facilities imply a rehabilitative role. For this discussion, corrections will refer to the prison system and its role in rehabilitation and penology will refer to the administration of the confinement system.

"The housing of offenders and suspected criminals in local detention facilities is a practice as old as the definition of crime," Allen and Simonsen writes. But only recently has corrections attempted to provide treatment programs for inmates (Allen and Simonsen, p. 162).

In 1974 Robert Martinson conducted a study of 231 correctional treatment programs, referred to as the "Nothing Works" research, to identify the reasons for a general lack of confidence in correctional programming. Martinson concluded that, with few exceptions, the correctional programs he reviewed had little or no effect on recidivism (Cromwell and Carmen, p. 312).

Public demands for correctional programs that both punish and satisfy public safety objectives must be balanced with the reality that not all criminals can be imprisoned. Community-based correctional programs are, therefore, utilized (Cromwell and Carmen, p. 320), despite recidivism rates.

SUMMARY

An understanding of the criminal justice system is essential in criminology in order to determine what works and what does not. The organization, operations, and procedures of law enforcement, prosecution, pre-trial release, the courts, probation, corrections and penology, and parole and clemency help us research how we are dealing with crime, delinquency, and criminals. It also helps us research new ways to better deal with these social problems.

CONCLUSION

Criminology has developed as a marriage between physical science and behavioral science with the goal of detecting and understanding crime. Criminology as a physical science, *criminalistics*, seeks to detect and solve crime. Criminology as a social science studies the *sociological* causes of crime and criminal behavior. Criminology also studies the criminal justice system as a process involving the police, courts, corrections, and related services and their operations.

By developing new technologies and theories we may better prepare ourselves to serve society in the detection, prevention, and correction of criminal social problems. This is the study of criminology.

REFERENCES—CHAPTER 1

Allen, Harry E., and Clifford E. Simonsen. **Corrections in American: An Introduction** (Eighth Edition). Upper Saddle River, NJ: Prentice-Hall, Inc., 1998.

Cromwell, Paul F., and Rolando V. Del Carmen. **Community–Based Corrections** (Forth Edition). Belmont, CA: Wadsworth Publishing Company, 1999.

Gibbons, Don C.. **Society, Crime, and Criminal Careers: An Introduction to Criminology** (Third Edition). Englewood Cliffs: New Jersey: Prentice-Hall, Inc., 1997.

Goddard, Kenneth W. **Crime Scene investigation.** Reston, VA: Reston Publishing Company, Inc. (A Prentice-Hall Co.), 1977.

Inbau, Fred E., Andre A. Moenssens, and Louis R. Vitullo. **Scientific Police Investigation**. Philadelphia, PA: Chilton Book Company, 1972.

Killinger, George G., Hazel B. Kerper, and Paul F. Cromwell, Jr.. **Probation and Parole in the Criminal Justice System**. St. Paul, Minn.: West Publishing Co., 1976.

Mannle, Henry, and J. David Hirschel. **Fundamentals of Criminology**. Englewood Cliffs, NJ: Prentice Hall, 1988.

Monk, Richard C. **Taking Sides: Clashing Views on Controversial Issues in Crime and Criminology** (Forth Edition). Guilford, Connecticut: Dushkin Publishing Group, 1996.

Quinney, Richard. **Criminology** (Second Edition). Boston, Mass.: Little Brown and Company, 1979.

Reid, Sue Titus. **Criminal Justice: Procedures and Issues**. St. Paul, Minn.: West Publishing Co., 1987.

Roberson, Cliff, and Harvey Wallace. **Introduction to Criminology**. Incline Village, Nevada: Copperhouse Publishing Company, 1998.

Senna, Joseph J., and Larry J. Siegel. **Essentials of Criminal Justice** (Second Edition). Belmont, CA: Wadsworth Publishing Company, 1998.

Siegel, Larry J. **Criminology** (Sixth Edition). Belmont, CA: West/Wadsworth Publishing Co., 1998.

Sutor, Andrew. **Police Operations: Tactical Approaches to Crimes in Progress.** St. Paul, Minn.: West Publishing Co., 1976.

Thorwald, Jurgen. **Crime and Science; The New Frontier in Criminology.** New York, NY: Harcourt, Brace & World, Inc., 1966.

Vold, George B., and Thomas Jo. Bernard. **Theoretical Criminology** (Third Edition), New York, NY: Oxford University Press, 1986.

Chapter Two

THE SOCIOLOGY OF DEVIANCE

INTRODUCTION

Deviance has been studied by sociologists since Dr. Marshall B. Clinard, Professor of Sociology (Ret.) at the University of Wisconsin, wrote *Sociology of Deviant Behavior* in 1957. These studies have largely been defined as studies of violations of rules and norms established and presumed harmful to society at large.

Allen E. Liska says these violations of rules and norms range from socially harmful behavior, such as homicide, to relatively minor behavior, such as spitting in public. These may encompass rules or norms adhered to by society at large, small groups, or particular organizations (Liska, p. 2).

The study of norm violations can be divided into two classifications: violation rates and individual violations. *Violation rates* may study the number of murders for a year in a particular city (such as those reported in the FBI's Uniform Crime Reports). *Individual violations* could study mass murders by postal employees. An infinite number of examples could apply to both classifications.

Violation rates are useful for studies involving sociopolitical units and are generally expressed as a number of violations per 1000 population. *Individual violations* characterized the violators' norms, demographics, motives or causal factors, etc.

The disciplines that study deviance are actually overlapping or multidisciplinary fields. Academic courses entitled "Deviance," "Social Problems," "Criminology," "Mental illness," etc. all study areas of deviance. The study of norm violations or deviance, therefore, may involve studies of social problems, crime, and/or psychological abnormality.

THE NATURE OF DEVIANCE

Erich Goode declares that it is both naive and misleading to define deviance by absolute criteria, statistical rarity, social and individual harm, or an act's criminal status (Goode, p. 17).

The normative definition of deviance suggests that violations of the norms of a culture or subculture in which the act(s) takes place is the objective view of deviance. The interjection of culture, time, and place make this normative definition one of relativity. What makes an act "deviant," then, is a violation of a custom, rule, law, or norm at the time and place the violation occurs.

The reactive definition of deviance views deviance in actual examples of *negative reactions* to behavior, individuals, and conditions. In other words, a deviant act must be known and result in condemnation or punishment to be classified as "deviant." By this definition, undetected acts do not exist socially and, therefore, are not deviant.

Erich Goode provides a working definition of "deviance." He defines it as:

> ...behavior or characteristics that some people in society find offensive or reprehensible and that generates—or would generate if discovered—in these people disapproval, punishment, of condemnation of, or hostility toward, the actor or possessor (Goode, p. 37).

Defining an action, a trait, or a person as deviant does not involve condemnation, but merely taking note of the condition or circumstances. Such definitions are descriptive, rather than stigmatizing.

When groups or segments of society believe strongly that an act is violative of norms it is assumed to be *deviant*. Seeking political action may transform these beliefs from informal sanctions (such as negative reactions) into formal sanctions (such as criminal laws). Instituting such sanctions against acts, believed to involve harmful behavior, exerts considerable political influence on the social control apparatus (Goode, p.48).

Explanations for deviance and deviant behavior have taken the form of biological, psychological, and social theories (Liska, p. 7). But in the case of making deviant behavior a criminal act, Allen E. Liska writes that the probability of becoming a criminal violation depends largely on the behavior violating *both* legal *and* cultural norms (Liska, p. 177). An example of this would be laws (legal norms) which also violate the police subculture (cultural norms of the authorities) are more likely to be strictly enforced and, therefore, considered *criminal behavior*.

DEVIANCE AND CRIME

The "authorities" referred to by Liska includes political, educational, religious, and other authorities. The police are a "subculture" of the political authority. The law is the political instrument that empowers social control.

"Radical criminology" asserts that some crimes are a result of cultural conflicts in which groups conflict over what is proper behavior. In such conflict, this theory proposes, some groups have the power to transform their cultural norms into laws (Liska, p. 182).

Based on Goode's definition that *deviance* is something "for which there is a probability of negative sanctions subsequent to its detection," criminal behavior is one form of deviance (Goode, p. 49). Not all deviance, it is important to remember, however, is criminal behavior.

Because not all laws have general cultural support, not all crimes are *deviant* norm violations. Some deviant behavior, therefore, is not criminal (such as adultery, homosexuality, or alcoholism) and some criminal behavior is not deviant (such as many forms of "white-collar crime"). Some behavior is considered *both* deviant and criminal, while some, of course, is considered neither.

Sociologists study deviance from three perspectives. There are those who study "soft" deviance which carries little formal sanctions, such as alcoholism, marijuana use, homosexuality, prostitution, nudism, or mental illness. A second focus of study involves the development of laws, with the behavior being a secondary consideration. The third sociological emphasis is made up of criminologists who study "hard" deviance, such as violent crimes, property crimes, etc.

Although the sociology of deviance is not criminology, the two sociological fields often overlap. The study of deviance also frequently overlaps with the psychological fields of social, forensic, and abnormal psychology.

Although deviance and crime can be distinguished conceptually, in practice and reality they are often inter-related. Because deviance involves social norms, the definitions are not always clear or permanent.

CRIME AND DELINQUENCY

While sociologists refer to less formal rules and norms as folkways and mores, formal societal rules are embodied in laws. Maintenance of social order involves the enforcement of these formal social rules or laws.

Most societies have laws regulating and prohibiting physical actions such as murder, rape, robbery, etc. Modern societies with private and corporate structures and property also have property protections against theft, burglary, fraud, misappropriation, and other larcenies. Property crimes also include prohibitions against destructive acts, such as arson, vandalism, and so forth.

Other laws regulating social behavior involve economic and regulatory or "white collar" crime and vice violations. Vice laws relate to "public morals" offenses such as pornography, prostitution, alcohol, gambling, etc. Drug and narcotics violations are sometimes included in this category, but are sometimes accorded a separate status.

Delinquency is not necessarily a crime. It usually includes acts which would be a crime if committed by an adult. It also includes status offenses, which are violations by virtue of one's age. These include under-aged alcohol and tobacco offenses, curfew, truancy, and similar violations.

Sociological theories of crime generally apply to both crime and delinquency. Such theories include:

1.   *Strain or motivational theories* in which people have legitimate desires that cannot be satisfied by legitimate means.

2. *Control or bond theories* in which the person's bonds to conventional society are weak or broken.
3. *Cultural deviance* in which the deviant conforms to a set of standards not accepted by society at large (Endelman, p. 29-30).

Major categories of crime include *crimes against persons* (violence), discussed in more depth later, *crimes against property, public morals crimes* (vice and narcotics), and *crimes against the public* (public corruption, obstructing justice and order, and crimes against the public administration).

Crimes against property include theft, burglary, arson, auto theft, economic crime, etc. It does not include robbery, which is a crime against persons. Crimes against property only involve theft, destruction, or deprivation involving property or profits.

Goode says that, while stealing is widespread in society, the vast majority of "serious" property crime is committed by a very small proportion of persons (Goode, p. 341). Though corporate crime involves, for the most part, much larger losses than most thefts, it generally carries less severe penalties than shoplifting thefts. Both are included as property crimes.

SEXUAL DEVIANCE

Dr. Robert Endelman reiterates that the terms "deviant," "deviance," and "deviant behavior" do not make value judgments, imply agreement or disagreement, or infer negative connotations. The sociological reference to deviance and associated terms refer to conduct which society regards as "going against the norms" (Endelman, p. 51).

By this definition both prostitution and homosexuality, Endelman says, constitute deviant behavior and sexual deviance. While this is a controversial issue, there is little agreement among social scientists concerning this form of deviance. Dr. Endelman writes:

> Homosexual behavior, consummating sexual behavior with a partner of the same sex, by preference and choice (and not under duress), *is* considered in this society as deviant, going against the norms of proper conduct, by *most* people of this society. It is considered "abnormal" in one sense or another (Endelman, p. 51).

This statement is supported by the facts that:

- to the law such behavior is (in some locations) criminal,
- to most religions it is sinful and against the Word of God, and
- many describe it as "unnatural" behavior.

Because heterosexual mating is necessary for reproduction and survival of the species, homosexual activity is viewed as "going against the demands of nature." Other views observe that such behavior is statistically abnormal and many, though not all, mental health professionals view such behavior as clinically abnormal and psychologically "sick" (Endelman, p. 51).

While homophile protesters contend that homosexuality is an "alternative lifestyle" that does not conflict with religious doctrine, they view it as an "equally valuable form of love" (Endelman, p. 51). While they criticize religious groups' belief systems as "homophobic," they are often violent in espousing their "love" doctrine. While morally objecting to such behavior, most religions are not hostile to such homophiles and follow a "hate the sin, love the sinner" doctrine.

Most homosexual objections are based on moral beliefs that are peacefully held. Yet, society does consist of isolated individuals who act out their objections violently, which is another form of deviance. By definition, whether we like the definition or not, *deviance consists of behavior that goes against the norms of most people.*

Still others, mostly homophile-supporting sociologists, reject the use of the term "deviant" in favor of the term "variant." Other supporters in the psychological arena, such as the American Psychiatric Association, have publicly supported both homosexuality and pedophelia, declaring both same-sex relationships and adult-child sex "normal". Yet, this is still a controversial area among behavioral and social scientists and practitioners.

Dr. Endelman points out the biased agenda of some behavioral and social scientists, however, using the much quoted Kinsey studies as an example. The Kinsey studies, conducted in the 1940s, reported that about 35% of the males in the "sample" had experienced "homosexual contact at some point in their lives." This definition included those who had only one "contact" in their life and included a questionable "sample" source (Endelman, pp. 53-4).

Endelman writes that it is appropriate to study homosexuality and prostitution "side by side" because both involve a prevalent form of sexual deviance. He writes, "Both are seen as immoral, degrading, disgusting, sinful, and invariably, against the law" (Endelman, p. 76). Both are commonly associated with each other in the form of lesbian prostitutes, transvestite prostitutes, and male/same-sex prostitution.

Other areas of sexual deviance include:

1. sadism—being aroused by inflicting pain,
2. masochism—being aroused by receiving pain,
3. transvestism—sexual thrills or arousal by cross-dressing,
4. sexual asphyxia—stimulation by denying one's own body of oxygen by choking or strangling oneself to the point of near-unconsciousness,
5. pedophilia—sexual activity with prepubescent children,
6. **voyeurism**—habitual "peeping" to see others undress or engaging in sex,
7. exhibitionism—displaying oneself sexually to others without their consent,
8. frotteurism—rubbing against nonconsenting persons,
9. bestiality—sex with animals, and
10. sex with non-human objects (Goode, p. 22).

The fourth area, *asphyxia,* includes **autoerotic asphyxia**, which usually leads to death by accidental or intentional asphyxiation during such sexual conduct (Auto-self, erotic-sexual, asphyxia-death by oxygen deprivation). This and other areas are commonly associated with *bondage* (binding with chains, ropes, etc.).

(See Chapter Six, Section VIII, for a discussion of profiling sex crimes).

SUBSTANCE ABUSE

Whether or not substance abuse is deviant is sometimes controversial. Some classify "alcohol" in the same category as "drugs," though most differentiate "alcohol abuse" and "controlled substance abuse" based on the legality and illegality of use and possession. Alcohol, narcotics, and illicit drugs will be categorized here, however, as included in the broad scope of "substance abuse," which also includes legally obtained or over-the-counter (OTC) drugs.

Based on the definition of "deviant," the inclusion of substance abuse may depend upon the time and place in which it is used or abused. The cultural norms of both alcohol and drug use vary greatly.

Endelman writes, "The patterns of drug use are too diverse for any one sociological formulation to fit them all," noting that age may also determine the norms of a generation (Endelman, p. 113).

Endelman also suggested that drug-using criminals are not psychologically or sociologically distinct from non-drug using criminals. He says that both demonstrate the same patterns that are rebellious, unconventional, lying, deceitful, predatory, and exploitative (Endelman, p. 115).

Substance abuse has objective, measurable consequences and subjectively generates public concern (Goode, p. 170). These consequences (norms) and public concerns (objections) constitute the defining elements of deviance. They are formally instituted in most countries by laws. Alcohol, as a psychoactive drug, also has similar consequences and concerns.

VIOLENT BEHAVIOR

Because the term "violence" implies illegitimate, deviant action, many people do not label certain actions, which they approve of, as violent, no matter how much damage or harm they inflict. Therefore, any study of violence requires an understanding of how behavior is viewed and classified by members of society. This may not only involve the harm, but the perception of whether an act is justified or unjustified (Goode, p. 277).

Criminal violence involves homicide, rape, battery, robbery, and other *crimes against persons*. Murder is nearly universally recognized as both illegal and deviant. Yet classifying any killing as a "murder" involves a judgment and is not automatically a fact.

The determination of whether a killing is a criminal or non-criminal homicide involves both a legal definition and a subjective evaluation. Extenuating circumstances, such as who did it, who was killed, why, when, and where it occurred, must all be considered.

Deviant forms of violence range from murder and rape to domestic battery and stalking. Sometimes this "range" overlaps and in all cases the consequences are tragic.

EXAMPLES OF DEVIANT VIOLENCE

For deviance to be a public fact, deviant categories (such as mores and laws) must exist, someone must be perceived as violating them (the "deviant"), and someone must attempt to enforce the consequences of these violations (society or the government).

All societies confront the social problem of crime and criminality. Because the acts characterized as crimes change with time and place, their form changes and the deviance of crime and criminality are not uniformly or universally applied (Kelly, p. 51).

Domestic battery was not always considered violent, criminal, or deviant. The expression "rule of thumb" comes from a custom that asserted that a man may not beat his wife with anything larger than his own thumb. Even today spousal battery and domestic violence is not universally accepted in all cultures as criminal or deviant.

As late as 1979 social writers noted that domestic battery and spousal abuse had only recently gained public attention as social problems. Over the past twenty years now, however, a great deal of information and public education has been made available about the causes and consequences of domestic battery and spousal abuse (Kelly, p. 537).

A 1975 study by the Ann Arbor, Michigan, Chapter of the National Organization of Women reported the following as the major causes of domestic assault as perceived by victims:

Money	35%	Jealousy	21%
Bad Temper	15%	Sex	7%
Children	5%	Household Care	4%
Pregnancy	4%	Assailant's job frustration	2%
Other	6%		

(Kelly, p. 544).

Another example of deviant violence or criminal deviance is *stalking* or "obsessional following." Lenore E. Walker and J. Reid Meloy write that domestic violence has been viewed as "an abuser's attempt to use physical, sexual, or psychological force to take away a woman's power and control over her life" (Meloy, p. 140).

One method of controlling is the systematic isolation of women from friends, family, and community support systems. Patterns of psychological manipulation may go unnoticed and appear normal at first. Using his knowledge of a woman's thoughts and feelings, however, the manipulator's intent to control soon becomes apparent and often leads to stalking (Meloy, p. 140).

Domestic battery and spousal abuse also can lead to murder. Homicides resulting from domestic violence may take the form of either the abused victim being killed by the abuser or the battery victim killing the batterer to escape the abuse (Meloy, p. 141).

Comparing the causes of domestic violence to the motives for murder may merely be interesting, but is worth noting. John M. MacDonald reports that more than one-third of criminal homicides are a result of "an altercation of relatively trivial origin such as an insult, curse or jostling (36.6 percent)," a domestic quarrel (13.4 percent), jealousy (11.1 percent), and altercations over money (10.3 percent) (MacDonald, p. 22). Not all murders, of course, involve domestic violence. Both stalking and murder will be discussed in greater depth as forms of deviant behavior.

STALKING AS DEVIANT BEHAVIOR

Stalking involves the unwanted pursuit of a victim over a period of time and is usually threatening or dangerous to the victim. In the case of public officials, dignitaries, or well-known personalities, stalking may even pose the threat of assassination.

Criminality and legal definitions vary from state to state, but usually the elements of the crime include an unwanted pattern of behavioral intrusion, an implied or explicit threat, and reasonable fear on the part of the victim. All fifty states have stalking statutes and the Violent Crime Control and Law Enforcement Act of 1994 (PL 103-322) makes it a federal crime as well.

J. Reid Meloy identifies a variety of findings from recent studies regarding stalkers and their victims. These findings include:

- Stalkers and victims are older than most other criminals and their victims, usually occurring in their fourth decade of life.
- Stalkers often have prior criminal, psychiatric, and/or drug abuse histories. Stalkers may be characterized by Axis I mental disorders, such as drug and alcohol abuse, mood disorders, or schizophrenia.
- Stalkers may also be characterized by Axis II personality disorders, such as paranoid personality disorder and dependent personality disorder.
- Most stalkers are not psychotic at the time of their stalking.
- Research indicates that stalking is a pathology of attachment, evidenced by early childhood attachment disruptions and recent adulthood losses prior to the stalking.
- At least one-half of stalkers threaten their victims, and even though most threats are not carried out, the risk of violence increases when threats are articulated (Meloy, pp. 4-5).

Stalking seems to involve *obsessional following*, though not in compliance with the DSM-IV definition of *obsessional*, and is characterized by the object-related thinking of the stalker (Meloy, p. 13). Obsessed stalkers constantly think and/or fantasize about their victims. These fantasies may be oriented toward love, anger, or vengeance (Internet: http://www.fiu.edu/~victimad/stalkprof.htm).

Though stalkers rarely demonstrate violence, when they do it is most often directed first at the object (victim) of the stalking and second toward anyone perceived as interfering with access to the victim (Meloy, p. 15).

The *psychodynamics* of stalking refer to the thoughts, emotions, and defenses in the mind of the stalker that are related to the victim (object of pursuit). Meloy identifies the characteristics of the stalkers' fantasies:

- **idealizing**—thoughts of being loved or loving or admired or admiring the object (victim),
- **mirroring**—being exactly like the object (victim),
- **twinship**—complementing the object (victim), or
- **merger**—sharing a destiny with the object (victim) (Meloy, p. 18).

PROFILE OF A STALKER

Stalkers may have had an intimate relationship with their victims or merely the desire to have had one. The latter may focus on a classmate, coworker, or mere acquaintance. Stalkers often have obsessive fantasies of love, anger, or vengeance about their victims. Many stalkers have a history of failed relationships, have difficulty communicating with people, and may be overwhelmed by real or perceived *rejection* (Internet: http://www.fiu.edu/~victimad/stalkprof.htm).

Though stalkers have poor communication and social skills, they have good planning behaviors that help them master their stalking terrorism, while staying on the edge of the law. They may be of surprisingly high *intelligence*. They may be male or female, but female stalkers are just as dangerous in many cases. Again, stalkers may be *motivated* by "love," anger, or to avenge a perceived wrong (Internet: http://www.fiu.edu/~victimad/stalkprof.htm).

Meloy coined the term "obsessional follower" to describe individuals who pursue abnormal or long-term patterns of threatening or harassing a specific individual (Meloy, p. 51). This obsessional behavior may be linked behaviorally to the *attachment theory* commonly associated with early childhood bonding with caregivers (Meloy, p. 52).

A national sample of 16,000 individuals interviewed in a random telephone survey indicates that approximately 1.4% of Americans are stalked annually and that 8% of women and 2% of men have been stalked at some time. This survey, by the Center for Policy Research in Denver, Colorado, also suggests that, though most stalkings last for less than a year, some have lasted beyond five years (Internet: http://www.fiu.edu/~victimad/statstalk.htm).

In 1997 I worked a stalking case in which a female stalked a male victim for nearly ten years. In that case the victim and stalker had "dated" for a year or two, though she (the stalker) was married. The stalking pattern included showing up at the victim's job each pay-day, following him to his credit union and standing with him as he made deposits, following him home and forcing her way into his home.

The stalker called the victim so often that the victim's answering machine wore out twice. She would mysteriously show up when he was on dates and sit with him and his date at restaurants and other public places. The stalker finally discontinued the "obsessive following" only after numerous police reports and a plea arrangement with the prosecutor's office.

According to the survey of the Center for Policy Research 87% of stalkers identified in the survey were men while 13% were women. Approximately 80% of the victims were women while 20% were males. Nearly 45 % of the victims were threatened and 75% were followed. While only half of the victims filed police reports, only 24% of the female victims had their cases prosecuted and a mere 54% of these resulted in convictions (Internet: http://www.fiu.edu/~victi-mad/statstalk.htm).

Though stalkers are characterized by a variety of disturbed attachment styles and mental disorders, research indicates they may share at least two similarities. First, *early attachment disturbance* may be a predisposing factor in stalking and, second, *adult recent loss* may precipitate stalking (Meloy, p. 65).

Thought disorders from Axis I (*Clinical Syndromes*), from the Diagnostic and Statistical Manual of Mental Disorders or DSM-IV, affecting the ability to discern the real from the unreal is common in stalkers. Symptoms include hallucinations, delusions, and disorganized thought. This may be manifested as *schizophrenia* or one of a variety of other delusional disorders (Meloy, p. 70).

Other diagnostic characteristics of stalkers may include a symptom known as "*ideas of reference*," in which ordinary events are interpreted by the delusional person to have a special personal meaning. Another symptom may involve some type of *mood disorder* such as a manic or depression disorder. Depression related relationship discord and schisms may lead the stalker to suicide or homicide, particularly associated with work place violence (Meloy, p. 72).

Stalkers may also be identified with the Axis I category substance use (abuse or dependence) disorder (Meloy, p. 72). Stalkers may also be identified with Axis II, (*Developmental Disorders and Personality Disorders*) from the Diagnostic and Statistical Manual of Mental Disorders or DSM-IV, Cluster A, B, and C disorders. But most typically are characterized by antisocial, borderline, histrionic, and narcissistic personality disorders (Meloy, p. 73).

Stalking may lead to more serious problems than obsessional following. It, as we will see, can lead to murder and assassination.

VICTIMOLOGY AND STALKING

There are numerous examples of stalking leading to murder or the assassination of public figures. The 1989 stalking—murder of actress Rebecca Schaeffer by her stalker Robert Bardo brought national attention to stalking violence.

Following this incident the Los Angeles Police Department developed a database for use in profiling stalkers for threat assessment or threat management.

The diagnostic categories in the DSM-IV has limited use, therefore the *stalker/victim types* were developed. These include:

1. the *simple obsessional* in which the victim and perpetrator have prior knowledge of each other;
2. the *love obsessional* which is characterized by the absence of an existing relationship between the perpetrator and victim; and
3. *erotomanic groups* which are characterized by the suspect's delusional belief that he/she is loved by the victim (erotomania) (Meloy, p. 76-78).

An additional category of stalker types is the *false victimization syndrome*. This category is characterized by the creation of elaborate scenarios to falsely support reports of being stalked. The "victims" are usually female, usually exhibit histrionic personality disorder (described in DSM-IV), and this type is usually motivated by an attempt to resurrect a perceived failing relationship (Meloy, p. 79).

The 1980 murder of John Lennon and the 1981 attempt to assassinate President Ronald Reagan by John Hinkley, Jr. brought the seriousness of stalking to public attention. Studies of victim/stalker profiles have been developed to help with threat assessment and management. This is relevant not only for the protection of public officials and figures, but for clinicians targeted by their patients.

Such stalking incidents as threats, assassination attempts, and murders of public officials, celebrities, and executives have lead to greater awareness of the need for threat assessment and management. The U.S. Secret Service undertook an ongoing research program called Exceptional Case Study Project (ECSP) to help profile such threats.

ECSP data to help profile was developed through **archival review** and **interviews**. The interview protocol included sections on:

- idea to action,
- target selection,
- communications,
- pre-incident behaviors,
- planning,
- symptoms of mental illness and violence, and
- key developmental experiences (Meloy, pp. 180-181).

This lead to the development of threat assessment and management conclusions.

THREAT ASSESSMENT AND MANAGEMENT

One of the greatest threats by stalkers, particularly to public personalities, is the potential for assassination. The findings of the U.S. Secret Service Exceptional Case Study Project (ECSP) includes the identification of three "myths about assassins."

The *first* myth identified by ECSP research data is that there is a "profile" of "the assassin." The fact is that there are no accurate descriptive or demographic "profiles" of American assassins, attackers, and near-lethal approachers (Meloy, p. 181). Although there is no "profile," the ECSP did identify "common denominator" behaviors and activities.

The *second* myth is that assassination is a result of mental illness or derangement. The fact is that mental illness is rarely involved, although most attackers had some type of psychological problems (Meloy, p. 183).

The *third* myth is that explicit threateners are the most likely to carry out attacks. The fact is that persons who *pose* threats most often do not *make* threats, especially explicit threats (Meloy, p. 183). While some threateners pose a threat, most of those who pose a threat do not threaten.

The ECSP findings made three observations about assassins and their behaviors:

1. Assassination is the end result of a discernible and understandable process of thinking and behavior;
2. Most attackers perceive their violence as a means to a goal or a way to solve a problem;
3. There is a direct connection between the assassin's motives and their selection of target(s) (Meloy, p. 184).

Stalking methods may range from obsessional following to Internet e-mail stalking. Erotomania has come to be recognized as a delusional disorder, identified in DSM-IV (Diagnostic and Statistical Manual of Mental Disorders, Fourth Edition) as a variation of pathological mourning, an attachment disorder, an identity disturbance, and a reflection of poor reality testing (Meloy, p. 213).

Functional analysis is an assessment technology that may aid law enforcement and mental health officials in identifying stalking behavior. Functional analysis is a broad behavioral approach to understanding behavior in general (Meloy, p. 275).

Functional analysis is used to identify those variables that *precede* a behavior (*antecedents*) and those that *follow* it (*consequences*). It also identifies the *relationship* between antecedents, behaviors, and consequences. The **functional relation** between behavior, antecedents, and consequences hinges on the antecedent that triggers the behavior that has been reinforced in the past (Meloy, p. 281).

Functional relations "imply a contingent covariance as opposed to direct causality" and the presence of one functional relation "does not preclude the presence or impact of other functional relations potentially involved in a given behavior (Meloy, p. 281). *Reinforcement* occurs when a tangible or intangible stimulus maintains or increases a behavior. The reinforcer functionally strengthens the behavior (Meloy, pp. 281-2).

Positive reinforcement occurs when a stimulus strengthens a behavior. *Negative* reinforcement strengthens behavior by removing something aversive. The manner in which reinforcement is related to behavior has an important effect on that behavior and is referred to as the "reinforcement schedule." Behavior is influenced by the *rate* at which reinforcement occurs, though even occasional reinforcement may result in persistent behavior (Meloy, p. 282).

When behavior is no longer reinforced, *extinction* occurs, however, a phenomenon called *extinction burst* may occur when behavior is no longer reinforced but the behavior actually accelerates before ceasing altogether. *Punishment* is a stimulus that weakens the behavior, rather than reinforces it (Meloy, p. 282).

An **assessment protocol** begins with selection of a *targeted behavior*, (e.g. behavior that is most problematic, most amenable to change, and most dangerous). An operational description and topography (what a behavior looks like and how it is enacted) must be identified. Next, functional analysis identifies the *antecedents* of the behavior,)e.g. the settings or triggers, etc.). Finally, the *consequences* of the behavior are assessed in terms of how people respond to the behavior and what happens when it occurs. Other elements considered in a functional analysis protocol includes the amount of time between stalking behaviors, the consequences, and how the target responds, etc. (Meloy, pp. 283-4).

To recapitulate, an example of the steps in a functional analysis protocol might include:

1.   Identify the behavior.
2.   Identify the antecedents to the behavior.
3.   Identify the consequences to the behavior.
4.   Consider several functions of the behavior (e.g. getting attention) (Meloy, pp. 286-7).

Stalking or obsessional following is both a psychological and a sociological phenomenon. Its characteristics have a broad range, as do its consequences. Stalking is a potentially serious form of deviance and deviant behavior.

MURDER AS DEVIANCE

Murder is the most extreme form of deviance and committing a homicide is the most serious manifestation of deviant behavior. Murder is nearly universally regarded as unlawful and a deviant act.

While mass, serial, and ritualistic/cult murders receive a great deal of attention in the media, television, and movies, these are the exception rather than the rule. In my experience as a homicide investigator, most have involved random crimes (robbery, burglary, drug deals gone bad, etc.) and violence between persons known to each other.

Dr. John M. MacDonald, a forensic psychiatrist, reported in 1986 that 40 percent of homicides in the United States involved disagreements between friends, neighbors, and acquaintances. Half of these involved killings within the family and about half of those family killings involved a spouse killing a spouse (nearly 10 percent) (MacDonald, p. 11).

About 10 percent of homicides occurred during robberies and another 10 percent during other felonies, such as narcotics offenses, sex offenses, arson, etc. (MacDonald, p. 11). The Public Health Policy Advisory Board (PHPAB) reported in May, 1999, that while the overall mortality rate among U.S. children has decreased 33.5% between 1979 and 1995, the number of homicides and suicides among American children has dramatically increased (Internet: http://taxa.psyc.missouri.edu/abnormal/1999/msg00474.html). Other sources suggest that juvenile homicides are decreases. (The FBI UCR is considered the authoritative source of crime statistics).

The PHPAB cites the five leading causes of death among American children from birth to age 19 as:

- unintentional injury (42%),
- homicide (14%),
- suicide (7%),
- cancer (7%), and
- birth defects (5%).

(Internet: http://taxa.psyc.missouri.edu/abnormal/1999/msg00474.html).

These statistics make homicide and suicide the second and third leading causes of death, respectively, for our children for an alarming total of 21% of those deaths.

MacDonald states that in 1986 murderers tended to be younger than those they killed, male offenders out numbered female offenders six to one, and the murder was often not the offenders first crime. He also reports that though mental retardation, coupled with defects in temperament and character, weakens control over homicidal impulses, mentally retarded persons rarely commit murder (MacDonald, pp. 20-23).

HOMICIDAL BEHAVIOR

Kruglanski, Bar-Tal, and Klar write that the behavior of individuals in conflict situations depend on *general knowledge (categorical knowledge)* of what "conflict" means and *specific knowledge* of whether a particular situation actually represents a conflict (Larsen, p. 45). In contrast to this rather esoteric statement, MacDonald says that even with confessions and statements of the circumstances of the crime an adequate explanation of violent conflict will never result. He says that external circumstances are often not the motive for incomprehensible acts (MacDonald, p. 82).

MacDonald writes that the urge to kill another human being is the ultimate form of aggression, which Freud regarded as an instinct and, therefore, inevitable. Dr. MacDonald says the psychoanalytic concept of the mind's id, ego, and super-ego personifies passion, common sense, and conscience (MacDonald, p. 85).

The **id** is the source of the instincts and constantly seeks expression of asocial drives. The psychoanalytical view, therefore, views everyone as potential criminals (MacDonald, p. 85). Aggression may lash out when one is aroused and not sufficiently self-restrained (Berkowitz, p. 142).

Dr. Leonard Berkowitz agrees with Dr. MacDonald's earlier comments that murderers often have prior criminal offenses. Berkowitz cites that nearly two-thirds of the killers identified in the Wolfgang Philadelphia study had been arrested before and, predominantly, for crimes against persons (Berkowitz, p. 282).

It is a popular assumption that murderers are mentally ill (i.e. only one who was mad would do such an insane act). Yet, MacDonald observes, studies have shown that the only psychiatric disorders found more often among criminal offender populations than the general population were sociopathic (antisocial) personality disorder, alcoholism, and drug dependence. Schizophrenia accounted for only one percent of criminals' psychiatric disorders (MacDonald, p. 177).

The motives for homicidal behavior are sometimes difficult to specify. There may be criminal motives that are readily apparent in some cases, such as robbery, but the behavioral causes are much more complex. Violence may indeed be instinctive to humankind, but submitting to such antisocial/psychopathic urges results in the ultimate expression of deviance and deviant behavior.

SENSATIONAL DEVIANCE

Sensational crimes are a special form of deviance. These include mass murder, serial homicides, serial sexual crimes and sexual homicide, ritualistic and cult crimes, the murder of or by public figures, etc. Though these are sensationalized in the media and capture the attention of the public, they account for a relatively small percentage of violent crimes.

Mass murderers are offenders who kill many persons at the same time and place. Serial murderers are offenders that kill repeatedly at different times and places. Sexual homicide involves murders in which a sexual factor is clearly involved. *Sexual homicide* may be apparent in mass or serial murders, as well as ritualistic and cult crimes. Ritualistic and cult crimes involve a ceremony, ceremonial purpose, or group that follows a cult belief.

Underlying psychiatric disorders involved in *mass murder* include sociopathic (psychopathic) personality, schizophrenia, and paranoid disorders (MacDonald, pp. 140-1).

In September, 1949, **Howard Unruh**, a paranoid with no prior criminal record, went on a twelve minute shooting spree that killed fourteen and wounded three. Unruh, a twenty-eight year old pharmacy student, was a loner who was "preoccupied" with religion and lived with his parents in Camden, New Jersey. Unruh thought his neighbors were making derogatory remarks about him and became upset when a gate was stolen from a fence he had built around his parent's yard (MacDonald, p. 141).

In March, 1966, **Charles Whitman**, a twenty-five year old architectural engineering student at the University of Texas in Austin consulted a psychiatrist because he was upset over his parent's separation. MacDonald writes, "In a two-hour interview he stated that he had beaten his wife several times and although he was making intense efforts to control his temper, he was worried that he might explode." Whitman revealed at that time that he was thinking about taking a rifle to the University Tower to start shooting people (MacDonald, p. 142).

In August, 1966, Whitman stabbed and shot his mother in her apartment, returned home, and stabbed his wife. In a note addressed to "To whom it may concern," he recorded the deaths of his first two victims and expressed love for his mother and hatred for his father. The next day he took three rifles, a shotgun, and other firearms to the observation deck of the 307-feet-tall University Tower where he shot forty-four people, killing fourteen, before being killed himself by the police. Whitman left a note requesting an autopsy. A small brain tumor was found, but considered to be irrelevant to his homicidal behavior (MacDonald, p. 142).

In July, 1984, Etna Huberty called two mental health clinics in San Ysidro, California, to see if her husband had made an appointment. **James Huberty,** a forty-one year old unemployed security guard, told his wife that he had guns and was going to kill someone. Both clinics told Mrs. Huberty to call the police, but she did not take the threat seriously (MacDonald, p. 142).

After spending the next day at the zoo with his wife and daughters, James Huberty changed into camouflage fatigue pants and a black tee shirt. He told his wife, "I'm going to hunt humans," and left with a rifle, shotgun, and pistol. At 4:00 p.m. Huberty entered a nearby McDonald's and shouted, "I'm going to kill you." He killed twenty-one persons and wounded nineteen before being killed himself by a police marksman at 5:15 p.m. (MacDonald, p. 143).

There are a number of other examples of mass murders, including several school shootings that have occurred in 1998-1999 (see Chapter Nine). There are also numerous examples of serial murders. Multiple murderers often confess only to those crimes that have already been detected by the police, but sometimes exaggerate the "total score" with hopes of substantiating an insanity plea. The examples provided involve serial murders involving thirty or more victims.

Examples include Gilles de Rais (1404-1440), William Burke (1792-1829), Henri De'sire' Landru (1869-1922), Fritz Harmann (1879-1925), and Marcel Petiot (1897-1946). (MacDonald, p. 148-155). A more recent example is **John Wayne Gacy.**

In 1980 John Wayne Gacy, a 37 year old building contractor, was convicted of murdering thirty-three young men and boys in his home at Des Plains, Illinois, outside of Chicago. Gacy had a criminal record and was a "police buff," carrying a portable red light in his car. He invited youths to his home for alcohol and homosexual activities, once handcuffing and forcing one youth to perform oral sex on him at knife-point. After being arrested for this, Gacy hired another youth to beat up and possibly kill this victim (MacDonald, pp. 155-6).

Gacy was an *antisocial personality* of bright normal intelligence (IQ 118). His wife divorced him while he was in the reformatory. He was diagnosed as a passive-aggressive personality and recommended for release by a psychiatrist. Gacy was active in both the Jaycees, receiving a "Sound Citizen Award," (MacDonald, p. 156) and the Democratic Party, even being photographed with Rosalyn Carter.

Dennis Nilsen, an English homosexual murderer strangled his victims between 1978 and 1983. **Henry Lee Lucas** claimed to have killed about 360 persons between 1975 and his arrest in Texas in 1983 at age 46. His illiterate homosexual lover, **Ottis Elwood Toole,** claimed 125 murders. Both are believed to have exaggerated their claims (MacDonald, pp. 157-9).

Sexual murders may involve a rape-murder, sadism, necrophilia, etc. Ritualistic and cult murders usually involve a ceremonial sacrifice or retribution.

If murder is the ultimate expression of deviance, mass, serial, and ritualistic homicides are the ultimate expression of deviant murder.

OTHER CRIMINAL DEVIANCE

Violence and aggression seem to be the same whether they are self directed or directed toward others. Studies of youthful murderers reveal histories of abuse, humiliation, terror or neglect, and evidence of psychiatric disorders or neurological abnormalities. Such offenders are characterized by a deadening of human feeling, an inability to feel remorse, love or empathy, and a dissociation from reality (Internet: http://taxa.psyc.missouri.edu/abnormal/1999/msg00465.html).

PETA (People for the Ethical Treatment of Animals) has released a study that suggests the lack of empathy exhibited among those who abuse animals is one of the most frequently ignored warning signs that a person is at risk for violent behavior. Each of the school shootings occurring in 1998-1999 revealed that the perpetrators had histories of abusing, torturing, and killing animals before moving on to humans. (Internet: http://www.peta.online.org/pn/599humaneed.html). PETA also reports that several high-profile killers have also shared a history of animal cruelty, including Jeffrey Dahmer, Ted Bundy, Carroll Edward Cole, and David Berkowitz. (Internet: http://www.peta-online.org/alert/viol.html).

Self-directed violence, pathological aggression, and cruelty to animals are all dangerous forms of deviant behavior. Such deviance is dangerous due to its potential to lead to homicidal behaviors such as those described in the previous sections.

CHARACTER DISORDERS AND DEVIANCE

The systematic study of behavior is based on the scientific development of classifications and/or typologies. Types of deviants, types of criminals, and types of phenomena may provide for systematic observations that assist in the formulation of hypotheses and guide research. (Clinard, et al., pp. 1-2).

A strict *classification* (composed of classes) consists of a set of *variables* or *attributes* that are linked to form a number of possible classes. A *typology* (composed of types) attempts to specify the ways in which the attributes of observable phenomena are *empirically connected* in the formation of particular types (Clinker, et al., p. 10).

Dr. MacDonald writes, "Murder is not confined to any one personality type but the sociopathic personality is disproportionately represented in the ranks of murderers." *Sociopathic* personalities, also known as *psychopathic* and *antisocial* personalities, are social misfits that are problems to themselves and to society (MacDonald, p. 203).

Sociopaths—psychopaths—antisocials appear at first to be plausible or even impressive persons, but consistently disappoint their families and associates. They do not have the capacity to *feel* and may be callous, cynical, and devoid of affection. They fail to conform to accepted social customs and lack persistence. Such persons are impulsive, intolerant of frustration, egocentric, immature, rebellious, and are intolerant of discipline and legal and social restrictions (MacDonald, pp. 203-4).

Sociopaths do not generally benefit from current mental health treatments and seem unable to learn from experience or punishment. The sociopath's disregard for the truth, unreliability, irresponsibility, immaturity, and lack of restraint is not exhibited in everything they say or do and is, therefore not always evident. In fact, sociopaths are capable of charm and are able to impress others (MacDonald, p. 204).

It is this lack of conformity to accepted social customs and problematic behavior that makes the sociopath/psychopath/antisocial a *deviant* and his or her behavior acts of *deviance*. Although such deviant behavior is not always criminal, often sociopathic behavior leads to criminal activity of varying degrees.

CONCLUSION

The sociology of *deviance* and the criminology of criminal *deviant behavior* have been of concern to sociologists and criminologists for some time, but are a comparatively new field of specialization in the behavioral sciences.

Definitions of deviance and deviant acts may differ from one time and place to another. This is because the nature or working definition of deviance involves a deviation from accepted social norms or noncompliance with accepted social customs, including laws. Violations of societies' laws by definition usually makes such deviance also a criminal act and offense. Thus, deviance is not always criminal, but some deviant acts are criminal acts and most criminal offenses are regarded as deviant.

Criminal deviance may involve substance abuse and offenses, vice (morality) and sexual offenses, crimes against property, crimes against persons, etc. Crimes against persons are deviant acts of violence and aggressive behavior. Stalking or obsessional following are regarded as deviant behavior because of the harm caused and the potential for violent behavior.

Murder, the ultimate expression of violent deviance, usually involves a known victim or an attendant underlying crime, such as robbery. Mass, serial, and ritualistic murder, however, is the ultimate expression of deviant homicide because of the inherent bizarre characteristics, motives, and "multicide" behaviors.

The seriousness of criminal deviance makes the study of deviant behavior a vital research issue for sociologists, criminologists, and forensic psychologists. Other fields of mental health, social science, and behavioral science, such as psychiatry, behavioral neurology, and social anthropology are also involved in this research issue. Such research is vital to the success of law enforcement and mental health professionals in dealing with dangerous and disruptive deviant behavior.

REFERENCES—CHAPTER 2

Berkowitz, Leonard. **Aggression: Its Causes, Consequences, and Control**. Philadelphia, PA: Temple University Press, 1993.

Clinard, Marshall B., Richard Quinney, and John Wildeman. **Criminal Behavior Systems: A Typology** (Third Edition). Cincinnati, OH: Anderson Publishing Co., 1994.

Endleman, Robert. **Deviance and Psychopathology: The Sociology and Psychology of Outsiders**, Malabar, FL: Robert E. Krieger Publishing Co., 1990.

Internet: Deeper Truths Sought in Violence by Youths (N.Y. Times, May 4, 1999, Erica Goode): http://taxa.psyc.missouri.edu/abnormal/1999/msg00465.html

Internet: Homicide, Suicide Rates Rise in US children: http://taxa.psyc.missouri.edu/abnormal/1999/msg00474.html

Internet: School Shootings Preventable with Humane Education: http://www.peta-online.org/pn/599humaneed.html

Internet: PETA Action Alerts: http://www.peta-online.org/alert/viol.html

Goode, Erich. **Deviant Behavior** (Fifth Edition). Upper Saddle River, NJ: Prentice Hall, 1997.

Kelly, Delos H., **Deviant Behavior: Readings in the Sociology of Deviance**, New York: St. Martin's Press, Inc., 1979.

Larsen, Knud S. (Editor). **Conflict and Social Psychology**. London: SAGE Publications, 1993.

Liska, Allen. **Perspectives on Deviance**. Englewood, NJ: Prentice-Hall, Inc., 1981.

MacDonald, John M.. **The Murderer and His Victim** (Second Edition). Springfield, IL: Charles C. Thomas Publisher, 1986.

Meloy, J. Reid. **The Psychology of Stalking: Clinical and Forensic Perspectives**. San Diego, CA: Academic Press, 1998.

Profile of a Stalker: http://www.fiu.edu/~victimad/stalkprof.htm

Chapter Three

ABNORMAL PSYCHOLOGY

INTRODUCTION
ORIGINS, GROWTH, AND DEVELOPMENT

Individuals are what they are because of their particular heredity and environment. Individuality begins when a sperm cell from the father penetrates the wall of an ovum (egg) from the mother and fertilizes it. Each sperm has twenty-three **chromosomes**, which carry heredity.

Each chromosome bears many sets of deoxyribonucleic acid (DNA) molecules. These sets of DNA molecules are called **genes**. Genes determine inherited characteristics. Genes do not always stay in their chromosomes but, because of "crossing-over," sometimes break off and are exchanged with a corresponding segment from a homologous chromosome. The number of possible combinations are infinite.

The **genotype** is the genetic potential that an individual possesses and can in part transmit to his offspring. This potential may be only partially expressed in his phenotype. The **phenotype** is the observable characteristics of an individual that are only partial manifestations of his genetic potential or genotype.

(**NOTE:** Fundamental psychological theories and definitions may be found in most undergraduate psychology texts or even good encyclopedias. For more information on these subjects and definitions you may refer to such texts as:

Bootzin, Richard R., Gordon H. Bower, Jennifer Crocker, and Elizabeth Hall, **Psychology Today: An Introduction**, New York, NY: McGraw-Hill, Inc., 1991.

Kretch, David, Richard S. Crutchfield, and Norman Livson, **Elements of Psychology**, New York, NY: Alfred A. Knopf Books, 1974. Matlin, Margaret W., **Cognition**, Orlando, FL: Harcourt Brace Publishers, 1994.)

Almost every topic involving the developmental process involves psychology—perception, learning, motivation and emotion, intelligence, personality, and social behavior. Because human development is characterized by almost continuous change, i.e. maturity and aging, the study of psychology is predominantly a developmental study.

When anatomical structures and physiological processes that are related to psychological events are studied, major attention is given to the nervous system—the brain, the spinal cord, and the nerves. Nerve cells conduct information. The activity of neurons can be measured by an electroencephalogram (EEG). The study of these processes is usually referred to as physiological psychology.

THINKING AND LANGUAGE

Swiss psychologist Jean Piaget's theory of cognitive development dominates modern views of the development of thinking. This theory involves the belief that human mental growth (cognitive development) is the result of infants' interaction with his or her physical world.

Jerome Bruner theorized that education and experience play a greater role than environment in cognitive growth. Bruner's theory of cognitive development involves three stages:

1. The **enactive** stage or **mode**—Knowledge is represented in terms of motor schemata.
2. The **iconic mode**—Knowledge is represented in terms of images or perceptions.
3. The **symbolic mode**—Knowledge is represented by symbols, particularly words, that can represent abstract notions as well as concrete information.

Early Gestalt psychologists extended their perceptual processes analysis to the development of thinking and cognitive development.

Linguistic knowledge does not refer to the ability to cite the rules of a language. Rather, it refers to the sound structure (**phonology**), word structure (**morphology**), meaning of words (**semantics**), and the ability to differentiate tones of voice (**intonation patterns**). To make sense of these utterances, we must also understand the ways in which the order of words determines the meaning of a sentence (**syntax**).

The study of **sociolinguistics** involves the use of appropriate linguistic forms to communicate social meanings. This requires an understanding of the social rules governing language use in communicative settings. **Psycholinguistics** explores the processes of linguistic knowledge and language–processing skills that allows perception and comprehension.

The process of thinking consists of the manipulation and interplay of symbolic elements such as words, images, and concepts to represent aspects of reality. Productive thinking, which requires new and original solutions, produces creative problem solving. **Autistic** thinking is predominantly influenced by personal desires and needs at the expense of its adaptability to objective reality.

INTELLIGENCE, PERCEPTION, MOTIVATION, AND EMOTION

Mental tests developed out of a need to classify individuals in terms of their abilities. Because mental age and chronological age do not increase at exactly the same rate, an intelligence quotient (IQ) can be computed to identify the ratio. The more intelligent an individual is measured to be (mentally advanced) relative to their age, the higher their IQ.

Information about our surroundings comes through our senses. This, of course, involves our sight, hearing, smell, taste, and touch which sense light and sound waves, pressures, and chemical stimuli.

To understand emotions, a brief review of motivation is necessary. Motivational arousal depends upon both internal states of bodily imbalance and external stimulus. Maslow's "hierarchy of needs" addresses these through a prioritized list of needs: physiological, safety, belongingness and love, esteem, and self-actualization.

Emotional experiences vary in their degree of pleasantness or unpleasantness, referred to as their **hedonic tone**. Grief, shame, fear, and remorse are examples of unpleasant emotions, while joy, pride, contentment, and reverence are examples of pleasant emotions.

CONFLICT AND AGGRESSION

Frustration is inevitable when individuals desire something that is denied them due to circumstances. Frustration may result from the conflict between personal desires and societal restraints and prohibitions. Because societal standards internalize as we mature, this conflict also turns inwards. The direction of the effects of frustration and conflict may be either constructive or disruptive.

When **cognitive narrowing** occurs, the individual focuses his or her attention on inaccessible goals or blocked pathways and does not see alternate goals or paths. Aggression may be the result of reaching what is known as the threshold of frustration tolerance. This is a form of attack on the obstacle or barrier and, in a sense, adaptive behavior.

Frustration may not be the result of identifiable barriers, but an experience of loss, lacking, or conflict with another motive. Because there is no logical object to attack, aggression may be diffused over several objects that are unrelated to the frustration. This **displacement** may be manifested negatively toward entirely innocent objects or people.

Another disruptive effect of conflict and frustration is escape. Chronic frustration and chronic **escape reactions** may lead to defense mechanisms such as

regression, reaction formation (exaggerated expression of behavioral tendencies exactly opposed to underling repressed impulses), **rationalization, insulation,** and **projection**.

MENTAL DISORDERS AND BEHAVIOR PATHOLOGY
FUNCTIONAL DISORDERS

The *Diagnostic and Statistical Manual of Mental Disorders* (DSM-IV), published by the American Psychiatric Association, classifies schemes for mental disorders. **Functional disorders** refer to disorders which have no specific organic basis and in which the patient's past experience has played an important part. These are classified as neurosis, personality disorders, and psychosis.

Persons suffering from a **neurosis (psychoneurosis)** are not as severely disorganized in behavior as psychotics are and they maintain reasonably appropriate responses to reality. *Neurotics* may experience periods of acute panic with no discernible source of anxiety. They often entertain *obsessive* thoughts or perform *compulsive* actions that seem irrational. *Neuroses* are emotional disorders that generally center on anxiety.

Personality disorders or **character disorders** refer to patterns of developmental antisocial behavior that are disapproved of by others or are harmful to the self or others. This may include illegal behavior (such as sexual deviance, alcohol offenses, drug abuse, etc.) or maladaptive behavior that is not illegal. Pervasive behavioral styles permeate most or all of the person's reactions to his or her environment. He or she may be unaware of the annoying or self-destructive behavior or rationalize it in moral terms.

A **psychosis** involves a relatively high degree of disorganization. *Psychotic* individuals display severe thinking, emotional, and behavioral aberrations. *Psychotics* may appear to have lost contact with reality and display emotional reactions that appear inappropriate for the situation. He or she may experience delusions and hallucinations.

NEUROSES

Anxiety is the primary characteristic of neuroses. Though symptoms may shift, a pattern is usually discernible. Generally recognized **psychoneurotic** reactions include:

1. **Anxiety Neurosis** is characterized by the appearance of periods of anxiety that may erupt in short periods of acute panic or be chronic and pervasive.

2. **Hysterical Neurosis** involves a) the **conversion reaction** in which physical disturbances in the sensory systems are characteristic and b) the **dissociative reaction** that is characterized by disturbances of memory or identity known as *amnesia.*

3. **Phobic Neurosis** is characterized by excessive fears of objects, places, or situations.

4. **Obsessive—Compulsive Neurosis** compels individuals toward thoughts and/or actions that they are unable to resist. *Obsession* usually applies to *thoughts* that may be troublesome or disgusting. *Compulsion* usually refers to *actions* that the person feels forced to perform.

5. **Existential Neurosis**, though not listed in the DSM-IV, asserts that people define themselves through choices and awareness of their finite existence. A failure to find meaning in this existence may result in existential frustration. An existential neurosis may result from the attempt to deal with or deny this frustration. Guilt may be associated with an awareness of unfulfilled expectations.

6. **Other Neuroses** include *depressive neurosis* (characterized by chronic sadness), *neurasthenic neurosis* (characterized by chronic fatigue), and *hypochondriacal neurosis* (characterized by an intense preoccupation with one's own physical symptoms, which have no basis in organic pathology).

PERSONALITY DISORDERS

Personality disorders consist of behaviors which are believed to be pervasive personality styles developed in response to conflict in one's early life. Although there are approximately ten personality disorders listed in the DSM-IV, the main ones include:

1. **Obsessive—Compulsive Personality** is similar to obsessive-compulsive neurosis but the obsessive-compulsive personality disorder is not characterized by anxiety. Individuals affected by this are extremely and irrationally concerned about neatness, orderliness, and conformity to well-defined rules. Though the neurosis also exhibits these traits, the personality disorder does not demonstrate the dramatic and obvious obsessions and compulsions of the classical neurotic pattern, nor the associated bizarre and disturbing symptoms of the neurotic.

2. **Hysterical Personality** disorder is somewhat related to hysterical neuroses in which overly dramatic behavior and feigned seductiveness are characteristic. Both the emotions and behavior of the affected individual are overly dramatic.

Behavior may appear to be highly seductive sexually, though the person (usually women) is actually sexually frigid. Sexual advances in response to this seductiveness may take the individual by surprise.

3. **Antisocial Reaction** or **Psychopathic Personality** disorder is a form of character disorder in which individuals show a chronic and socially incapacitating tendency to seek immediate need gratification. *Antisocials* or *psychopaths* tend to be poor judges of the consequences of their social actions and fail to learn from such experiences.

Antisocials/psychopaths display a diffuse and chronic incapacity for persistent, ordered living. They behave impulsively to obtain immediate gratification, are unable to anticipate the consequences of such actions, and fail to learn from experience. They do not seem to plan ahead or follow-through with long-range goals.

Antisocials/psychopaths are insensitive to the needs of others, live for the moment, are unable to tolerate frustration and demonstrate erratic, irresponsible, and unpredictable behavior. Though they make good first impressions and their intelligence is unimpaired, they use flattery, charm, and glib, articulate words to manipulate situations. Appearing friendly, they are usually isolated because of an incapacity to form lasting relations.

Antisocials/psychopaths suffer from a failure to develop moral standards or a conscience, having failed to internalize the standards of society. They have little guilt or anxiety, shallow or no emotions, and little capacity for real love or attachment.

FUNCTIONAL PSYCHOSES

Functional Psychoses involve a significant impairment in the capacity to meet the ordinary demands of life. DSM-IV identifies three primary classifications of functional psychoses: affective disorders, schizophrenia, and paranoid states.

1. **Affective Disorders** are characterized by exaggerations of mood, often involving fluctuation between extremes. There are three subclassifications: the manic, the depressive, and the manic-depressive.

- a) The **manic** tends to progress from normal moods to excessive elation, possibly becoming so excited that he/she may explode into violent and unrestrained behavior (i.e. become a *maniac*).
- b) The **depressive** may shift from a normal mood to extreme depression, possibly become suicidal, or even experience a condition of bodily immobility.
- c) The **manic-depressive** *psychotic* or **bipolar** alternates between extreme elation and depression. The manic-depressive cycle varies in length and regularity. Severe character changes may range from despondence, apathy, and listlessness to elation, grandiosity, enthusiasm, and energy, then back to the other extreme again.

2. **Schizophrenia** is the most prevalent *psychosis.* It is characterized by extreme emotional withdrawal and diminished contact with reality. There is a marked deterioration in social behavior, often accompanied by hallucinations, and a split or incompatibility between emotion and behavior (i.e. "split personality").

Schizophrenics appear to have distorted feelings and emotions that render them insensitive to things that would normally be expected to evoke an emotional response. Their conduct, dress, hygiene, and social interactions usually show severe deterioration. They are excessively withdrawn and out of touch with the external world. The hallucinations may involve hearing voices, seeing visions, and/or distortions of normal perceptual experiences.

The DSM-IV classifies ten types of schizophrenic reactions. Making a distinction requires a procedure called *differential diagnosis* which is usually difficult and sometimes unreliable.

3. **Paranoid States** or **paranoid reaction** is a psychosis characterized by serious *delusions* (i.e. false beliefs). These delusions may take many forms. The most common forms of delusions are *persecution* and *grandeur.*

Paranoids demonstrate little impairment of tested intelligence and often maintain good contact with reality with the exception of the limited area(s) of their delusions.

PERSONALITY

The study of personality is a difficult challenge. All psychological knowledge ultimately contributes to the understanding of personality, what shapes it, why and how it differs between individuals, and how it develops and changes throughout life.

The two methods of describing personality involve:

1. **Traits**—enduring characteristics of individuals manifested in consistent ways of behaving in a variety of situations.

2. **Personality Types**—the qualitatively different categories into which personalities may allegedly be divided.

The choice of personality measurement method depends upon the purpose to be served. Measurement techniques have taken a variety of forms: ratings, Q-sorts, rating data, interviews, self-ratings, situational tests, personality inventories, response sets, projective techniques, Rorschach inkblots, thematic apperception tests (TAT), etc. The Minnesota Multiphasic Personality Inventory (MMPI) and the California Psychological Inventory (CPI) are examples of personality measurement methods.

Personality development is subject to a myriad of influences, such as heredity, somatic factors (physical characteristics), childhood experiences, social and cultural determinants. Somatic factors include hormonal levels, sensory acuity, body build, etc., which can influence the rate and direction of the individual's personality development and functioning.

Personality theories are general theories of behavior that attempt to account for a full range of human behavior, thought, and emotion. *Psychodynamic* theories seek to understand personality in terms of mental functions, rather than behavior acts alone. This may involve rational and irrational, conscious and outside of conscious awareness, and/or internal (intrapsychic) conflict and attempted resolution.

Sigmund Freud's theory of psychoanalysis is a theory of personality, a method of therapy, a research tool, and, to some, a philosophical view of life. Freud viewed man as a dynamic system of energies. The personality is composed of three systems:

1. The **id**—that division of the psyche from which blind, instinctual impulses that demand immediate gratification of primitive needs come.

2. The **ego**—that aspect of personality that is in contact with the external world and constitutes what is usually defined as "the self." (Both the *id* and the *superego* affect the **ego** but are theoretically separate concepts).

3. The **superego**—a system within the total personality developed by incorporating parental standards the moral standards of society as perceived by the *ego*.
(See *Psychological Trait Theories* in the *Behavioral Criminology* section of Chapter One).

Freud conceived of the process of personality development as a sequence of psychosexual stages: the *oral stage*, the *anal stage*, and the *phallic stage*.

The **oral stage** involves the desire for nourishment of the senses (hunger, sensual stimulation, etc.). The **anal stage** (second and third years) is that stage where control of defecation is emphasized by the parents and certain personality traits are held to be associated with problems occurring during this period. The **phallic stage** involves an interest (at about age three to five) in pleasure attainable through and associated with the genital organs.

Freud believed psychological maturity is the end result of successful passage through the full sequence of these stages. His associate, Carl Jung, believed that a theory of personality could be enhanced by an understanding of the dreams, myths, and spiritual aspects of one's culture.

PESPECTIVES ON ABNORMAL BEHAVIOR

Throughout history, beliefs about mental disorders have been influenced and characterized by superstition, ignorance, and fear. Popular misconceptions include the beliefs that abnormal behavior is bizarre, that "normal" and "abnormal" behavior are notably different, and that former mental patients are unstable and dangerous. Other misconceptions include the beliefs that mental disorders are shameful, that mental disorders are magical or awe-inspiring, and an exaggerated fear of one's own susceptibility to mental disorders (Coleman, Butcher, and Carson, pp. 10-14).

Several professional fields are concerned with the study of abnormal behavior and mental health. Abnormal psychology has long been concerned with understanding, treating, and preventing abnormal behavior. Clinical psychology is the field that is concerned with the study, assessment, treatment, and prevention of abnormal behavior. Psychiatry is the medical field concerned with abnormal behavior. Social work is concerned with the analysis of social environments and providing services to assist patients with adjustment to family and community settings.

The characteristics of abnormal behavior include deviation from social norms, maladaptation, and classifiable mental disorders.

RESEARCH IN ABNORMAL PSYCHOLOGY

Facts and ideas pertinent to the study of abnormal behavior have resulted from research organized around direct observation and constructs based on inference or hypothesis, sampling and generalization, correlation and causation, methodological constraints, and retrospective and prospective strategies (Coleman, Butcher, and Carson, p. 22). To better understand abnormal psychology it is important to be familiar with the following concepts.

Direct Observation and Constructs involve the observation of behavior and the observation of the effects of unseen phenomena, respectively. Constructs are based inferences or hypotheses.

Sampling and Generalization rely on research studies employing groups of individuals that display roughly equivalent abnormalities. This requires the use of a representative sample comprising a control group and an experimental group.

Correlation and Causation relies on more than mere association of two or more variables as evidence of a causal relationship. Techniques, such as path analysis, statistically account for how variables are related and "predict" one another.

Methodological Constraints rely on the experimental method of controlling all factors that could be a variable, except one which is actively manipulated to test that factor.

Retrospective versus *Prospective Strategies* is an important development in research. "Retrospective" research looks backward from the present, while "prospective" strategies look forward.

MULTIDISCIPLINE VIEWPOINTS

Abnormal psychology draws from a variety of disciplines. The early *biological* viewpoint focused on neurological brain damage as a model for understanding abnormality. This model has limited application, though research in the field of biochemical brain functions show promising results.

The *psychosocial* viewpoint of abnormal behavior is oriented toward psycho-analysis. The *behavioristic* viewpoint, once dominated by psychodynamics, is now a reputable field of cognitive psychology.

The *humanistic* viewpoint focuses on the conditions that maximize superior functioning in individuals. The *interpersonal* viewpoint emphasizes the importance of human personality on social and interpersonal origins. The *sociocultural* viewpoint is an anthropological, multidiscipline perspective.

The etiology of each theoretical perspective is to identify a causal pattern. The primary cause for each disorder is classified in terms of biological factors, psychosocial factors, sociocultural factors, etc.

MALADAPTIVE BEHAVIOR

When overwhelming stress makes the going too tough, even previously stable individuals can break down with temporary or transient psychological problems. This breakdown of adaptive functioning may be sudden and prolonged.

Stressors may involve frustrations, conflicts, and pressures or a combination of these. An individual's stress tolerance is influenced by the perception of the threat and one's external resources and supports. Stress may result in *adjustment disorders* and/or *post-traumatic stress disorders* (PTSD).

In contrast to other types of abnormal behavior, specific problems may be the result of gross structural defects of the brain. Such defects impair the normal physiological functioning of the brain, producing deficiencies in thoughts, feeling, and actions.

Organic disorders may involve *organic symptom syndromes* such as delirium, dementia, amnestic syndrome, hallucinosis, organic delusional syndrome, organic affective syndrome, organic personality syndrome, etc. They may also include *general paresis* (an invasion of the central nervous system), *brain tumor disorders, head injury disorders, senile and presenile dementias, and cerebral arteriosclerosis disorders.*

Mental retardation is also an organic brain dysfunction but is usually given independent classification. Other independently classified disorders are commonly associated with childhood and adolescence, such as attention deficit disorder (ADD), conduct disorders and delinquency, anxiety disorders of childhood and adolescence, pervasive developmental disorders, etc.

NEUROSES: ANXIETY—BASED DISORDERS

Neuroses or **psychoneurosis** disorders include, as previously outlined, a variety of **neurosis** types:

1. Anxiety Neurosis
2. Hysterical Neurosis
3. Phobic Neurosis
4. Obsessive—Compulsive Neurosis
5. Existential Neurosis
6. Other neuroses

Because some researchers believe the concept of a causal pattern and reaction is too theoretical, "neuroses" as a general category was eliminated. The new categories include *anxiety, somatoform,* and *dissociative disorders.* Other researchers, however, still believe there is significant research and clinical evidence to support the theory that anxiety produces inner conflict.

The *neurotic process* involves a severe fear response and inadequate or misdirected attempts to manage and control the painful feelings associated with this anxiety (Coleman, Butcher, and Carson, p. 188). Anxiety is one of the most painful emotions, resembling fear without an identifiable cause.

Dealing with anxiety consumes neurotics, leaving little or no energy or enthusiasm for anything else. Neurotics usually "…have trouble establishing or maintaining satisfying interpersonal relationships, feel vaguely guilty for trying to avoid rather than cope with reality, and are dissatisfied and unhappy with their way of life" (Coleman, Butcher, and Carson, p.189).

Thomas R. Coleman (1974) identified seven characteristics of neurosis:

1. Excessive use of *ego* defense mechanisms.
2. Weak *ego,* associated with low tolerance for stress.
3. Anxiety and fearfulness.
4. Egocentricity or self-centeredness.
5. Stubborn conscious attitudes or lack of open mindedness.
6. Unhappiness.
7. Somatic and psychological symptoms (Coleman, pp. 37-39).

Phobic Neuroses or **disorders** involve persistent fears of objects or situations that are of no real danger or are out of proportion to it's actual seriousness. Such phobias include:

Acrophobia—high places.
Agoraphobia—open places.
Algophobia—pain.
Astraphobia—storms, thunder, and lightning.
Claustrophobia—closed places.
Hematophobia—blood.
Monophobia—being alone.
Mysophobia—contamination or germs.
Nyctophobia—darkness.
Ocholophobia—crowds.
Pathophobia—disease.
Pyrophobia—fire.
Syphilophabia—syphilis.
Zoophobia—animals or some particular animal (Coleman, Butcher, and Carson, p. 204).

Obsessive-Compulsive Neurosis involves thoughts, actions, or feelings the individual cannot control. An obsession is a preoccupation with something. A compulsion is an impulse that is irresistible. (Obsessive—Compulsive Disorders are a less severe Personality Disorder).

Somatoform Disorders relate to anxiety—based neurotic patterns in which the individual complains of bodily symptoms for which no organic reason can be found. One form of **somatization disorder** is **hypochodriasis**, which is character-ized by multiple complaints of illness.

Psychogenic pain disorder is characterized by reported severe, long-lasting pain with no physical cause or exaggerated complaints.

Conversion Disorder or **hysteria** is a neurotic pattern with symptoms of phys-ical malfunction or loss of control lacking any organic pathology. Any one of the senses can be affected by *sensory conversion reactions.* The most common of the sensory symptoms are:

Anethesia—loss of sensitivity.
Hypesthesia—partial loss of sensitivity.
Hyperesthesia—excessive sensitivity.
Analgesia—loss of sensitivity to pain.
Paresthesia—exceptional sensations, such as tingling (Coleman, Butcher, and Carson, p. 213).

Dissociative Disorders are ways of avoiding stress while gratifying needs in a way that denies personal responsibility for unacceptable behavior. This denial is an escape from stress by dissociating.

Multiple Personality is a dissociative reaction, usually due to stress, in which the individual displays two or more personalities. Each personality system has distinct emotional and thought processes. The individual may change from one personality to another over periods ranging from minutes to years. Various relationships may exist between the various personalities and when alternating between them the individual does not remember what happened while in another personality.

Depersonalization Disorder involves a "loss of the sense of self." The individual may believe that they are someone else or report an "out of body experience." Such experiences may be the result of acute stress involving a toxic illness, an accident, or a traumatic event (Coleman, Butcher, and Carson, p. 222).

Russell and Beigel note that while personality disorders are generally characterized by maladaptive behavior patterns that evolve throughout life, neurotics constitute a group whose abnormal behavior is more commonly characterized by episodic anxiety or depression. Neurotics, they observe, are not divorced from reality as are psychotics. They are merely unable to resolve their conflicts and develop neurotic symptoms as a result (Russell and Beigel, p. 70).

Personality disorders result from aberrations in the developmental process that influence patterns of "perceiving, relating to, and thinking about the environment and the self" (Russell and Beigel, p. 61).

PERSONALITY DISORDERS AND CRIME

Coleman, Butcher, and Carson say that the developmental process is in a continuous state of change throughout one's life. Healthy adjustment through the entire cycle is, they say, "…a matter of flexibly adapting to changing demands, opportunities, and limitations" at each stage of life (Coleman, Butcher, and Carson, p. 233).

Traits, coping styles, and ways of interacting in social environments are representative of individuals' **personality**. For most of us compliance with societal expectations and demands is normal. For others, personality formation is warped, making them ill-equipped to be a functioning member of society (Coleman, Butcher, and Carson, p. 233).

Personality disorders or **character disorders** are a product of immature and distorted personality development. Maladaptive perceptions, thinking, and relation to the world impair functioning and result in subjective distress.

Most individuals with personality disorders do not demonstrate obvious mental disorders, therefore these categories are among the most misdiagnosed.

While earlier categories discussed *obsessive-compulsive, hysterical personality,* and *psychopathic/antisocial* personality disorders, Coleman, Butcher, and Carson group them as follows:

Cluster I—*Paranoid, Schizoid,* and *Schizotypal;*
Cluster II—*Histrionic, Narcissistic, Antisocial,* and *Borderline;*
Cluster III—*Avoidant, Dependent, Compulsive* and *Passive-Aggressive*
(Coleman, Butcher, and Carson, p. 237)

Paranoid Personality Disorder is generally characterized by suspicious, hypersensitive, rigid, envious, and argumentative tendencies. Persons with this disorder also tend to hold themselves blameless for their mistakes and failures, blaming others instead (Coleman, Butcher, and Carson, p. 237).

Schizoid Personality Disorder is associated with a lack of genuinely relating to others and apathy (Turkat, p. 52). Individuals with this disorder seem unable to form social relationships and have no apparent interest in doing so. They lack social skills, are unable to express their feelings, and are viewed as cold, distant, loners.

Schizotypal Personality Disorders are characterized by odd thoughts, appearance, and behavior and are viewed as "a less severe but genetically related form of schizophrenia" (Turkat, p. 55). Individuals with this disorder are "seclusive, oversensitive, and eccentric…" (Coleman, Butcher, and Carson, p. 239).

Histrionic Personality Disorder is associated with patterns of immaturity, excitability, emotional instability, the need for excitement, and attention-seeking dramatization. Sexual adjustment and interpersonal relationships are poor.

Narcissistic Personality Disorder involves exaggerated self-importance and the need for attention. It is also characterized by an inability to share others' perspectives.

Antisocial Personality Disorder refers synonymously to *antisocial personalities, psychopaths,* and *sociapaths*. This disorder is associated with aggressive, antisocial behavior without remorse or loyalty for anyone. This will be discussed in greater detail later.

Borderline Personality Disorder is sometimes associated with both personality disorders and affective disorders (psychosis). This is the source of the definition "*borderline*." Here behavior is characterized by instability, dramatic mood swings, and behavior problems, such as unprovoked outbursts.

Avoidant Personality Disorder is characterized by hypersensitivity to rejection or social derogation. The fear of criticism prevents meaningful social relationships, despite a strong desire for affection.

Dependent Personality Disorder is characterized by an extreme dependence on other people and a fear of being alone. Affected individuals usually build their lives around others to keep them involved with them.

Compulsive Personality Disorder involves excessive concern for rules, order, efficiency, and work, along with an insistence that everyone do likewise. It is also characterized by a lack of warm feelings and difficulty relaxing.

Passive-Aggressive Personality Disorders is usually expressed through indirect, nonviolent hostility, such as procrastinating, pouting, "forgetting," stubbornness, intentional inefficiency, or obstructionism. Individuals with this disorder resent and resist the demands of others. Resentment of authority and a lack of assertiveness are typical.

CRIMINAL BEHAVIOR

Serious crime is an extreme form of "acting out" against others or society in general. Causal factors of criminal behavior have been thought to include pervasive personal pathologies, pathogenic family and peer patterns, and sociocultural factors that foster antisocial behavior.

Biological factors (heredity) have been the basis for a variety of theories ranging from stigmatizing features to phrenology. More recent theories include the possibility that criminal behavior is associated with men of the XYY chromosomal type (the "extra Y chromosome) (Coleman, Butcher, and Carson, p. 260).

Personal and Family pathology (antisocial personality, alcoholism, and drug dependence) are associated strongly with those who commit serious crimes. Borderline and psychotic personalities also make up a disproportionate group of criminals, while others come from dysfunctional families characterized by parental rejection and inconsistent punishment.

Sociocultural influences involve the values and attitudes individuals are exposed to. Factors such as low social class or socioeconomic level may also be associated with developmental psychological problems. Viewing violence on television or in movies is also thought to influence aggression, particularly in children with a predisposition to engage in violent behavior.

PSYCHOPATHY AND ANTISOCIAL PERSONALITY

Psychopaths are characterized by a "stunning lack of conscience" and self-gratification at the expense of others (Hare, p.1). Nathaniel J. Pallone says that criminologists frequently "disdain the fine conceptual discriminations made" by psychologists and psychiatrists, arguing that psychopathic behavior should be regarded as social deviance, rather than a mental illness, as indicated by "real-time data on criminal offending" (Schlesinger, p.195).

The term *psychopath* has been controversial and used to describe a range of attitudinal, emotional, and behavioral characteristics. In 1930 G.E. Patridge considered *psychopathy* a social, rather than mental, maladjustment and proposed the term *sociopath*. The American Psychiatric Association adopted this term in 1952, but again changed the label in 1968 to **antisocial** *personality disorder* (ASP) (Bartol, p. 58).

In 1970 Dr. Robert Hare suggested a clarification of the term *psychopath* by outlining three categories: the **primary psychopath,** the **secondary psychopath,** and the **dyssocial psychopaths** (Bartol, p. 58).

Only the *primary psychopath* is a "true" psychopath. The primary psychopath is distinguished from secondary or neurotic psychopaths in behavioral, cognitive, and neurophysiological features. He or she is neither neurotic, psychotic, nor emotionally disturbed (Bartol, pp. 58-9).

Secondary psychopaths commit *antisocial* or violent acts because of severe emotional problems or inner conflicts. They are often referred to as "acting-out neurotics, neurotic delinquents, symptomatic psychopaths, or simply neurotic characters" (Bartol, p.58).

Dyssocial psychopaths display aggressive, *antisocial* behavior that has been learned from their subculture, such as family or gangs. Both secondary and dyssocial psychopaths are incorrectly called psychopaths, Bartol says, because of their high recidivism rates (Bartol, p. 58).

Criminologists and sociologists predominantly use the term *sociopath* to identify repetitive offenders who do not respond appropriately to treatment, rehabilitation, or incarceration. Psychiatrists and psychologists predominantly use the term *antisocial personality disorder* to identify offenders who fail to conform to social norms, such as unlawful behavior. The term *criminal psychopath* has been used to identify *primary psychopaths* who engage in repetitive antisocial or criminal behavior (Bartol, pp. 58-9).

Dr. Hare and two of his graduate students conducted an experiment using a biomedical recorder to monitor electrical activity in the brains of several groups of men while they performed a language task. Recordings were traced on an electroencephalogram (EEG). They were surprised to find that the readings did not resemble human brain activity. These individuals were identified as psychopaths. They were characterized by a "stunning" lack of conscience and dominated by self-gratification at the expense of others (Hare, p.1).

Daniel A. Martell notes that the *neurobehavioral* components of violence and criminality are becoming increasingly important to forensic behavioral science. Though there is great divergence between clinical experience and empirical evidence, research seems to clearly indicate a significant influence of brain damage and dysfunction on violent and criminal behavior (Schlesinger, p.170).

Martell writes:

> Most of the research on the brain and violence or criminality can be organized under four broad headings: (1) studies documenting the prevalence of brain abnormalities in various criminal and forensic populations; (2) correctional and group-difference studies associating brain impairment with violent behavior in criminal and forensic populations; (3) studies showing the incidence of violent and/or criminal behavior in populations of individuals with specific neurobehavioral disorders; and (4) localization studies that attempt to isolate specific brain sites in which lesions may produce violent behavior.
> (Schlesinger, p.170).

There is at this time, however, no conclusive indication of the cause(s) of psychopathy, antisocial behavior, or the criminal behavior of sociopaths. Hare reports that there are conservatively at least 2 million psychopaths in North America and approximately 100,000 in New York City alone (Hare, p. 2).

Hare also reports that the prevalence of psychopathy in our society is about the same as that of schizophrenia. He says that though many psychopaths are criminals, many others stay out of prison using their charm and "chamelonlike abilities" (Hare, p.2). Unlike Schizophrenics and psychotics, however, psychopaths are neither delusional, nor out of touch with their behavior.

Psychopaths consider the rules and expectations of society unreasonable inconveniences and obstructions to the expression of their desires. They are impulsive, deceitful, and make their own rules. Childhood antisocial behavior has been shown in research to be indicative of life-long psychopathic behavioral traits (Hare, pp. 67-8).

PSYCHOSIS AND THE PSYCHOTIC PERSONALITY

Individuals who experience gross distortions of reality are referred to a "psychotic" and such distortions are classified as psychoses or a psychosis. Extreme pressure of "the emotional forces deranges the orderly operations of the mind, the memory, reason, and the grasp of reality…" which causes disorientation to time and place, illusions, delusions, and hallucinations (Saul and Warner, p.9).

Saul and Warner categorize eight types of *psychotic personality disorder* (PPD): 1) diffuse, 2) regressive withdrawal, 3) hostile, 4) schizoid, 5) paranoid, 6) depressive, 7) criminoid, and 8) criminal (Saul and Warner, p.40).

Because psychoses take many forms while having commonalities, described above, psychotic personalities also take many forms. The basic psychodynamics and diagnostic characteristics of psychotic personalities are not always readily identifiable.

Two essential dynamics of psychotic personalities are the direction of reason, rationality, and sense of reality and the *diffusion* of the psychotic dynamics throughout the personality (thinking, feeling, and behavior). Two of the PPD (*psychotic personality disorder*) types require further discussion.

The **criminoid** personality is characterized by "committing crimes *within* the law" or having goals that are infantile, irrational, hostile, and paranoid (Saul and Warner, p.161). Criminoids are further characterized by self-love, self-absorption, a rigid superego, and prudish, self-defined sense of "morality." Infantile fixation and intolerance for human closeness are also descriptive of the criminoid.

The *criminal personality* involves "the three D's"—deprivation, domination, and depreciation—and is characterized by impatience, irritation, overcontrol, domination, physical violence, hostility, and cruelty (Saul and Warner, p. 33). Such psychotic personalities may become incorrigible criminals.

Though the term "incorrigible criminal" stems from legal and moral roots, rather than a psychodynamic understanding of human personality, it accurately describes the extreme PPD (psychotic personality disorder) that is situated in the vague areas between neurosis, psychosis, and criminality.

To give a comparative description, repressed hostilities that cause physical symptoms are categorized as psychosomatic or a *neurosis*, while those that result in a break down of orderly socialized functioning is referenced as *psychotic*. If such hostility is acted out in criminal, antisocial behavior, then *criminality* would be an accurate description.

Though the causes of psychotic disorders are unknown, they are characterized by disturbances in thinking, thought content, perception, judgment, mood, emotions, and regression. It is uncertain whether these are of organic or functional origin (Russell and Beigel, pp 93-94).

CONCLUSION

An understanding of abnormal psychology begins with an understanding of human origins, growth and development. Ones heredity and environment are factors in the complex psychological makeup of individuals. Genetic factors, beginning with the DNA molecules, is the starting point of human development.

Language, linguistics, perceptions, motivation, and emotions are all components of human behavioral makeups. An understanding of these components is essential to an analysis of conflict and aggression. Such conflict and aggression often leads to abnormal behavior and even violence.

Abnormal behavior results from mental disorders and behavioral pathology. Functional disorders include neurosis, personality disorders, and psychosis.

The relationship between personality disorders and crime are very important to the fields of criminology and forensic psychology. A better understanding of the criminal mind and associated abnormal behavior may help criminal justice and mental health professionals prevent or solve crime and rehabilitate or treat offenders.

Understanding abnormal psychology helps prepare us to better understand the criminal mind and to profile criminal behavior. It is particularly important to understand psychopaths and psychotics and the differences between them.

REFERENCES—CHAPTER 3

Bortol, Curt R. **Criminal Behavior: A Psychosocial Approach** (Fourth Edition). Englewood Cliffs, NJ: Prentice-Hall, 1995.

Coleman, James C., James N. Butcher, and Robert C. Carson. **Abnormal Psychology and Modern Life** (Seventh Edition). Glenview, IL: Scott, Foresman and Company, 1984.

Coleman, Thomas R. **Abnormal Psychology**. New York, NY: MSS Information Corporation, 1974.

Hare, Robert D. **Without Conscience: The Disturbing World of the Psychopaths Among Us**. New York, NY: The Guilford Press, 1993.

Russell, Harold E., and Allen Beigel. **Understanding Human Behavior for Effective Police Work** (Third Edition). New York, NY: Basic Books, 1990.

Saul, Leon J., and Silas L. Warner. **The Psychotic Personality**. New York, NY: Van Nostrand Reinhold Company, 1982.

Schlesinger, Louis B. (Editor). **Explorations in Clinical Psychopathology: Clinical Syndromes with Forensic Implications**. Springfield, IL: Charles C. Thomas Publisher, 1996.

Turkat, Ira Daniel. **The Personality Disorders: A Psychological Approach to Clinical Management**. New York, NY: Pergamon Press, 1990.

Chapter 4
Forensic Psychology

INTRODUCTION

Forensic psychology is the psychology of legal matters and issues. This includes both civil and criminal legal matters, but is more commonly associated with criminal law and jurisprudence.

To the general public, forensic psychology is commonly associated with *police psychology* where astute sleuths deduce crimes and outwit criminals. Police psychology is a subdivision of forensic psychology and is further divided into specialty areas, such as interviewing and interrogation, forensic hypnosis, criminal profiling, and those techniques used in daily police operations.

Forensic psychology is also of interest to attorneys, psychologists, and psychiatrists who are concerned with *competency* and other courtroom issues.

Forensic psychology also deals with *criminal behavior* (the criminal mind) and the treatment, rehabilitation, and correction of criminals. Correctional forensic psychology also involves the diagnostic classification of incarcerated offenders.

Forensic psychology is of value in both civil and criminal practice. The emphasis here will be on criminal practice, police operations, and criminal behavior.

POLICE PSYCHOLOGY

Police psychology deals with interviewing and interrogation, forensic hypnosis, criminal profiling, and operational aspects of police work. This also involves hostage negotiations, stress management, and other specialty areas.

Other experimental and controversial areas of study include "backward masking" truth detection, scientific content analysis (SCAN) linguistic truth detection, voice stress analysis, and polygraph examination.

The study of human relations seeks to understand how to interact with others, why individuals respond the ways they do, and what personality is and how it develops. This study ranges from public relations and crowd control to the more advanced subject listed above.

Psychology as a whole uses four main classifications of investigative techniques. *Experimental* findings are controlled laboratory studies which remove "extraneous variables." *Clinical* studies are based on information gained from patient interviews, but not under lab conditions. *Naturalistic observation* makes observations of individuals and events in their natural environment to arrive at facts or hypotheses. *Statistics* aid in the classification of facts and summarizes trends (Wicks, pp. 15-16).

A *nomothetic* approach to rating human behavior attempts to describe characteristics for all individuals and rate them on a single scale. An *idiographic* approach measures only the characteristics unique to each individual in order to evaluate them (Wicks, p. 17).

INTERVIEWING AND INTERROGATION

Interviewing is the process of gathering information with the goal of purposeful communications (Wicks, p. 114). *Interrogation* is also a method of gathering information and is a form of interviewing. Its methodology differs in regard to its purpose and who employs it. An interrogation seeks to illicit an admission or to clarify or elaborate upon certain facts. It has a specific goal (Wicks, p. 133).

Don Rabon suggests the difference between the interview and the interrogation is determined by the willingness of the subject (Rabon, 1992, p. 6). Various strategies exist to move a subject from "unwilling" to "willing" and influence the actions of the subject (Rabon, 1992, p. 8). As agents of this change we not only mani pulate individuals into desired behavior but do so in a manner that would withstand scrutiny and evaluation and even be met with approval (Rabon, 1992, p. 14).

Prior to an interrogation the interrogator should become familiar with all known facts and circumstances of the incident in question (Inbau and Reid, p. 13). The interrogator/investigator should project an attitude of truth seeking, avoid overt note taking, and use milder, less realistic words (Inbau and Reid, pp. 17-18) that the subject can better deal with.

The interrogation environment should have no psychological barriers (tables, desk, etc. between interrogator and subject). The interrogator should remain close, seated, avoid smoking and "fumbling with a pencil, pen, or other room accessories" (Inbau and Reid, pp. 18-19).

The interrogator should adapt his or her language to that used and understood by the subject. The subject should be treated with decency and respect (Inbau and Reid, p. 20). When catching a subject in a lie, do not scold or reprimand, but convey the impression that it was known all along that the subject was not telling the truth. Occupy a fearless position and face the subject "man to man." Think in terms of what you would be thinking and remember the subject will probably react as you would (Inbau and Reid, pp. 22-23).

Inbau and Reid categorize interrogation subjects as: 1.) *emotional offenders* who have committed crimes against persons, such as heat of passion, anger, revenge, and accidental/negligent offenses and 2.) *non-emotional offenders* who have committed crimes for profit, such as theft, burglary, robbery, or killings and injuries for financial gain (Inbau and Reid, p. 25).

Inbau and Reid suggest that the most effective tactics and techniques to use with *emotional offenders* involve the *sympathetic approach*. For *non-emotional offenders*, a *factual analysis* that appeals to the subject's common sense and reasoning is recommended. The latter convinces the subject that guilt is already established or soon will be (Inbau and Reid, pp. 25-26).

Zulawski and Wicklander identify three methods of interrogation:

1. **Good Guy/Bad Guy Approach** (commonly known as "good cop/bad cop") which they consider ineffective due to movie and television exposure, unprofessional employment, and potential for allegations of intimidation and coercion (Zulawski and Wicklander, p. 2).

2. **Factual Approach** (associated with *non-emotional offenders)* which requires extensive preparation and investigation. Zulawski and Wicklander feel this is ineffective because the known facts from the investigation are often not sufficient to counter the suspects' explanations or stories and may lack the inclusion of "rationalization" (Zulawski and Wicklander, p. 2).

3. **Emotional Approach** (associated with emotional offenders) in which the subject is confronted, not with the circumstances or details, but with the *reasons why* the subject did what he did. Zulawski and Wicklander write, "It is here that the interrogator rationalizes with the suspect by offering reasons or excuses that allow the suspect to save face while admitting his involvement in the incident" (Zulawski and Wicklander, p. 3).

Zulawski and Wicklander emphasize the *emotional approach* and assert that it is effective with "all but the most street-hardened individuals." By incorporating *factual* components (sometimes called a combined approach), the interrogator establishes credibility to the investigation and reduces suspect resistance. Even when using the *factual approach*, using rationalizations to justify and minimize the seriousness of the suspects' involvement helps (Zulawski and Wicklander, p. 3).

Inbau and Reid make a number of suggestions for interviews and interrogations:

1. Display an air of confidence in the subject's guilt (Inbau and Reid, p. 26).
2. Point out some, but by no means all, of the circumstantial evidence indicative of a subject's guilt (Inbau and Reid, p. 31).
3. Call attention to the subject's physiological and psychological symptoms of Guilt (destroy or minimize the suspect's confidence) (Inbau and Reid, pp. 33-38).

4. Sympathize with the subject by telling him that anyone else under similar conditions or circumstances might have done the same thing (particularly the *emotional* offender) (Inbau and Reid, p. 38).

5. Reduce the subject's guilt feeling by minimizing the moral seriousness of his (or her) offense (Inbau and Reid, p. 40).

6. Suggest a less revolting and more morally acceptable motivation or reason for the offense than that which is known or presumed (accident, intoxication, self-defense, for another's benefit, etc. to save face) (Inbau and Reid, pp. 43-47).

7. Sympathize with the subject by
   a) condemning the victim,
   b) condemning the accomplice, or
   c) condemning anyone else upon whom some degree of moral responsibility might conceivably be placed for the commission of the crime (Inbau and Reid, p. 47).

8. Utilize displays of understanding and sympathy in urging the subject to tell the truth (Inbau and Reid, p. 59).

9. Point out the possibility of exaggeration on the part of the accuser or victim or exaggerate the nature and seriousness of the offense itself (Inbau and Reid, p.64).

10. Have the subject place himself at the scene of the crime or in some sort of contact with the victim or the occurrence; if the suspect makes an *admission*, a *confession* may not be far off (Inbau and Reid, p. 70).

11. Seek an admission of lying about some incidental aspect of the occurrence; thereafter as the suspect attempts to assure his/her truthfulness he/she can be reminded that he/she was not telling the truth before (Inbau and Reid, p. 71)

12. Appeal to the subject's pride by well-selected flattery or by a challenge to his/her honor; it is a basic human trait to seek and enjoy the approval of others (Inbau and Reid, p. 73).

13. Point out the futility of resistance to telling the truth; not only convince the subject that his/her guilt has been detected, but that it can be established by currently available evidence (Inbau and Reid, p. 77).

14. Point out to the subject the grave consequences and futility of a continuation of his/her criminal behavior (Inbau and Reid, p. 77).

15. Rather than seek a general admission of guilt, first ask the subject a question regarding some detail of the offense or inquire about the reason for its commission (Inbau and Reid, p. 79).

16. When co-offenders are being interrogated and the previously described techniques have been ineffective, play one against the other (Inbau and Reid, p. 84).

Inbau and Reid suggest special techniques for interrogating **suspects whose guilt is uncertain**. These include:

1. Ask the subject if he/she knows why he/she is being questioned (Inbau and Reid, p. 94).
2. Ask the subject to relate all he/she knows about the occurrence, the victim, and possible suspects (Inbau and Reid, p. 95).
3. Obtain from the subject detailed information about his/her activities before, at the time or, and after the occurrence in question (Inbau and Reid, p. 94).
4. Where certain facts suggestive of the subject's guilt are known, ask him/her about them rather casually and as though the real facts were not already known (Inbau and Reid, p. 101).
5. At various intervals ask the subject certain pertinent questions in a manner which implies that the correct answers are already known (Inbau and Reid, p.102).
6. Refer to some non-existing incriminating evidence to determine whether the subject will attempt to explain it away; if he/she does, that fact is suggestive of guilt (Inbau and Reid, p. 103).
7. Ask the subject whether he/she ever "thought" about committing the offense or one similar to it. If the subject "thought" about committing the offense, this may be suggestive of guilt (Inbau and Reid, p. 104).
8. If a suspect offers to make restitution in theft cases, it is indicative of guilt (innocent persons will not agree to pay any part of it back); ask about paying back another, fictitious, lesser loss (the suspect will probably refuse) (Inbau and Reid, p. 106).
9. Ask the subject whether he is willing to take a lie-detector test. The innocent person will almost always agree to prove his/her innocence but the guilty person is more likely to refuse, find excuses not to take it, or back out of it (Inbau and Reid, p. 106).
10. A subject who tells the interrogator, "All right, I'll tell you what you want, but I didn't do it," is probably guilty. A guilty person may attempt to placate the interrogator by expressing a willingness to admit the offense while still denying that he/she committed it (Inbau and Reid, p. 108).

Interviewing

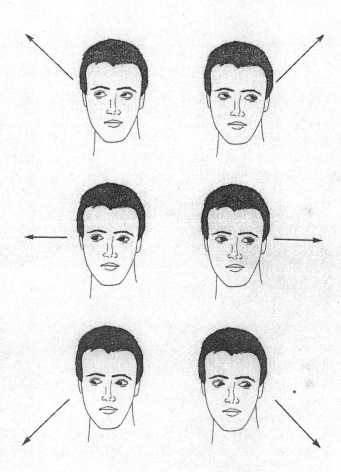

(Top left) Individual is creating visually. (Top right) Individual is recalling visually something that he actually experienced. (Middle left) Creating an auditory memory. (Middle right) Recalling sounds actually experienced. (Bottom left) Kinesic or touch position. (Bottom right) Internal dialogues, getting in touch with one's feelings.

Reprinted with permission of CRC Press

Interviewing and Interrogation

Channel Eye Movements

VISUAL MEMORY:

VISUAL CONSTRUCTION:

Reprinted with permission of Carolina Academic Press

Rapport: The Foundation Process

Auditory Memory:

Auditory Construction

Reprinted with permission of Carolina Academic Press

Rapport: The Foundation Process

FEELING:

Reprinted with permission of Carolina Academic Press

Zulawski and Wicklander identify seven parts of the *interview and interrogation process:*

- Preparation and Strategy.
- Interviewing—nonaccusatory fact gathering:
  - a.) **cognitive interviewing**, which is a method of enhancing witness recollection and
  - b.) **selective interviewing**, which is a means of evaluating the truthfulness of potential witnesses or suspects (e.g. *neurolinguistics*).
- Establishing Credibility (interrogation of the guilty suspect and convincing him/her that he/she has been clearly identified as the perpetrator).
- Reducing Resistance (interdiction of emphatic and explanatory denials).
- Obtaining the Admission (move from behavioral submission with *rationalizations* to an admission).
- Developing the Admission into an acceptable confession.
- Professional Close—the written statement and treatment of the suspect (Inbau and Reid, pp. 7-11)

Don Rabon suggests that "people tend to communicate in the language of the senses." He writes, "Our language usage will reflect the vocabulary of the five senses. However, we usually tend to think in one of three senses: sight, hearing, or touch." He says that in order to establish rapport it is necessary to communicate on the same channel or in the same sensory language (Rabon, 1992, p. 17).

Rabon says that while the subject's terminology provides insight into the dominant sensory mode, there are terms that are neutral. Because the eyes are the "windows to the soul," there are corresponding eye movements and positions for each of the senses of sight, hearing, and touch. The eye movements, therefore, are revealing of sensory mode of neutral terms (Rabon, 1992, p. 25).

When subjects recover data stored in *visual memory* there are eye-movement patterns that correspond to "visual" vocabulary (Rabon, 1992, p. 25). Rabon writes that in response to a visual question ("look back" and "show me") visually oriented subjects "should display one or both of a pair of eye-movement patterns" indicative of visual memory processing:

- the eyes move upward and to the subject's left and
- the eyes look straight ahead.

When the subject begins to speak "he looks straight ahead and then his eyes move upward and to his left" (Rabon, 1992, p. 27).

Rabon says that in this case the subject's eye movement to that *spatial quadrant* allows the mind to recover visually stored data. The subject is recalling a past event that is remembered visually (Rabon, 1992, p. 27).

Visual construction is the building of an image. The subject constructs (builds) the suggested image, evaluates what he/she sees, and then answers the question. "The corresponding eye movements for a visually oriented person," writes Rabon, "would most likely be looking upward and then to his right." Because the event has not occurred, it must be constructed (Rabon, 1992, p. 27).

Watch for visual memory processing and vocabulary that corresponds to the eye movements. Watch for visual construction. Watch for *changes* in speech patterns and the employment of "false sounds," such as "uh...let's see...uh." Finally, watch for a "qualifier" such as "that's about it" (Rabon, 1992, pp. 28-29).

Auditory eye movements indicate a subject is remembering sounds and are indicated by a) both eyes down and to the left or b) horizontally to the left. When the eyes are down and to the left, the subject is remembering what he/she has heard or *external sounds*. Eyes horizontally to the left indicate *internal sounds* (what the subject thought or said) (Rabon, 1992, p. 31-32).

Sensation eye movements involve the "feeling" or "sensation channel." Eye patterns associated with emotion or sensation are eyes

- down,
- down and to the right,
- eyes closing, and
- eyes fluttering or blinking rapidly

(Rabon, 1992, p. 34). The investigator or interrogator should use the vocabulary of sensation to encourage the subject. While no eye patterns are consistently associated with feeling or sensation construction, it is possible to identify changes in speech patterns, qualifiers, and hedges (Rabon, 1992, pp. 36-37).

While there is no single behavioral clue that is a reliable indicator of truth or deception, behavior symptoms do not occur by chance and have meaningful clues about truthfulness. *Verbal* communication (spoken words, the choice of words, tone of voice, and speed) and *Nonverbal* communication (facial expressions, body position, posture, movements, gestures, etc.) are the two styles of communication behavior.

Nonverbal communication accounts for 55 to 65% of communication between persons, while 39 to 40% involves the tone and less than 10 % actually involves spoken words (Zulawski and Wicklander, p. 52). There are six **rules for evaluating behavior:**

1. Evaluate the suspect against himself—identify behavior norms or a baseline for the subject;
2. Evaluate the suspect's behavior against that of the average population—what most people would do under similar circumstances;
3. Evaluate behavior in the context of the situation or circumstances;
4. Behavior clusters are more likely to be valid;
5. Interviewer behavior should not project his/her beliefs or disbeliefs to a subject;
6. Evaluate behavior based on their timing and consistency in relation to a stressful question (Zulawski and Wicklander, pp. 54-58)

The entire body must be considered when observing and interpreting nonverbal behavior. The body is divided into zones:

- the trunk, shoulders, and posture,
- hand and arm positions,
- leg and feet positions,
- head and neck positions,
- mouth positions,
- the nose, and
- eye movements.

Truthful people usually make good eye contact and are able to maintain eye contact when asked emotional questions. However, many liars recognize that poor eye contact is an indicator of deception. Eye contact may also be broken by closing the eyes or placing a hand over the face when making a denial. Deceptive subjects may turn their entire head to look away (Zulawski and Wicklander, pp. 90-91).

Verbal communication involves both the verbal quality and verbal content. *Verbal quality* communicates the emotional state of an individual and includes the voice pitch, volume, rate of speech, and clarity (Walters, p. 17). Tension or stress can be revealed by a change in the pitch of a subject's voice or a cracking of the voice (Walters, p. 18).

The interviewer must determine a "baseline" to determine the subject's general rate of speech. Additionally, *speech dysfunctions* are "speech dysfluencies" or errors that represent uncharacteristic speech flaws that indicate stress. This is more prevalent in deceptive subjects who are under stress (Walters, p. 19).

The "baseline" is necessary to identify groups or clusters of symptoms for more reliable analysis. Responses include:

1. **Anger**—*focused anger*, which is an open frontal attack on the interviewer, victim, or witness, and *covert anger*, which is conducted on an intellectual level to attack case facts (Walters, pp. 23-25).
2. **Depression**—aggression is focused inward or reflected back onto the subject (Walters, p. 27).
3. **Denial**—the subject's effort to reject reality through *memory lapses, denial flag expressions, weighted expressions, modifiers* (but, however, etc.), *guilt phrases, blocking statements, bridging phrases, vocabulary shifting, displacement, stalling maneuvers, specific denials,* and/or *deceptive "No's"* (Walters, pp. 28-39).
4. **Bargaining**—manipulation that permits the selling of "substitute solutions;" this includes the subjects *complaining for sympathy,* use of *substitute words gray statements* (vague), *religious statements* and *personal moral statements, overly courteous* or polite behavior, and *name dropping* (Walters, pp. 40-47).
5. **Acceptance**—the point where subjects no longer deny the reality of events. This is indicated by a.) *"buy out" statements*, which indicate a desire by the suspect to by their way out of the problem, b.) *fantasy— reality statements*, which are comments that indicate acceptance of reality that a crime has occurred, and c.) *punishment statements*, which involve inquiries about penalties or punishments (Walters, pp. 47-51).
    Other verbal behavior includes unsolicited, premature excuses or explanations, uncheckable sources, focusing on irrelevant points, delays, verbal slips, etc. (Zulawski and Wicklander, pp. 95-107).

Rabon writes that it is critical to understand the subject's motivational process, rationalization process, and thought process for making choices (Rabon, 1992, p. 54). The *persuasion process* involves moving the subject from being unwilling to being willing in a manner that will withstand scrutiny (Rabon, 1992, p. 99).

FORENSIC HYPNOSIS

Another method or tool of forensic psychology is *forensic hypnosis*. Forensic hypnosis is the use of the psychological tool of hypnosis for legal purposes or those dealing in civil and criminal law and jurisprudence. To understand forensic hypnosis it is first essential to understand the mind and how the brain functions.

The brain, which weighs about 3.5 pounds, is a electro-chemical system, which produces electricity by "burning" sugar. Its 10-12 billion cells can store and process 10-quadrillion facts, ideas, images and items of information. The brain is divided into three basic systems: 1. the **sensory input** from the senses, 2. the **modulation or**

control system which evaluates information (incoming, outgoing, memories, and experiences), and 3. the **motor output system** (Reiser, p. 7).

Normal wakefulness is characterized by **beta** waves with a frequency of 18-30 cycles per second. **Alpha** waves of 7-13 cycles per second are associated with relaxation, which can be consciously controlled with biofeedback techniques. **Theta** waves of 4-8 cycles per second are associated with "an introspective, restful state conductive to creativity." Electroencephalograph tracings during hypnosis are similar to the waking state (beta) (Reiser, p. 8).

The **left hemisphere** of the brain deals with logical thinking processes involving language (except in the case of most left-handers). It processes information in an orderly, *sequential* manner, one bit after another. The **right hemisphere** specializes in *simultaneous* processing of holistic, relational information, including meditation, intuition, imagery, art and creativity (Reiser, p. 8). Information is recorded in the temporal cortex of each hemisphere.

The mind is made up of the *conscious mind,* which contains about one-eighth of the mind's total capacity, and the *subconscious mind,* which contains the remaining seven-eighths. The conscious mind involves cognitive functions and external reality using logic and reason. The subconscious (*preconscious* and *unconscious*) controls the sympathetic division of the autonomic nervous system (involuntary muscles, organs, glands, and metabolism) (Reiser, p. 11).

Hypnotic induction begins with rapport building and the pre-induction orientation. Induction techniques include eye fixation or direct suggestion for eye closure, breath and muscle relaxation methods through progressive tensing and relaxation of specific muscle groups. Dr. Martin Reiser suggests the following methods:

- Traditional eye-fixation method,
- hand-levitation technique,
- relaxation technique,
- Chiasson's technique (using the subject's hand 12 inches from his nose as the focal point),
- Spiegel eye roll-levitation technique (simulating a floating experience through breath control, relaxation, and concentration),
- imagery of "going deeper" via an elevator, escalator, or stairs (Reiser, pp. 52-56)

Hypnosis has military, intelligence, therapeutic, clinical, educational and other uses. Because it includes increased susceptibility to suggestion, it must be used carefully and without biased leading in forensic practice. Legal issues must be considered as they currently exist in the practitioner's area.

Forensic hypnosis can be a valuable tool, particularly when used in conjunction with a composite artist or compu-sketch (generically) operator. The field of forensic hypnosis is a comprehensive study in the broader topic of forensic psychology.

TRUTH DETECTION (POLYGRAPH AND VOICE STRESS ANALYSIS)

Two major methods of *truth detection,* or more accurately *deception detection,* are the **polygraph** (commonly referred to as a "lie detector") and the **voice stress analysis** (VSA) test. The polygraph measures four to six points of stress during "yes" and "no" questions, including pulse, blood pressure, breathing, and galvanic skin response. The voice stress analysis tests measures only one—a stressful change in the voice pattern.

Both test (polygraph and VSA) measure stress responses. Each requires careful analysis by highly trained examiners. Both are comprehensive studies related to forensic psychology and are beyond the scope of this discussion. A brief mention of these subjects, however, is necessary to the study of forensic psychology.

The interviewing and interrogation techniques discussed earlier can be used to help in the detection of deception. This includes the use of traditional psychological disciplines, such as body language and psycholinguistics (Lieberman, p. 11).

STATEMENT ANALYSIS

There is a variety of research and theoretical practice in this field. Dr. David J. Lieberman, for example, discusses advanced techniques of deception detection such as "psycholinguistic emphasis and neural linguistic choice perception." His research has involved both hypnosis and a system he calls "Trance-Scripts." The latter is a method of truth persuasion (Lieberman, pp. 3-5).

Stan B. Walters also promotes a method of "analyzing verbal behavior" and using the same techniques to "analyze statements…for truth and accuracy." Walters says that his methods of "practical Kinesic statement analysis" is not a substitute for an interview, but helps detect deception (Walters, pp. 55-56).

Walters method is not reliable with subjects classified as mentally deficient, psychotic or mentally disturbed, suffering from brain disease, under the influence of alcohol or drugs, or who use language functions unfamiliar to the interviewer (Walters, pp. 55-56).

A review of the basic *grammatical rules* and terms is essential for **statement analysis** or what Don Rabon refers to as **investigative discourse analysis.** "Investigative Discourse Analysis" is the "close and systematic study of the basic linking components of spoken or written communication in order to determine" (Rabon, 1994, p. 11)

- **Process**—how something is accomplished (Rabon, 1994, p. 22).
- **Occurrence**—when something happened or the manner in which it happened (Rabon, 1994, p. 12).
- **Descriptions**—(Rabon, 1994, p. 12).
- **Individuals Involved**—who did what and when (Rabon, 1994, p. 12).
- **Evaluation**—good/bad or right/wrong (Rabon, 1994, pp. 12-13).
- **Relationships**—(Rabon, 1994, p. 13).
- **Reasons for specific word selections**—(Rabon, 1994, p. 13).
- **Truthfulness and deception**—what the form and semantic quality of the narrative indicates about its truthfulness or deceptiveness (Rabon, 1994, p. 13).

A sentence is developed by combining some or all of the eight parts of speech:

1. *Verbs* express action, existence, or occurrence; they denote what is done in the present, past, and future *tense* (Rabon, 1994, p. 2).
2. *Pronouns* are relationship or signal words that assume the functions of nouns within *clauses*; they are either:
   a) *personal*—I, him, you, he, she, it, they, we, them;
   b) *demonstrative*—those, this, that, these;
   c) *relative*—whoever, what;
   d) *interrogative*—who, which, what;
   e) *indefinite*—one, some;
   f) *first person*—the speaker;
   g) *second person*—the one spoken to; or
   h) *third person*—the one spoken about (Rabon, 1994, p. 3).
3. *Adjectives* are words used to limit or qualify a noun and answer *"how many"* or *"what kind."* Nouns and pronouns can function as adjectives (Rabon, 1994, p. 3).
4. *Adverbs* are used to modify a verb, an adjective, another adverb, a phrase or a clause by expressing time, place, manner, degree, cause, etc. Adverbs answer the questions:
   a) when (time),
   b) where (place),
   c) how (manner),
   d) how often (frequency), and/or
   e) yes or no (affirmation or negation).
   (Rabon, 1994, p. 4)

5.   *Conjunctions* connect words, phrases, clauses, or sentences and may be:
      a) *coordinating* (and, but, or),
      b) *subordinating* (if, when, as, because, through, etc.), or
      c) *correlative* (either…or, both…and, etc.).
      (Rabon, 1994, p. 4-5)
6.   *Prepositions* are relation or function words that connect a *lexical* word (usually a noun or pronoun) or a *syntactical construction* to another element of the sentence (a verb, noun, or adjective), e.g. at, by, in, for, from, off, on, above, around, before, behind, between, over, through, until, etc. (Rabon, 1994, p. 5).

Within discourse, *words* are the smallest unit or analysis and each one is a **sign** that can be "read" and interpreted. A "sign" is "any linguistic unit that is the symbol of an idea" (Rabon, 1994, pp. 14-15).

Each word that a speaker uses is based on choice and analysis seeks to determine the meaning and primary aim of the narrative: to *convince* or to *convey*. The next unit of analysis is the *sentence* (Rabon, 1994, p. 16). The words in a sentence are chosen for specific reasons:

- *Introjection*—the "process by which aspects of the external world are absorbed into or incorporated within the self." "My" refers to the speaker, or self, and indicates possession or possessiveness. These include "I, we, my, our, your, his, her, their," etc. (Strandberg, p. 52).
- *Marker Words*—words which label or modify the word being marked (e.g. a, her, this). Heavy use of "me" may "indicate that the subject perceives himself, or wishes to portray himself, as the passive object of external actions or events…"
- *Abjuration Terms*—serve to withdraw assertions made in previous clauses of a sentence (usually conjunctions, such as "but").
- *Repression*—the mental process in which "anxiety—producing mental content is forcefully removed from consciousness and prevented from reemerging." Repression is indicated by phrases like "have no recollection," etc.
- *Temporal Lacuna*—a blank space or missing elements within the discourse, such as "later on," "after that," or "by and by."
- *Modifying or Equivocating Terms*—allow the speaker to "evade the risk of comment," for example "I believe," "I guess," "It was kind of," "sort of," etc.
- *Explanatory Terms*—used to give the reason for or cause of or justification and rationale, e.g. "so."
- *Denial or Negation*—a defense mechanism that "disavows or denies thoughts, feelings, wishes or needs that cause anxiety, e.g. "I didn't even know…"

- *Stalling Mechanisms*—allow the speaker to hold back or pause, e.g. see."
- *Second Person Referencing*—occurs when the speaker refers to himse. with the second-person pronoun "you" and thereby diverts attention from him. This signals that he/she feels no personal accountability or responsibility for what happened.
- *Weakened Assertions*—when the speaker feels a need for additional support for what he/she has said, e.g. "to tell the truth…"

(Rabon, 1994, pp. 17-22).

Investigative Discourse Analysis can be implemented with written narratives or accounts from the subject, transcribed records, or written dictation from the subject (Rabon, 1994, p. 29). The investigator should begin with open-ended, non-specific questions, such as, "what happened?" (Rabon, 1994, p. 30).

The investigator should first attempt to determine truth or deception through the **form** or **structure** of the subject's narrative (Rabon, 1994, p. 34). This involves:

1. Identification of the formal organization of the narrative in terms of *balance* or *proportion* (prologue, event, epilogue) (Rabon, 1994, p. 35).
2. Identification of nonconforming statements (those in which the subject alludes to some action, procedure, or activity without saying he/she actually performed any of these). Watch for *weakened assertions* (Rabon, 1994, p. 42).
3. Identification of any nonsequential statements (those that are out of place or chronological order) (Rabon, 1994, p. 44).

Next, the investigator conducts a **semantic analysis** (meaning). Semantic indicators of deception include:

1. Lack of conviction about one's own assertions (often indicated by *modifying* or *equivocating* terms).
2. Use of present tense when describing a past occurrence (reluctance to refer to past events in the past tense if it is the subject of the investigation).
3. Use of more generalized statements (vague narratives of a series of actions or blocks of time).
4. Reduced or eliminated self-references (indicated by sentences that begin with verbs or descriptions of activities in which the speaker was a participant, but avoids reference to his/her involvement).
5. Reduced mean length of utterance (MLU) in relation to a particular unit of narration. The MLU consists of the number of words in a sentence

and/or number of sentences in a passage of a narrative. The formula for this is: MLU = *Words* divided by *sentences*.
(Rabon, 1994, pp. 48-55)

Once analysis is completed, it can be used to amplify the narrative by eliciting more details in the areas identified in this analysis (Rabon, 1994, p. 89). Investigative discourse analysis provides new directions and supplements the interview process by further identifying areas of deception. Strandberg writes, "Statement analysis gives law enforcement officers insight to use during the follow-up interview." He says, "With practice, statement analysis will pay off as you find inconsistencies that lead to more crimes solved" (Strandberg, p. 54).

CRIMINAL PROFILING

The forensic psychology specialty of *criminal profiling and behavioral analysis* is an extensive study in itself. No study of forensic psychology would be complete, however, without at least a cursory review of its elements. Criminal profiling actually involves a multidisciplinary approach to behavioral analysis. It involves the fields of psychology, sociology, criminology, anthropology and forensic science.

The *goals* of criminal profiling include:

1.　Providing the Criminal Justice System with a social and psychological assessment of an offender;
2.　Providing the Criminal Justice System with a psychological evaluation of belongings found in the possession of an offender; and
3.　Providing interviewing suggestions and strategies.
(Holmes, p. 10-12)

Personality profiling, says Dr. Ronald M. Homes, is the "sum total of what a person is" or that person's total set of values and attitudes (Holmes, p. 34). This is comprised of five personality components: biology, culture, environment, common experiences, and unique experiences (Holmes, p. 35).

The crime scene contains clues about mode of operation (modus operandi). The criminal's *signature* is evidenced by the crime scene rather than the crime itself. Thus, the crime scene reflects the pathology of the offender's personality.

Profiling reduces the number of suspects by providing nonphysical evidence indicative of race, sex, employment, residence, etc. After examining the nonphysical evidence, physical evidence is reintroduced in an "interrelationship" approach to reconstructing the crime (Holmes, p. 43).

The FBI developed a "typology of lust offenders" consisting of two categories: Disorganized *Asocial* and *Organized Nonsocial.*

Disorganized Asocial Typology refers to an offender who is disorganized in his/her daily activities, including his/her home or apartment, place of employment (if applicable), vehicle, clothing, demeanor, general appearance, lifestyle, and psychological state (Homes, p. 43).

Research suggests that this personality type is typically of a non-athletic, **white, male,** introverted personality. Many have been victims of physical or emotional abuse, the father was either absent or, if employed, his work was unstable. He/she is a loner and may be described by neighbors as strange. This personality has solitary hobbies, few extracurricular activities, and had difficulty in school (a below average IQ and probably a high school drop out) (Holmes, pp. 43-44).

The *disorganized asocial* has limited intelligence, usually has unskilled, menial jobs, and rarely dates. He/she is a loner because of societal segregation, rather than choice. This offender's crimes are spontaneous, lacking in planning, and not far from home or work. Because he/she does not feel comfortable venturing far, he/she will often walk or ride a bike to the crime scene (Holmes, p. 45).

Post-offense personality action or behavior usually includes the need to return to the crime scene, envisioning and reliving the crime, and perhaps even attending the funeral or placing a memorial in a newspaper. He/she may keep a diary of these activities and the victims. He/she may keep photographs or videotapes of these offenses (Holmes, p. 45).

Interviewing or interrogation for this personality type will more likely be effective if a relationship-motivation strategy and empathy are employed. Dr. Holmes says, "it may be beneficial to keep up a constant stream of conversation and perhaps introduce something into the conversation which has been found at the crime scene itself (Holmes, p. 46).

Organized Nonsocial Typology refers to an organized personality which is reflected in a subject's lifestyle (home or apartment, vehicle, appearance, etc.). The opposite of the *disorganized asocial,* the **organized nonsocial** insists upon organization; everything has a place and everything must be in its place (and personality) (Holmes, pp. 46-47).

This personality type is nonsocial by choice and a loner because there is no one good enough for him/her. This subject is of average intelligence and may have done well in school. They are socially competent, have sex partners, may be married and most are intimate with someone. Many are from middle-class families and are high in the birth order. The father held a stable job but his discipline was inconsistent (Holmes, p. 48).

The organized offender feels more comfortable venturing from home, has no trouble making new (superficial) friends, and is able to change employment. This offender's personality is often masculine, dresses flashy, and drives a car reflecting his personality (Holmes, p. 48).

Post-offense personality action or behavior often includes returning to the scene of the crime to relive it. In interviewing, this personality type respects competency and should be confronted directly. Using "false evidence" will make this subject know there is no case (Homes, pp. 49-50).

The *organized nonsocial* will be organized in the perpetration of their crimes by taking great care in the perpetration of violence, destroying evidence, and possibly killing at one location and disposing of the body at another. The *disorganized asocial* commits acts of sudden violence with little planning. The "blitz attack" reflects a violent scene with a great deal of physical evidence (Holmes, p. 50).

Both offenders select "strangers" for victims. The *organized nonsocial* targets a victim-stranger while the *disorganized asocial* may be aware of the victim's existence, but does not have a personal relationship with them (Holmes, p. 52).

Minimal conversation occurs between the *disorganized* offender and the victim, while the *organized* offender intimidates the victim once in the offender's comfort zone. Prior to death vicious attacks may occur, restraints may be used to make the victim helpless, and the offender may attempt to elicit fear reactions in the victim (Holmes, p. 53).

In a *Organized nonsocial* scene the weapon belongs to the offender and is taken to and from the scene. This, along with movement of the body from the scene, indicates organization and at least minimal planning (Holmes, p. 54).

HOSTAGE NEGOTIATIONS

Hostage negotiations is another in-depth study in forensic psychology and behavioral science. The purpose is obvious—to gain the safe release of hostages taken by criminals, terrorists, or even hostile governments. For this reason hostage negotiations can take a variety of forms and be of interest to the police, military, and diplomatic organizations.

For the hostage, adjusting to captivity may involve dealing with fear, the living conditions, boredom, or illness (USAF OSI, pp. 6-10). Negotiators must be mature (mentally and emotionally), good listeners, experienced in communication techniques, sincere, flexible, and physically fit (HQTRADOC, pp. 9-12 and 9-13).

This subjects bears more in-depth study of its own, but any study of forensic psychology must at least acknowledge this specialty field.

STRESS MANAGEMENT

Although stress management is not a specialty of forensic psychology, forensic, police, and correctional psychologist and psychiatrists should be familiar, if not proficient, in counseling for stress management.

Stress management may be preventive or reactive, as in the case of post-traumatic stress disorder (PTSD). The latter may involve post-shooting stress, a traumatic loss or experience, post-hostage experiences, or personal stress.

Stress is a natural condition, but the presence of eustress (good stress, such as a game, sexual intercourse, exercise, etc.) must be differentiated from distress (bad stress, such as fatigue, anger, fear, physical injury, etc.).

Personal stress management should include a proper diet and nutrition, exercise, hypnosis or bio-feed back, massage or muscle therapy, and various forms of relaxation. When stress becomes unmanageable, one must seek medical or psychological assistance for one's overall mental and physical health.

COMPETENCY AND COURTROOM ISSUES

Another area of forensic psychology involves competency determination and other courtroom issues, such as insanity defenses and culpability. Other courtroom issues include the process of jury selection, known in jurisprudence as *voir dire*, body language, and "the gentle art of persuasion" or "verbal judo.".

COMPETENCY

Free will is the primary theme on which the tenets of punishment for crimes and punitive damages for torts (civil wrongs) are based (Gordon, p. 35). The issue of free will hinges on the psychological factors of freedom of choice versus manipulated behavior. Free will is a primary determinant of competency in legal issues.

Competency determination is based upon professional evaluations of the subject's history, physical condition, neurologic state, psychiatric condition, etc. (Davidson, pp. 371-373). This is based upon a series of tests in each of these fields.\

JURY SELECTION

Jury selection is a function that forensic psychologists can be very effective in helping with. Physician-Psychologist William Bryant, Jr., for example, helped attorney F. Lee Bailey in selecting the jury for the trial of Dr. Sam Sheppard, the neurosurgeon accused of killing his wife (the basis for *The Fugitive*) (Gordon, p. 76).

BODY LANGUAGE

Robert Gordon suggests that behavioral science research invalidates *physiognomic* approaches (based upon physical characteristics) in jury selection (Gordon, p. 81). He suggests that body language is a more reliable method of conducting *voir dire* (jury selection; French for "speak the truth") for example:

- Open hands—sincerity and openness.
- Unbuttoning coat—agreement is possible.
- Arms crossed on chest—defensiveness.
- Arms crossed on chest—indifference.
- Female crossing legs with a slight kicking motion—boredom.
- Hand to cheek or chin stroking—evaluation.
- Nose rubbing—negative reaction.
- Joining fingertips—confidence or egotism.
- Leaning back with hands laced behind head—relaxed aggressiveness.
- Throat clearing—nervousness.

(Gordon, p. 82-83)

VERBAL JUDO—THE GENTLE ART OF PERSUASION

George Thompson, a former professor of English literature, a police officer, and a black belt in judo and tae kwondo karate, developed a technique known as verbal judo. He believes his techniques can help avoid "unnecessary conflict, tension, and abuse" (Thompson and Jenkins, p. 12).

Thompson and co-author Jerry B. Jenkins write that to master "the gentle way of persuasion" and become a "communication samurai," one must develop new habits of the mind and become a "consciously competent speaker" (Thompson and Jenkins, p. 17 and p. 32).

They say that "truly enlightened communication does not come naturally to anyone" and we should never use words that readily come to mind or lips (Thompson and Jenkins, p. 32). They say the secret to success is simple: If someone insults, resists, or attacks you, laugh it off and show that it has no meaning (Thompson and Jenkins, p. 37).

Thompson and Jenkins list *Eleven Things Never to Say to Anyone* (and what to say to someone who says them to you):

1. "**Come here!**"—usually implies an order to move when told to move. Instead, "I need to chat with you..." is clear, but gives a feeling of choice. A response might simply be "why?" (Thompson and Jenkins, pp. 47-48).

2. **"You wouldn't understand"**—is insulting. It might be better to say, "This might be difficult to understand, but…" or "let me try to explain this…" A response might be "yes I would. Try me. I want to help" (Thompson and Jenkins, p. 48).

3. **"Because those are the rules."**—Explain the rules, instead of sounding weak or without logic. A response might be "Could you please tell me why this rule was created? It doesn't make sense to me, and if you could help me understand why it was made, it would be much easier for me to follow" (Thompson and Jenkins, pp. 48-49).

4. **"It's none of your business."**—Explain *why* it is or is not (Thompson and Jenkins, p. 49).

5. **"What do you want me to do about it?"**—Explain that you have no solutions or you would offer to help (Thompson and Jenkins, p. 50).

6. **"Calm down!"**—implies criticism and no right to be upset. It might be better to say, "It's going to be all right. Talk to me. What's the trouble?" A response might be, "I'm obviously not calm and there are reasons for it. Let's talk about them" (Thompson and Jenkins, p. 51).

7. **"What's your problem?"**—It might be better to say, "What's the matter? How can I help?" A response might include, "It's not a problem, it's just something I need to discuss. Can we talk?" (Thompson and Jenkins, p. 51).

8. **"You never…"** or **"You always…"**—are absolute generalizations. Instead, "you make me feel…" might be better. A response might be "I know it seems…" (Thompson and Jenkins, p. 52).

9. **"I'm not going to say this again."**—Instead, "It's important that you understand this, so let me say it again and please listen carefully." A response might be, "Okay, I got it" (Thompson and Jenkins, p. 53).

10. **"I'm doing this for your own good."**—Offer reasons. A response might be to remind them that you are the best judge of what is for your own good (Thompson and Jenkins, p. 53).

11. **"Why don't you be reasonable?"**—Instead try "Let me see if I understand your position." A response might be "…apparently I see this issue differently than you do" (Thompson and Jenkins, p. 54).

Thompson and Jenkins say that the most powerful word in the English language is **empathy**—the ability to understand and see through the eyes of another. They say empathy absorbs tension (Thompson and Jenkins, pp. 63-64). They refer to the **Five—Step Hard Style** of persuasion as the ability to generate compliance:

1. Ask—ethical appeal.
2. Set context—reasonable appeal.
3. Present options—personal appeal.
4. Confirm—practical appeal.
5. Act—determination of appropriate action (Thompson and Jenkins, p. 95)

BEHAVIORAL COURTROOM ISSUES

The forensic psychiatrist's function is to match a defendant's mental state to a formula that is accepted by the courts to help juries determine responsibility (Davidson, p. 3). A number of other medico-legal psychiatric evaluation responsibilities are involved in both civil and criminal cases.

The forensic psychologist has an interest in a variety of psychological-legal issues in both the civil and criminal courts. Behavior of witnesses and juries are often as important as the evaluation of defendants.

Dr. Robert Sadoff points out that an evaluation of an offender's mental status at the time of the commission of a criminal act is impractical and must be determined after the fact, such as after an arrest. The offender is assumed to possess a normal mental capacity to form *mens rea* (guilty intent) unless proven otherwise by expert testimony (Sadoff, p. 76).

Competency is an "all-encompassing term" that refers to an individual's ability to handle his/her own affairs (Sadoff, p. 149). This may not only involve a determination of "guilty mind," but may also involve a myriad of civil affairs.

CRIMINAL BEHAVIOR
NEUROTIC DISORDERS AND NEUROTICISM

Neurotic Disorders encompass three major categories which were once grouped together as merely **neuroses** in the DSM-II (*Diagnostic and Statistical Manual of Mental Disorders*). These three categories are: 1. **anxiety disorders**, which include phobias, generalized anxiety disorders, and obsessive compulsive disorders; 2. **somatoform disorders**, including somatization and conversion disorders; and 3. **dissociative disorders**, such as amnesia, fugues, and multiple personality (Bartol, p. 143).

Behavior which is commonly referred to as "crazy" usually does not refer to neurotic disorders. These disorders usually do not cause problems, discomfort, or disorder in society, except for the affected person. Neurotic disorders distress the individual and possibly those directly involved with him or her (family, friends, etc.). Usually only the affected individual is distressed by associated emotional reactions (Bartol, p. 143).

Neurotic symptoms are present to a certain degree in everyone and the degree to which these symptoms exist is what differentiates the "normal" from the abnormal individual (Wicks, p. 41). These symptom patterns are characterized by anxiety, phobia, depression, obsessions, asthenic reaction (neurasthenia), and hysteria (Wicks, p. 45).

Neuroticism and the term *neurotic* as it is associated with neuroticism are distinct from the neurotic classification of mental disorders. Neuroticism is a "significant variable in the relationship between personality and crime." Reflected in a biological reaction to stressful events, neuroticism is also referred to as *emotionality* because it involves the intensity of emotional reactions (Bartol, pp. 44-45).

Neuroticism results in intense, long-lasting reactions to stress. Even exposure to low-stress conditions may result in the individual being "moody, touchy, sensitive to slights, anxious" and complaints of "physical ailments like headaches, backaches, and digestive problems." Such individuals overreact to stress and have difficulty returning to a normal, calm state. They are also prone to phobias and obsessions (Bartol, p. 44).

Neuroticism or emotionality is a strong drive that encourages the performance of behavior previously acquired during childhood. It amplifies existing behavior. For example, one who is not conditioned to avoid stealing, but has frequently and successfully engaged in stealing will experience a strong drive or force toward the *habit* of stealing (Bartol, p. 50). Bartol, however, suggest that the relationship between neuroticism and criminal or antisocial behavior is not supported by research (Bartol, p. 53).

PSYCHOSIS AND PSYCHOTICISM
Psychosis

Psychosis was a major section in the DSM-II which included:

- schizophrenia,
- paranoid states, and
- major affective disorders (severe depression) (Bartol, p. 144)

The DSM-III reclassified psychosis as separate major categories:

- schizophrenic disorders,
- paranoid disorders,
- affective disorders, and
- psychotic disorders "not elsewhere classified" (Bartol, p. 144)

The previous term "psychosis" was defined as "the denial of major aspects of reality" (Wicks, p. 49). The reclassified categories are elaborated further here.

Schizophrenic Disorder

Schizophrenic disorders are the first major reclassification of psychosis. **Schizophrenia** is manifested by bizarre actions and associated with what is commonly called "crazy." It is characterized by a breakdown of thought patterns, emotions, and perceptions. Extreme social withdrawal and disorganized thoughts and cognitive functions are typical. Thoughts become fragmented, bizarre, and delusional and are reflected in inappropriate emotions (Bartol, p. 145).

Hallucinations, particularly auditory, are common and typically manifested by hearing voices or sounds that no one else does (Bartol, p. 145). A "split mind" personality is associated with inconsistent thoughts, emotions, and behavior. The schizophrenic becomes preoccupied with his or her fantasy perceptions and tends to withdraw from others (MacDonald, p. 177-178).

Schizophrenia is characterized by 1. delusions, 2. hallucinations, 3. disorganized speech, 4. grossly disorganized behavior, and 5. inappropriate affect (Bartol, p. 145). The *paranoid schizophrenic* may believe he or she is being followed (MacDonald, p. 178).

Paranoid Disorder

Paranoid disorders are characterized by similar persecutory delusions, but the individual's personality is "better preserved" than in schizophrenia. Persons experiencing *paranoid delusions* may believe it is necessary to protect his or her life by killing or attempting to kill imagined persecutors (MacDonald, p. 178).

The paranoid spectrum ranges from the *simple paranoid character* through full-blown *paranoia* (delusional disorder) to *paranoid schizophrenia* (Palermo and Scott, p. 3).

Simon suggests that a significant number of murderers have been acquitted by reason of insanity. These people are more likely to have killed a parent, child, spouse, or stranger (Simon, p. 284). Samenow, however, asserts that, despite his or her delusions of persecution, such homicides are carried out with deliberation and an awareness of consequences (Somenow, p. 137).

Affective Disorders

Affective disorders do not have a great deal of influence on criminal behavior. *Affective reactions* are manifested by a "seriously unrealistic" *mood* disorder (Wicks, p. 53).

Psychotic Disorders

Psychotic disorders "not elsewhere classified" cover other "psychoses" not covered elsewhere or neatly fitting into one of the previous categories.

Antisocial Personality Disorder

Antisocial personality disorder (ASP) is characterized by "a history of continuous behavior in which the rights of others are violated" (Bartol, p. 147). Though antisocial behaviors are typical for *psychopaths*, Dr. Robert I. Simon says people who commit antisocial acts are not necessarily, psychopaths (Simon, p. 21). Dr. John M. MacDonald, however, notes that the terms **antisocial**, **sociopathic**, and **psychopathic** are often used interchangeably (MacDonald, p. 203).

Psychoticism

Psychoticism is characterized by "cold cruelty, social insensitivity, unemotionality, disregard for danger, troublesome behavior, dislike of others, and an attraction to the unusual." This type of psychotic is distinguishable from the clinical psychotic who is out of touch with reality (Bartol, p. 47).

PSYCHOPATHY AND PSYCHOPATHS

Sociologists and criminologists refer to repetitive offenders who do not respond to treatment, rehabilitation, or incarceration as **sociopaths**. Psychologists and psychiatrists refer to those who demonstrate a failure to conform to social norms repeatedly as individuals with **antisocial personality disorder** (ASP) (Bartol, p. 59).

The terms *sociopath, antisocial personality disorder,* and *psychopath* are sometimes used interchangeably (MacDonald, p. 203). **Psychopaths**, categorized as primary, secondary, and dyssocial psychopaths, are identified as engaging in "repetitive antisocial or criminal behavior" (Bartol, pp. 58-59).

Psychopaths are not mentally ill in the usual sense. They are not out of touch with reality, compulsive or socially dysfunctional (Baumeister, p. 137).

The **psychopath** is characterized by the following symptoms:

Emotional/Interpersonal

- glib and superficial,
- egocentric and grandiose,

- lack of remorse or guilt,
- lack of empathy,
- deceitful and manipulative, and
- shallow emotions (Hare, p. 34)

Social Deviance

- impulsive,
- poor behavior controls,
- need for excitement,
- lack of responsibility,
- early behavior problems, and
- adult antisocial behavior (Hare, p. 34)

Dr. Robert D. Hare notes the difference between *antisocial personality disorder* (ASP) and *psychopathy*. ASP refers to a "cluster of criminal and antisocial behaviors. Psychopathy is defined by a cluster of both personality traits and socially deviant behaviors (Hare, p. 25).

Dr. Hare describes psychopaths thus:

> Psychopaths are social predators who charm, manipulate, and ruthlessly plow their way through life leaving a broad trail of broken hearts, shattered expectations, and empty wallets. Completely lacking in conscience and in feelings for others, they selfishly take what they want to do as they please…(Hare, p. xi).

THE CRIMINAL MIND

Baumeister says that most people who perpetrate evil do not see what they are doing as evil. He says, "Evil exists primarily in the eye of the beholder, especially in the eye of the victim" (Baumeister, p. 1).

Simon has even darker observations. He writes, "One cannot listen for so many years to patients and to criminal defendants revealing their inner lives without coming to the conclusion that bad men and women do what good men and women only dream about doing" (Simon, p. 2). He goes on to suggest that there are no "good" and no "bad" people, but people who are both to varying degrees (Simon, p. 3).

Samenow, too, comments on the criminal, noting that criminals cause crime, *not* bad neighborhoods, inadequate parents, television, schools, drugs, unemployment, or social conditions. He says, "Crime resides in the minds of human beings" (Samenow, p. 6) and that only by changing their thinking patterns can they be "habilitated" (Samenow, p. 23).

CONCLUSION

Forensic psychology is a broad field of psychological practice, as is clinical, social, and educational psychology, to name a few. Specialties within forensic psychology include broad functional areas, which include police psychology, competency and courtroom psychology, and the study of criminal psychology or criminal behavior.

Police psychology includes a range of topics used to further police operations and investigations. Interviewing, interrogation, hypnosis, truth detection (polygraph, voice stress analysis, etc.), and statement analysis each deal with the psychology of communicating truth and deception. Criminal profiling draws a behavioral and descriptive portrait of unknown suspects and identifies communication strategies for them. Hostage negotiations and stress management also deals with behavioral issues of interest to the police behavioral scientist.

Competency is an issue which combines the legal system with the mental health system. Other court room issues involve forensic behavioral issues, such as jury selection (*voir dire*) and proxemics.

Of course forensic psychology deals with criminal behavior. Identifying and treating criminals and criminal behavior requires a practical knowledge of the criminal mind.

The field of forensic psychology is an interesting and important field. It is a practical field for not only behavioral scientists and the mental health professions, but provides essential tools to practitioners in law enforcement, the legal profession, corrections, and those concerned with and about the criminal mind.

REFERENCES—CHAPTER 4

Bartol, Curt R. **Criminal Behavior: A Psychosocial Approach** (Fourth Edition). Englewood Cliffs, New Jersey: Prentice Hall, 1995.

Baumeister, Roy F. (Ph.D.). **Evil: Inside Human Violence and Cruelty.** New York, NY: W.H. Freeman Company, 1999.

Clinard, Marshall B., Richard Quinney, and John Wildeman. **Criminal Behavior Systems: A Typology** (Third Edition). Cincinnati, OH: Anderson Publishing Co., 1994.

Davidson, Henry A. (M.D.). **Forensic Psychiatry.** New York, NY: The Ronald Press Company, 1952.

Gordon, Robert (J.D., Ph.D.). **Forensic Psychology: A Guide for Lawyers and Mental Health Professions.** Chicago, IL: Nelson-Hall, 1975.

Hare, Robert D. (Ph.D.). **Without Conscious: The Disturbing World of the Psychopaths Among Us,** New York, NY: The Guilford Press, 1993.

Holmes, Ronald M. **Profiling Violent Crimes: An Investigative Tool.** Newbury Park, CA: Sage Publications, 1989.

HQTRADOC. **Countering Terrorism on U.S. Army Installations** (TC19-16). Ft. Monroe, VA: 1983. (Unclassified)

Inbau, Fred E., and John E. Reid. **Criminal Interrogation and Confessions** (Second Edition). Baltimore, MD: Williams & Wilkens, 1967.

Lieberman, David J. (Ph.D.). **Never Be Lied to Again.** New York, NY: St. Martin's Press, 1998.

MacDonald, John M. **The Murderer and His Victim** (Second Edition). Springfield, IL: Charles C. Thomas Publisher, 1986.

Palermo, George B., and Edward M. Scott. **The Paranoid: In and Out of Prison.** Springfield, IL: Charles C. Thomas Publisher, Ltd., 1997.

Rabon, Don. **Interviewing and Interrogation.** Durham, NC: Carolina Academic Press, 1992.

Rabon, Don. **Investigative Discourse Analysis.** Durham, North Carolina: Carolina Academic Press, 1994.

Reiser, Martin (Ed.D.). **Handbook of Investigative Hypnosis**. Los Angeles, CA: LEHI Publishing Co., 1980.

Sadoff, Robert L. (M.D.). **Forensic Psychiatry: A Practical Guide for Lawyers and Psychiatrists**. Springfield, IL: Charles C. Thomas Publisher, 1988.

Samenow, Stanton E. (Ph.D.). **Inside the Criminal Mind**. New York, NY: Times Books, 1984.

Simon, Robert I. (M.D.). **Bad Men Do What Good Men Dream: A Forensic Psychiatrist Illuminates the Darker Side of Human Behavior**, Washington, DC: American Psychiatric Press, Inc., 1996.

Strandberg, Keith W. "**Guilty…In Their Own Words: Statement Analysis.**" Law Enforcement Technology March 1998.

Thompson, George J., and Jerry B. Jenkins. **Verbal Judo: The Gentle Art of Persuasion**, New York, NY: William Morrow and Co., Inc., 1993.

Walters, Stan B. **Principles of Kinesic Interview and Interrogation**. Boca Raton, FL: CRC Press, 1996.

U.S. Air Force Office of Special Investigations (USAF OSI). **Antiterrorism Commentary: Hostage Survival**. Washington, DC: undated. (Unclassified)

Wicks, Robert J. **Applied Psychology for Law Enforcement and Corrections Officers**, New York, NY: McGraw-Hill Book Company, 1974.

Zulawski, David E., and Douglas E. Wicklander. **Practical Aspects of Interview and Interrogation**. Boca Raton, FL: CRC Press, 1993.

Chapter 5
FORENSIC SCIENCE

INTRODUCTION

Forensic Science is the application of a variety of sciences to legal issues, particularly the detection and solution of crimes. Here "forensic science" will be divided into three areas: forensic medicine, specific forensic sciences, and criminalistics.

Forensic medicine deals with the medical sciences and related disciplines that deal with medico-legal issues. These include forensic pathology, forensic anthropology, forensic osteology, forensic odontology, and related fields. Although DNA typing and forensic toxicology are fields of forensic medicine, they will be included in the next section.

Specific forensic sciences are those specialties which overlap in the medical examiner's office (forensic medicine) and the crime lab (criminalistics). These include DNA typing and evidence, forensic toxicology (drugs and poisons), forensic chemistry (analysis of drugs, chemical substances, and serology/hematology), and forensic entimology (bugs).

Finally, *criminalistics* is the science of crime scenes and crime labs. Criminalistics is the physical science of criminology, which is also a behavioral science. Criminalistics includes, but is not limited to, firearms and toolmark comparison, questioned documents analysis (handwriting, typewriting, inks, papers, etc.), fingerprints, photography and video, trace evidence, and a number of other ever evolving scientific and technological specialties.

Together these sciences and technologies form a broad field commonly grouped together as "forensic science." These are the scientific methods and technologies used to detect and solve crimes and present evidence of what happened at a crime scene to a judge and jury in a court of law.

FORENSIC MEDICINE
FORENSIC PATHOLOGY

Forensic pathology is the specialty within *forensic medicine* that deals with the scientific diagnosis of illnesses and injuries. It involves the intersection of the legal field and the pathologic field (Eckert, pp. 93-94).

The forensic pathologists assists in the identification of the deceased, determination (estimate) of the time of death, conduct of the autopsy, and determination of the cause of death (Nickell and Fischer, p. 246).

Identification of the decedent involves an examination of the physical description, scars and marks, fingerprints, photographs, age determination, dental features, radiological evidence, blood factors (ABO grouping, Rh factor, blood characteristics, and DNA testing), medical indications, etc. (Nickell and Fischer, p. 248).

Time of death is estimated through body changes, such as temperature, lividity, rigor mortis, putrefaction, stomach contents, ocular changes, etc. (Nickell and Fischer, pp. 249-252). For example, rigor sets in between fifteen minutes and fifteen hours after death, the average being five to six hours. Rigor dissipates in eight to ten hours (usually within thirty-six hours after death) (Nickell and Fischer, pp. 249-250).

The *autopsy* is the postmortem examination which includes the preliminary examination, identification of the body, photography, x-raying, etc. (Nickell and Fischer, p. 252), but begins with an external examination (Eckert, p. 99).

The pathology of trauma examined in the autopsy attempts to determine:

1. the *modality* of violence (e.g. mechanical, thermal, chemical, electric, etc.),
2. the *manner* of its origin (homicide, suicide, accidental, undetermined), and
3. whether the victim *survived* (Adelson, p. 6).

The *cause of death* attempts to identify these four manners or modes of death. The types of cause includes asphyxia, blunt force, burns, electric shock, gunshots, motor vehicle fatalities, poisoning, and stabbing (Nickell and Fischer, p. 256). The pathology of homicide asks if the victim died of trauma, unlawful violence, and permits judicial proceedings to adjudicate guilt or innocence (Adelson, p. 7).

Homicide, the killing of another human being, may be criminal, justifiable, or excusable (accidental) in nature (Adelson, pp. 3-4). The forensic pathologist seeks to distinguish between *antemortem* and *post mortem* injuries (Perper and Wecht, p. 3) and asks six critical questions:

1. **Who** are you?
2. **When** were you hit, did you become ill, or, die?
3. **Where** did you get hurt or die?
4. Did you die as a **result** of violence, from natural causes or from a combination of both?
5. If violence was completely or partially **responsible** for your death, was it suicidal, accidental, or homicidal?
6. If someone killed you, **who** did it?

(Adelson, pp. 33-39).

Every wound found on or in a body must be explained and patterns or group-ings of wounds studied (Gresham, p. 188). Forensic pathologists attempt to find even the less obvious for causes or clues that may be latent to casual observation.

FORENSIC ANTHROPOLOGY

Dr. William R. Maples, a forensic anthropologist at the University of Florida (Florida Museum of Natural History) writes, "For me, every day is Halloween. When you think of all the horror movies you have seen in your entire life, you are visualizing only a dim, dull fraction of what I have seen in actual fact" (Maples, p. 2).

The human body consists of 206 bones. In the average male these bones weigh twelve pounds and in the average female they weigh about ten pounds. Together these artifacts form a picture of how a person lived, any illnesses they had (such as rickets or polio), healed fractures, whether they were right- or left-handed, clues about their occupation, etc. (Evans, p. 122).

Forensic anthropology may help determine a person's age at the time of death, their sex, race, height, etc. For example, Dr. Mildred Trotter devised a formula for studying the long bones within plus or minus three centimeters. For a male Caucasoid the formula is:

Length of femur x 2.38 + 61.41 cm = height;
Length of tibia x 2.52 + 78.62 cm = height;
Length of fibula x 2.68 + 71.78 cm = height
(Evans, pp. 122-123).

Forensic anthropologists or physical anthropologists trained in forensic anthropology help recover, clean, preserve and store bones from a crime scene or the scene of an investigation. This requires that no damage occurs to the bone that has not already been done by the incident under investigation (El-Najjar and McWilliams, p. 3).

The bones are unpacked carefully and any soil is brushed off. If this cannot be done, they are washed under slow running lukewarm water in a tub or sink stopped closed to prevent the loss of teeth, bone fragments, bullets, or other arti-facts (El-Najjar and McWilliams, p. 5).

The bones are air-dried in shade at room temperature to prevent cracking for twenty-four to forty-eight hours. An acrylic acetone-resin mixture can be used to preserve the bones by submerging them in the mixture until the bubbles stop. The bones should be removed and drained until the dripping stops. They should again dry for eight to twenty-four hours (El-Najjar and McWilliams, p. 5).

A variety of indicators exist to determine the **sex** in post-adolescents. The primary indicator is "an observable sex-related detail of a bone, like the little triangle on the inferomedial border of the body of the pubis which can be categorized as *present* (female), *absent* (male), or *indeterminate* (unknown) (Stewart, p. 86).

A single dimension of a bone, such as the diameter of the proximal joint surface of the humerus, may also be indicative of sex. Usually the largest figures indicate maleness and the smallest femaleness (Stewart, p. 86).

An *index* is also used to determine sex and involves the "ratio between two differently-directed dimensions selected to express the shape of some part of a bone" such as the sacrum. Again, however, overlaps between the sexes exist (Stewart, p. 86).

The skull and lower jaw are also indicative of sex. As the female moves from puberty into adulthood her skull retains much of the "gracility and smoothness characteristic of the prepubertal period," while the male's skull becomes "less gracile, relatively larger, and much rougher in the areas of muscle insertions" (Stewart, pp. 87-88). These differences are most noticeable along the jaw.

Other skeletal traits indicative of sex include the clavicle, sternum, scapula, humerus, sacrum, innominate, femur, multiple long bones, and tarsal bones. The teeth are also indicators (see **forensic odontology**).

Another indicator of forensic anthropology is the **age** of the person at the time of death. Dr. T. D. Stewart writes, "Following the cessation of growth and development, which signifies adulthood and occurs around age twenty-three to twenty-five, depending on sex, aging continues in the form of degenerative change." The degenerative aging is especially manifested after age forty (Stewart, p. 128).

The next aspect of anthropological identification is the **estimation of stature**. As mentioned earlier, Dr. Mildred Trotter devised a formula for such measurement (Evans, pp. 122-123) (Tables of formulas, the <u>Trotter and Gleser charts</u>, are used for this purpose and for reference) (Stewart, pp. 202-215).

Another area of forensic anthropological information involves **estimation of body weight**. Charts also exist for the consideration of bone, muscle, and fat relationships, but to a lesser extent than other areas (Stewart, pp. 222-226).

Determination of **race** is another attribute of anthropological identification. The term "race" refers to the zoological sub-division of a species based on appearance (phenotype). Stewart writes, "Among the phenotypic racial traits observed in the living that are identifiable still in the disarticulated skeleton are head shape, nose shape, face shape, stature, and the relative proportions of the extremities." Stewart notes that none of these are useful in determining the race of unknowns because none of these are unique to a particular racial group (Stewart, p. 227).

The attribution of race in skeletal remains is achieved by evaluating anatomical details and by "utilizing certain measurements in special regression equations." If available, microscopic analysis of head hairs supply a more reliable racial diagnosis (Stewart, pp. 228-229).

Anthropological classification of **handedness** categorizes individuals as right-handed, left-handed, or ambidextrous (Stewart, p. 239).

El-Najjar and McWilliams recommend that the reconstruction process determine the age, race, sex, and stature respectively (El-Najjar and McWilliams, p. 55). They note, "While most techniques used by physical anthropologists are borrowed from anatomy, biochemistry, genetics, medicine, pathology, and statistics," *anthroposcopy* and *anthropometry* are unique contributions of anthropology (El-Najjar and McWilliams, p. 106).

Anthroposcopy is the visual observation and description of biological characteristics (living or dead) which cannot be measured. These include the color of hair, skin, and eyes, form of lip and nose, and nonmetric traits. Anthropometry includes:

- *Somatometry*—the measurement of the body in the living and in the cadaver;
- *Osteometry*—the measurement of the skeleton parts; and
- *Craniometry*—the measurement of the skull (included in osteometry) (El-Najjar and McWilliams, p. 106).

Related to forensic anthropology are *forensic osteology* and *forensic odontology*, which are also discussed hereafter.

Forensic anthropologists and special agents assigned from the U.S. Army Criminal Investigations Command (USACIDC) are on staff at the Armed Forces Institute of Pathology. Here are they gather to confer in an anthropology lab about artifacts from a death scene.

Author, Captain Robert Girod, at AFIP while assigned to USACIDC.

FORENSIC OSTEOLOGY

Kathleen J. Reichs writes, "Physical anthropologists have applied their knowledge of osteology and human variation to the analysis of unknown skeletons for almost a century." She goes on to say, "Forensic anthropologists are no longer restricting themselves to the reconstruction of biological profiles from skeletal remains. They are addressing questions, and qualifying as experts, in areas considered outside the boundaries of forensic anthropology just a decade ago (Reiches, p. 10).

Osteologically trained physical anthropologists operating as forensic anthropologists specialize in the recognition and evaluation of skeletal details that might elude experts in other fields. Osteological anthropology deals with dried human bone specimens and their interpretation, including decomposed, incinerated, and skeletonized remains (Rathbun and Buikstra, p. 30).

Forensic archaeology is applied in forensic osteological anthropology to meet the modified requirements of crime scene processing (Rathbun and Buikstra, p. 53) where exhumation is required (Rathbun and Buikstra, p. 64).

The study of anthropology includes social (cultural) anthropology, archaeology, linguistics, and physical anthropology. Physical anthropology includes primatology (the study of living primates), paleontology (fossil primates), and *osteology*. Osteology is the study of the bones and skeleton (Killam, p. 3).

Forensic anthropology utilizes archaeological techniques to process scenes and artifacts, as mentioned earlier, and osteology to aid in the identification of human remains. An entire text of tables, equations, and data for osteological identification is found in *A Field Guide for Human Skeletal Identification* by Kenneth A. Bennett, Ph.D. of the University of Wisconsin, Department of Anthropology (Bennett).

The forensic osteological anthropologist can be of great assistance in the proper recovery of remains, estimation of the time interval of death, and identification of remains (Krogman and Iscan, p. 44). *Forensic odontology* is another field that can assist in the anthropological or osteological identification of remains.

FORENSIC ODONTOLOGY

Forensic odontology utilizes the "peculiarities of dental restorations" to provide dental identification of human remains (Rathbun and Buikstra, p. 37). The teeth also provide evidence of behavior patterns and biocultural interaction. Because of the durability of dentition, they are often the best preserved forms of evidence of evolutionary changes through time (El-Najjar and McWilliams, p. 40).

Evans Writes, "Of all the components of the human body, virtually nothing outlasts the teeth after death. This durability makes them ideally suited as a means of identification" (Evans, p. 142).

Because of their ability to resist erosion, heat, and mechanical damage, teeth are among the most durable and useful elements of human anatomy in forensic investigations. The teeth have several variable details, such as their hereditary form, size, and genetic characteristics. Some genetic characteristics are indicative of racial groups, such as the "shovel-shaped" incisors found among Mongoloid and American Indiana peoples (Rogers, p. 3).

Wear characteristics, pathological states, and distinctive dental work are sources of identification and forensic data. The dental code of designation is used for describing and diagramming the symbolism of this information.

Each tooth has five surfaces: 1. the **mesial** toward the midplane, 2. the **distal** away from the midplane, 3. the **buccal** toward the cheek or the **labial** on the outer surface of the front of the mouth, 4. the **lingual** toward the tongue, and 5. the **occlusal** in contact with teeth of the other jaw or the **incisal** which have little or no contact (such as the incisors) (Rogers, pp. 5-6).

The four *quadrants* are the upper right, upper left, lower right, and lower left. Based on these quadrants and the midplane of the mouth, systems of nomenclature have been developed that number each tooth in the dental array (Rogers, pp. 6-7).

Normal variations in the teeth can be indicative of sex (Rogers, p. 33) and race (Rogers, p. 41). Atypical variables may be noted in the structures of individual teeth and their placement in the jaws. These are determined by both genetics and various environmental factors (Rogers, p. 47).

Culturally created variations result from:

- Wear resulting from food preparation methods.
- Wear caused by holding implements, or by cutting, holding, or chewing materials used in industrial processes.
- Wear caused by personal habits.
- Staining of the teeth through contact with chemicals in the environment or taken into the mouth.
- Cosmetic and ritual mutilation of the teeth.
- Surgical manipulation of the teeth in alleviative and restorative dentistry. Such wear is categorized as either *attrition, abrasion,* or *erosion*.

(Rogers, pp. 61-62).

Environmentally and culturally induced alterations through decay, calculus build up, filing, and removal influence the anthropological value of dentition in identification and for forensic evidence (El-Najjar and McWilliams, p. 40).

Forensic investigations of human dentition involves thirty-two teeth and tooth locations, five tooth faces each, and a variety of evidence involving caries, fillings, crowns, indications of use, misuse, trauma, or vacant spaces. Carefully scrutinized observations and findings are the task of a trained dental examiner (Rogers, pp. 88-89) or forensic odontologist.

FORENSIC SCIENCES
DNA EVIDENCE

In 1992 Paul R. Billings noted that although forensic science data and the expert testimony of scientists and physicians can influence the judicial process, juries and the public draw incomplete conclusions about the controversy and limitations of "scientific truth". He cites a 1992 National Academy of Science (NAS) findings "near-final draft" which reported that "DNA identification systems were not adequately studied to be used safely in forensic settings." He suggests that these findings were contradicted the next day and then acknowledged again the day after that (Billings, p. 1).

Billings asserts that DNA identification techniques have not undergone the twenty-year scrutiny that fingerprints did before acceptance. He says that although thousands of cases have relied on DNA techniques, politics and marketing have brought these techniques to the courtroom (Billings, p. 2).

In 1996 the NAS observed that their 1992 report had taken a "moderate position" which created controversy and criticism from scientists and lawyers on both sides. By 1996 ten years had passed since DNA was first used in criminal investigation and trials and the committee updated and clarified their 1992 report (National Research Council, p. 1).

DNA *typing* has the capability of differentiating one human from another based on "a large body of scientific principles and techniques that are universally accepted." Contemporary *molecular* techniques differentiate human variability at the *genetic* level. If enough DNA *markers* are used for comparison the chances of two individuals sharing them becomes increasingly small (NRC, p. 9).

Yet Paul Rabinow suggests that DNA typing identifies individuals based on genetics which uses biological differences such as race and ethnic groups. Rabinow suggests that, rather than legitimizing DNA typing, efforts should be directed at finding individualizing markers not based on population differences (Billings, p. 5). He seems to suggest that it is more important to evade racial or ethnic typing than it is to validate this technology, regardless of the factual realities.

DNA typing for forensic, medical, and genetic purposes is based on the same principles and techniques. An individual's genetic makeup can be determined directly and is not subject to the shortcomings of blood group and enzyme testing (NRC, p. 11).

A *chromosome* is a very thin thread of **deoxyribonucleic acid** (DNA), surrounded by other materials, mainly protein. The total number of base pairs in a set of twenty-three chromosomes is about three billion. A *gene* is a stretch of DNA, ranging from a few thousand to tens of thousands of base pairs, that produces a specific product, usually a protein (NRC, pp. 12-13).

The position a gene occupies along the DNA thread is its *locus*. One group of DNA *loci* that are used extensively in forensic analysis are those containing Variable Numbers of Tandem Repeats (NRC, pp. 13-14).

Genetic types at VNTR loci are determined by a VNTR profiling. The DNA is extracted from the source and cut by a specific enzyme into fragments. Each fragment is placed in a small well of a semisolid gel. Both the subject samples and known samples are placed in an electric field and the DNA migrates away from the wells. Different fragments will have migrated different distances and are, in the process, *denatured* (double strands are separated into single strands) (NRC, pp. 15-16).

The fragments are transferred to a nylon membrane and exposed to a radioactive probe. The probe is attracted to specific VNTR and the probes are recorded when the membrane is placed on photographic film. This photo is called an *autoradiograph* or *autorad*. The two DNA samples are then compared (NRC, p. 16).

DNA testing can provide results where blood groups and proteins cannot. DNA testing can also withstand environmental conditions that destroy other evidence (NRC, p. 47). This is a more thumbnail sketch of the complex, yet efficient, techniques of DNA typing and analysis used in forensic science. Often referred to as "DNA fingerprinting," this science has proven equally reliable.

FORENSIC TOXICOLOGY

Forensic Toxicology involves the detection and identification of poisons and drugs in deceased persons and in medical emergencies of unknown cause in living patients. The *forensic toxicologist*, usually an M.D. or Ph.D., can be of great assistance to police detectives, the coroner, forensic pathologists, and other forensic scientists in solving mysterious deaths or illnesses.

Emergency toxicology begins with a determination of the symptoms. Rapid screening of the blood tests for metabolic studies, insulin and oral hypoglycaemics, salicylate, barbiturates and glutethimide, paracetamol, alcohols and aldehydes, carbon monoxide, methylpentynol, iron in the serum, lithium, organophosphorous pesticides, etc. (Curry, p. 18).

Other *toxicological* tests utilize analysis of the urine (Curry, pp. 35-38), stomach wash and aspirate, feces, hair and nails, and air form the lungs (Curry, pp. 38-41). Drug abuse screening is also the norm in emergency toxicology procedures (Curry, pp. 43-44).

In *postmortem examinations* test are conducted of the stomach wall and contents. Even when the stomach appears empty visually, the mucosa is usually inspected (Curry, p. 59). The forensic pathologist will then separate the intestine for the toxicologist to examine the contents (Curry p. 60).

Blood samples, histological samples of the liver, both kidneys, the brain, urine, and bile are also examined by the toxicologist (Curry, pp. 61-63). Hair samples are also utilized. For example, in deaths from arsenic, *atomic absorption* and *neutron activation analysis* (AA/NAA) identifies the concentration pattern along the lengths of hairs. In the case of thallium poisoning, detection can be made by microscopic examination of the hairs roots (Curry, p. 64).

The lungs are also submitted by the pathologist to the toxicologist. *Gas chromatography* may reveal gases, such as propane, butane, and other hydrocarbons (Curry p. 64).

Toxicological analysis may be grouped into categories based on what is sought or suspected:

Abortion inquiries (detection of pennyroyal and other herbs, ammonia vapors, isopropanol etc. and gas chromatography after esterification of the fatty acids) (Curry, pp. 147-148).

Agricultural chemicals and pesticides

- Chloralose,
- Dinitro-o-Cresol,
- Fluoroacetate,
- Malathion,
- Organochloro compounds,
- Paraquate and Diquat,
- Parathion and other organo phosphorous compounds,
- Pentachlorophenol,
- Trichlorophon, and
- Warfarin

(Curry, pp. 148-159).

Amanita (toxic, hallucinogenic mushrooms) (Curry, p. 159).

Amphetamine type compounds (Curry pp. 161-164).

Analgesics

- Acetaminophen (Paracetamol),
- Dextropropoxyphene,
- Diclofenac,
- Diflunisal,
- Ethoheptazine,
- Phenylbutazone, and
- Salicylates

(Curry, pp. 164-172).

Anions

- Bromide,
- Fluoride,
- Iodide, and
- Oxalate

(Curry pp. 172-178).

Antabuse (Tetraethyldithiuram Disulphide) is a acetaldehyde oxidation inhibitor and can be toxic when ethanol is ingested, even a week after drug therapy (Curry, p. 180).

Antiarrhythmic Drugs (Curry, pp. 181-182).

Antidepressants and Tricyclics

- Chlorpromazine,
- Clomipramine,
- Doxepin,
- Imipramine and Desmethy limipramine, and
- Thioridazine

(Curry, pp. 182-189).

Antiepileptics (Curry, p. 190).

Antimalarials

- Chloroquinine and Hydroxychloroquine,
- Pyrimethamine, and
- Quinine

(Curry, pp. 191-192).

Benzodiazepines (Curry, p. 192).

Beta-blockers (Curry, p. 195).

Cannabis (Curry, p. 196).

Canthardin (Curry, p. 201).

Carbon Monoxide (Curry, p. 202).

Cholinesterase (Curry, p. 207).

Cimetidine (Curry, p. 208).

Cocaine (Curry, p. 208).

Colchicine (Curry, p. 210).

Cyanide (Curry, p. 210).
Cyclizine (Curry, p. 212).
Dicyclomine (Curry, p. 213).
Digoxin (Curry, p. 213).
Dimethylnitrosamine (Curry, p. 216).
Diphenhydramine (Curry, p. 216).
Food and Beverages (poisoned) (Curry, pp. 216-217).
Hypnotics and Sedatives

- Barbiturates,
- Chlormezanone,
- Ethclorvynol,
- Glutethimide,
- Meprobamate,
- Methaqualone,
- Methylpentynol, and
- Methyprylon

(Curry, p. 217-239).
Insulin (Curry, p. 240).
Isonicotinyl Hydrazide (Curry, p. 242).
LSD and Hallucinogens (Curry, p. 244).
Laxatives (Curry, p. 248).
Monoamine Oxidase Inhibitors (Curry, p. 248).
Metals (aluminum, *arsenic*, beryllium, boron, cadmium, chromium, copper, iron, lead, magnesium, manganese, mercury, etc.) (Curry, pp. 250-269).
Narcotics (Curry, p. 270).
Oenanthotoxia (Curry, p. 272).
Quaternary Ammonium Compounds

- Tubocurarine,
- Suxamethonium, and
- Other compounds

(Curry, pp. 272-280).
Volatiles

- Camphor,
- Diethylene glycol,
- Ethanol,
- Ethylene Glycol,
- Halogenated Hydrocarbons,
- Hydrocarbons,
- Isopropanol
- Methanol,

- Paraldehyde, and
- Tetraethyl lead

(Curry, pp. 281-292).

Toxicology, then, is the study of poisons, the chemical and physical properties of toxic substances, and their effects on living organisms (Eckert, p. 107). These toxins are grouped as:

Group I	Gases
Group II	Steam Volatile
Group III	Metallic Poisons
Group IV	Nonvolatile Organic Poisons
Group V	Miscellaneous Poisons

(Eckert, pp. 118-119).

The variety of agents used in criminal poisoning continually expands. The increased complexity of analytical techniques and the variety of potential substances to be sought have increased the burden on forensic medicine (Mant, p. 213).

This variety of poisons found in forensic practice includes those potentially applied to homicides, suicides, or even accidental use. Post-mortem tests may be the key to unraveling these mysteries (Gresham, pp. 240-241).

FORENSIC CHEMISTRY

Chemistry is one of the five major classifications of science, along with biology, physics, earth science, and space science. Chemistry is the science that treats the composition of substances and their transformation (change reactions into other substances) (Nickell and Fischer, pp. 219-22).

Forensic chemists and toxicologists test drugs, narcotics, and associated substances. While toxicologists (See *Toxicology*) also analyze poisons and toxic substances, chemists also analyze a variety of other chemical evidence. Discussed in more detail above (See *Toxicology*) forensic chemists are also concerned with the identification of narcotics, depressants, stimulants, and hallucinogens (Nickell and Fischer, p. 220).

Forensic chemists exam arson evidence, such as solid and liquid accelerants (Nickell and Fischer, p. 230), and explosives evidence, such as high and low explosive compounds (Nickell and Fischer, pp. 233-234). The varieties of chemical evidence are as numerous as the number of compounds and chemical elements that exist.

FORENSIC ENTIMOLOGY

Forensic entomology is the use of insect information to assist in determining time and location of death or other information about deaths and injuries. For example, the development of maggots into flies follows a predictable time pattern and may be used to estimate the time larvae was deposited and the presumption of exposure or death.

When a dead body lies above ground, insects and their larvae destroy it. When weather conditions are favorable, a variety of insects lay their eggs in the body and produce a number of larvae (maggots). An adult body can be completely destroyed (to the skeleton) in less than two months or less than one month for a child (Fisher, Svensson, and Wendel, p. 441).

Fisher, Svensson and Wendel write, "It has been found that the insects that appear on a body, either to feed on it or to lay their eggs in it, always in a definite order, depending on the state of decomposition of the body." This makes it possible to make a good estimate to the time of death (Fisher, Svensson, and Wendel, p. 441).

Flies may begin to lay their eggs in the body, even before death actually occurs, in the mucous membrane (eyes, nose, mouth) and in wounds or bloody parts of the body. The eggs are white and about 1/16th inch long and laid in clumps (Fisher, Svensson, and Wendel, p. 441).

Indoors *Musca domestica* (common houseflies) may be prevelant while outdoors or buried bodies may have bluebottles (Calliphora erythrocephala), greenbottles (Lucilia caesar), and sheep maggot flies (Lucilia sericata). A body outdoors with houseflies may indicate that it has been moved (Fisher, Svensson, and Wendel, pp. 441-442).

Larvae of the fly come out of their eggs after only one or two days and change into pupae after 10 to 14 days. In another 12 to 14 days the flies come out to multiply again (Fisher, Svensson, and Wendel, p. 442).

This is one example of the use of forensic entimology.

CRIMINALISTICS
CRIME SCENE AND CRIME LAB TECHNOLOGY

The terms *criminalistics* and *forensic science* are often used interchangeably. Because forensic science often includes forensic medicine and other specialty fields, *criminalistics* will be used here to specify the science used in crime scene and crime laboratory technology.

Forensic science is the application of science to the law. Criminalistics includes, but is not limited to, fingerprints, photography, firearms and toolmark identification, handwriting and typewriting or questioned document examination, trace evidence, drug analysis, toxicology, chemistry, and serology.

Richard Saferstein, noted forensic author and retired Chief Forensic Scientist from the New Jersey State Police Laboratory, says, "Physical evidence encompasses any and all objects that can establish that a crime has been committed or can provide a link between a crime and its victim or a crime and its perpetrator" (Saferstein, p. 36).

Processing the crime scene involves these steps:

1. Secure and isolate the crime scene;
2. Record the scene through;
   a) photography and video,
   b) sketches,
   c) notes (including tape recordings);
3. A systematic search for evidence;
4. Collection and packaging physical evidence;
5. Maintenance of the chain of custody;
6. Collection (obtaining) of control samples;
7. Submission of evidence to the lab; and
8. Utilization of crime-scene safety precautions Saferstein, pp. 37-51).

Types of evidence examined by crime laboratories include, but are not limited to, the following:

1. Blood, semen, and saliva;
2. Documents;
3. Drugs;
4. Explosives;
5. Fibers;
6. Fingerprints;
7. Firearms and ammunition;
8. Glass;
9. Hair;
10. Impressions;
11. Organs and physiological fluids;
12. Paint;
13. Petroleum products;
14. Plastic bags;

15. Powder residues;
16. Serial number;
17. Soil and minerals;
18. Toolmarks;
19. Vehicle lights; and
20. Wood and other vegetative matter; etc., etc. (Saferstein, pp. 66-68).

Scientific crime laboratories evolved from bureaus of identification in major police departments (Eckert, p. 1). Labs utilize forensic evidence to help define the elements of crimes, provide leads, link crime scenes or victims to suspects, corroborate or refute suspect's statements or alibis, identify suspects, induce confessions, exonerate the innocent, and provide expert testimony in court (Eckert, p. 34).

Forensic science, then, is the application of all scientific disciplines that are utilized in investigations, with the goal of bringing criminals to justice, for the purposes of the law (Nickell and Fischer, p. 1).

FINGERPRINTS AND PHOTOGRAPHY

Fingerprint identification (collection, classification, and comparison) and *forensic photography* (still, video, etc.) are mainstays of criminalistics. The study of each is a class or multiple courses themselves.

The fundamental principles of fingerprints are:

1. A fingerprint is an individual characteristic, no two fingers have yet been found to have identical ridge characteristics.
2. A fingerprint will remain unchanged during the lifetime of an Individual.

(Saferstein, pp. 440-442).

Fingerprints are divided into three general patterns: loops, whorls, and arches. These are further subdivided into ulnar or radial loops, plain, central pocket loop, double loop, or accidental whorls, and plain or tented arches. Deltas and cores are used to determine ridge counts in classification (Saferstein, pp. 444-446).

The Automated Fingerprint Identification System (AFIS) is an automated system of searching scanned digital images of fingerprints. Latent print development utilizes powders and chemicals to recover prints at crime scenes for comparison by AFIS or traditional methods.

Photography is not only used for documenting and preservation of prints, but to document all aspects of a crime scene and physical evidence. Development and enhancement of photographic and video evidence is a part of forensic photography.

QUESTIONED DOCUMENTS AND VOICE IDENTIFICATION

Questioned document examination involves the analysis of handwriting, typewriting, or other examination of documents whose source or authenticity is unknown, in doubt, or questioned. This includes not only the analysis of the writing, printing, or type, but the paper, ink, or other printing artifacts.

Document experts compare handwriting, collect exemplars, and analyze alterations, erasures, and obliterations (Saferstein, pp. 503-510).

Training in questioned document examination typically takes up to two years in a large police lab (Eckert, p. 137). *Class characteristics* in questioned documents refers to those "common copy book characteristics" learned by beginning writers. Unique features that individuals knowingly or unconsciously interjects into their writing is referred to as *individual characteristics* (Eckert, p. 142).

Identification of handwriting is based on three categories of factors: form, line quality, and arrangement. Some characteristics will be unique and some will be obviously distinctive (Nickell and Fischer, pp. 171-173).

Voice examination involves the comparison of known and suspect voice patterns through the sound spectrograph (Saferstein, p. 518). Lawrence Kersta of Bell Telephone Laboratories held that "each voice has its own unique quality and character, arising out of individual variations in the vocal mechanism" (Saferstein, p. 520). Voice spectrograms or "voice prints,' therefore, are used as a means of personal identification.

FIREARMS AND TOOLMARKS

The term "ballistics" is often used to describe the examination of firearms and ammunition. *Ballistics* is actually the study of projectiles and their characteristics. The more accurate term is "firearms and toolmarks examinations" which examines the marks, trace evidence, and characteristics of firearms, ammunition, and tools.

Ordnance experts study four ballistic characteristics:

1. *Interior ballistics*—the motion of projectiles in the gun barrel and the conversion of propellant chemical energy in the cartridge to kinetic energy of the projectile;
2. *Exterior ballistics*—the flight of projectiles from the weapon to the target, under the influence of gravity and air resistance;
3. *Terminal ballistics*—the interaction of the projectile with its target; and

4. *Transition ballistics*—the passage of the projectile from the regime of interior ballistics to that of exterior ballistics, including lateral and vertical trajectory changes. (Saferstein, Volume II, p. 394).

Bullet comparison involves the examination of the rifling (lands and grooves), the caliber (caliber) or gauge, and microscopic characteristics of bullets (Saferstein, pp. 467-474). Cartridge cases are also examined for firing pin, breechblock, extractor, and ejector marks (Saferstein, p. 475).

Just as AFIS (the Automated Fingerprint Identification System) provides an automated search system for fingerprints, automated firearms search systems are now available. Computerized imaging technology is utilized in systems such as the Federal Bureau of Investigation (FBI's) DRUGFIRE system and the Bureau of Alcohol, Tobacco, and Firearms (BATF's) Integrated Ballistic Identification System (IBIS) (Saferstein, p. 476). Characteristics and striations are analyzed by microscope, captured by video imaging, digitized, and store in the databases for comparison.

Firearms and ammunition examination also involves gunpowder residue, primer residue, and other chemical analysis, as well as serial number restoration.

Saferstein describes the collection of swabs to test for gunshot residue (GSR), such as barium and antimony, for neutron activation analysis (NAA) and flameless atomic absorption spectrophotometry (AA) (Saferstein, p. 485). While such techniques are still available, the FBI laboratory issued a notice (Lab. No. 70319037 S RF) on April 16, 1987, that because "the presence of gun shot residue on a victim's hand(s) must also include the possibility that the victim was shot at close range by another person," such specimens are only accepted "if there are specific considerations" (Report of the FBI laboratory, Lab. No. 70319037 S RF, April 16, 1987). Many experts still believe GSR is a valuable form of evidence.

Tool marks include impressions, cuts, gouges, or abrasions caused by a tool contacting another object. Impressions and striations are compared for individual characteristics (Saferstein, p. 490)

"Minute imperfections" appear on a variety of items, including tools, tires, footwear, etc., that leave unique markings or distinctive impressions. These impressions are characterized as *compression marks* (when an instrument is pushed or forced into a material making an impression) or *scraping* or *striated marks* (which is produced by a combination of pressure and sliding contact by a tool) (Fisher, Svensson, and Wendel, p. 210).

Footprints not only produce an identifiable impression but a series of impressions may also provide a *gait pattern*. The gait pattern is comprised of the direction line, gait line, foot line, foot angle, principal angle, length of step, and width of step (Fisher, Svensson, and Wendel, p. 214).

Casting impressions can be accomplished with plaster of paris or Class I dental stone (Fisher, Svensson, and Wendel, p. 219), while dust prints may be photographed and lifted by techniques such as an electrostatic dust print lifter (Fisher, Svensson, and Wendel, p. 224). Other impressions may result from clothing, body parts, or tooth impressions, which may also be photographed and analyzed.

Author firing the John Lennon murder weapon at the NYPD crime lab.

ARSON AND EXPLOSIVES EXAMINATION

Arson and explosives examinations share some characteristics of both firearms and chemical examinations.

Arson investigation and forensic analysis begins with the chemistry of fire. This requires an understanding of the principles of oxidation, energy, combustion (exothermic versus endothermic), ignition temperature, flash point, flammable range, and spontaneous combustion (Saferstein, pp. 327-333).

The search for, collection, preservation, and analysis of residues and evidence are the main focus of crime scene investigation for arsons. Explosives and explosions are handled in similar fashion.

Explosives are classified by the speed at which they decompose. Low explosives are classified by the *speed of deflagration* (burning). High explosives are classified by the *speed of detonation* (Saferstein, p. 345).

GLASS AND SOIL EVIDENCE

Physical properties describe substances without reference to other substances. Chemical properties describe the behavior of substances when reacting to or combing with other substances (Saferstein, p. 97).

Physical properties include temperature, weight, mass, density, refractive index, etc. (Saferstein, pp. 100-107).

Because glass and soil are so prevalent in our environment, their value as physical evidence has great potential. Examination of physical and chemical properties aids in identification of trace evidence (See *Forensic Geology*).

ORGANIC AND INORGANIC EVIDENCE

Organic analysis involves the examination of the elements and compounds of matter. This may involve solids, liquids, and gases (vapors) (Saferstein, pp. 129-130).

Analytical techniques include chromatography or gas chromatography (GC), high-performance liquid. Chromatography (HPLC), thin-layer chromatography (TLC), electrophoresis, spectrophotometry (light and electromagnetic radiation), mass spectrometry (MS), etc.

Inorganic analysis involves substances that do not contain carbon (organic substances). Inorganic substances make up most of the earth's crust and only ten elements are included in this 99% composition (Saferstein, p. 164).

Analytical techniques designed to determine the elemental composition of materials include *emission spectroscopy* and *atomic absorption spectrophotometry*. The emission of light and resulting display of colors is called the emission spectrum (Saferstein, p. 169).

Another technique in inorganic analysis is *neutron activation analysis* which measures the atomic mass number (total number of protons and neutrons in a neucleous) (Saferstein, p. 176).

These techniques tell us what elements are present in a particular substance, but *x- ray diffraction* tells us how the elements are combined into compounds. Such analysis provides a series of light and dark bands known as a diffraction pattern which is unique in every compound (Saferstein, pp. 179-180). (See *Forensic Chemistry*).

HAIR, FIBER, AND PAINT EVIDENCE

Trace evidence transferred between individuals and objects at crime scenes may provide corroborative evidence or narrow the origin to include the suspect. The techniques used in organic, inorganic, and microscopic analysis are used in the examination of hair, fiber, and paint evidence.

Comparison of *hair* evidence usually establishes whether a hair is human or animal or to compare to a known suspect's specimen (Saferstein, p. 215). Microscopic examination helps establish the color, length, and diameter of a hair and is classified as *class evidence* (Saferstein, p. 217).

Comparison of *fibers* includes natural and man-made fibers. Natural fibers include vegetable, animal, and mineral fibers. Man-made include acetate, acrylic, anidex, aramid, azlon, fluorocarbon (teflon), glass, metallic, modacrylic, novoloid, nylon, nytril, olefin, polyester, rayon, saran, spandex, triacetate, vinyl, and vinyon (Saferstein, Volume II, pp. 211-213).

Fiber identification may reveal whether fibers are natural or man-made, the generic type or subtype, the color and shade, type of textile, and the manufacturer of the fiber or textile material (Saferstein, Volume II, p. 221). Examinations may include infrared spectroscopy, hot-stage mircoscopy, solubility tests, pyrolysis gas chromatography (PGC), etc. (Saferstein, Volume II, pp. 231-237).

Comparison of *paint* usually establishes common origins. Analysis can also provide identification of color, make, and model of automobiles and other objects (Saferstein, p. 239).

MICROSCOPIC ANALYSIS OF EVIDENCE

One of the earliest methods of evidence examination utilized the microscope to analyze the structure and composition of matter. Magnified images are known as *virtual images* versus *real images*. High-level magnification is obtained through the use of *compound microscopes* (Saferstein, p. 183).

Other tools for microscopic examination are the *comparison microscope*, the *stereoscopic microscope*, the *polarizing microscope*, and the *microspectrophotometer* (Saferstein, p. 184).

Hairs and fiber are valuable evidence that can be microscopically analyzed. These constitute a large proportion of the material mutually transferred between persons in contact at crime scenes. This is particularly valuable evidence in homicide and rape cases (Perper and Wecht, p. 337). Other microscopic evidence may include vegetable and synthetic fibers (Perper and Wecht, p. 377). These have been discussed in more detail above.

SEROLOGY (BLOOD, SEMEN, ETC.)

In 1901 Karl Landsteiner earned a Nobel Prize for developing the A-B-O blood typing system. By 1937 the Rh factor was demonstrated and soon more than one hundred blood factors were identified (Saferstein, p. 261).

Both blood and semen are used to identify individual characteristics through **deoxyribonucleic acid** (DNA) (Saferstein, P. 362). Additionally, saliva, perspiration, and fecal matter may be examined as evidence (Nickell and Fischer, p. 192).

Blood consists of plasma (fluid or water), serum (red and white cells and platelets), and antigens (blood chemicals). Blood is also Rh positive or negative, depending on the existence or nonexistence of D antigen (Saferstein, p. 363).

In addition to blood typing and DNA identification, serologists are concerned with the patterns of bloodstains. The location, distribution, and appearance of bloodstains and splatters may be valuable for interpreting and reconstructing crime scenes (Saferstein, p. 379).

Semen is of great evidentiary value, particularly in sexual offenses. The normal male releases 2.5 to 6 milliliters of seminal fluid during an ejaculation. Each milliliter contains 100 million or more spermatozoa (male reproductive cells) (Saferstein, pp. 389-890). The identification of semen follows the same analytical sequence as is used for bloodstain examinations (Saferstein, Vol. II, p. 348). (See *DNA*).

TOXICOLOGY, CHEMISTRY, AND DRUG TESTING

Toxicology and chemistry are covered in individual sections under "forensic science." Drug testing is covered in these sections.

OTHER SCIENCES AND TECHNOLOGY

Other sciences and technologies are continually emerging in forensic science and criminalistics. *Forensic engineering*, for example, involves failure analysis, accident reconstruction, and the cause and origin of fires and explosions (Saferstein, p. 23). This is also associated with *safety engineering*.

Forensic technology also involves evidence or information from computers, the Internet, and computer hardware and software. As science and technology evolves, so does crime and forensic science.

CONCLUSION

Physical evidence can:

- prove a crime has been committed or establish key elements of a crime,
- place the suspect in contact with the victim or the crime scene,
- establish the identity of persons associated with the crime,
- exonerate the innocent,
- corroborate the victim's testimony, and
- induce a suspect to make admissions or give a confession

(Fisher, Svensson, and Wendel, pp. 6-7).

Physical evidence is more reliable than eye witnesses, is expected by juries, and has become increasingly important due to recent court decisions. The absence of physical evidence may also provide useful information or stop defense arguments at the time of trial (Fisher, Svensson, and Wendel, pp. 7-8).

Forensic medicine has made invaluable contributions to criminology and forensic science. The specialty fields of forensic pathology, forensic anthropology, forensic osteology, and forensic odontology contribute to the identification of victims, the cause of death, and the circumstances surrounding the death.

Forensic sciences are a marriage between criminology and medical sciences. DNA evidence is an increasingly important subspecialty of forensic serology and hematology. Forensic toxicology identifies poisons and toxic substances that cause death, illness, or injury. Forensic chemistry involves the analysis substances and compounds that provide physical evidence. Both toxicology and chemistry are used in the identification of drugs. Forensic entimology utilizes insect evidence in the determination of time, place, and circumstances of death, illness, or injury.

Criminalistics is the scientific specialty of criminology. Criminalists are crime scene technicians and crime laboratory scientists that examine and analyze a wide variety of physical evidence. This ranges from fingerprints and photography to microscopic and chemical analysis.

The combination of forensic medicine, forensic sciences, and criminalistics comprise the broad category of *forensic science* that brings science and law together to detect crime.

REFERENCES—CHAPTER 5

Adelson, Lester (M.D.) and Cyril H. Wecht (M.D., J.D.). **The Pathology of Homicide: A Vade Mecum for Pathologist, Prosecutor, and Defense Counsel**. Springfield, IL: Charles C. Thomas Publisher, 1974.

Bennett, Kenneth A. **A Field Guide for Human Skeletal Identification** (Second Edition). Springfield, IL: Charles C. Thomas Publisher, 1993.

Billings, Paul R. (M.D., Ph.D.). **DNA on Trial: Genetic Identification and Criminal Justice**. Cold Salem, Mass.: Spring Harbor Laboratory Press, 1992.

Curry, Alan S. (Ph.D., D.Sc., C.Chem.). **Poison Detection in Human Organs** (Fourth Edition). Springfield, IL: Charles C. Thomas Publisher, 1988.

Eckert, William G. **Introduction to Forensic Sciences** (Second Edition). Boca Raton, FL: CRC Press, Inc., 1997.

El-Najjar, Mahmound Y. (Ph.D.), and K. Richard McWilliams (Ph.D., F.A.A.F.S.). **Forensic Anthropology: The Structure, Morphology, and Variation of Human Bone and Dentition**. Springfield, IL: Charles C. Thomas Publisher, 1978.

Evans, Colin. **The Casebook of Forensic Detection: How Science Solved 100 of the World's Most Baffling Crimes**. New York, NY: John Wiley & Sons, Inc., 1996.

Fatteh, Abdullah. **Medicolegal Investigation of Gunshot Wounds**. Philadelphia, PA: J.B. Lippincott Co., 1976.

Fisher, Barry A.J., Arne Svensson, and Otto Wendel. **Techniques of Crime Scene Investigation** (Fourth Edition). New York, NY: Elsevier, 1987.

Gresham, G. Austin. **Color Atlas of Forensic Pathology**. Chicago, IL: Year Book Medical Publishers, Inc., 1975.

Killam, Edward W. **The Detection of Human Remains**. Springfield, IL: Charles C. Thomas Publisher, 1990.

Krogman, Wilton Marion (Ph.D.), and Mehmet Yasar Iscan (Ph.D., D-ABFA). **The Human Skeleton in Forensic Medicine**. Springfield, IL: Charles C. Thomas Publisher, 1986.

Mant, A. Keith (Editor). **Modern Trends in Forensic Medicine–3**. London, England: Butterworths, 1973.

Maples, William R. (Ph.D.). **Dead Men Do Tell Tales: The Strange and Fascinating Cases of a Forensic Anthropologist**. New York, NY: Doubleday, 1994.

Nickell, Joe, and John F. Fischer. **Crime Science: Methods of Forensic Detection**. Lexington, KY: The University Press of Kentucky, 1999.

National Research Council, Committee on DNA Forensic Science and Commission on DNA Forensic Science. **The Evaluation of Forensic DNA Evidence**, Washington, DC: National Academy Press, 1996.

Perper, Joshua A. (M.D., LL.B., M. Sc.), and Cyril H. Wecht (M.D., J.D.). **Microscopic Diagnosis in Forensic Pathology**. Springfield, IL: Charles C. Thomas Publisher, 1980.

Rathbun, Ted A. (Ph.D.), and Jane E. Buikstra (Ph.D.). **Human Identification: Case Studies in Forensic Anthropology**. Springfield, IL: Charles C. Thomas Publisher, 1984.

Reichs, Kathleen J. (Ph.D., D.A.B.F.A.) (Editor). **Forensic Osteology: Advances in the Identification of Human Remains**, Springfield, IL: Charles C. Thomas Publisher, Ltd., 1998.

Rogers, Spencer L. **The Testimony of Teeth: Forensic Aspects of Human Dentition**.Charles C. Thomas Publisher, Springfield, IL: 1988.

Saferstein, Richard. **Criminalistics: An Introduction to Forensic Science** (Sixth Edition). Upper Saddle River, NJ: Prentice-Hall, 1998.

Saferstein, Richard (Editor). **Forensic Science Handbook, Volume II**. Englewood Cliffs, NJ: Prentice Hall, 1988.

Stewart, T.D. (M.D.). **Essentials of Forensic Anthropology**. Springfield, IL: Charles C. Thomas Publisher, 1979.

Chapter Six

CRIMINAL PROFILING
AND
BEHAVIORAL ANALYSIS

There is no hunting like the hunting the hunting of man, and
those who have hunted armed men long enough and like it,
never care for anything else there after.
- Ernest Hemingway -

_____

(Criminal Investigative Analysis)
INTRODUCTION

Criminal profiling and behavioral analysis, now referred to as "criminal investigative analysis," is often thought of as psychological profiling. Still others think of it as the methods used to stop probable drug smugglers or what the news media calls "racial profiling" in traffic stops. These are all misconceptions.

Criminal profiling, as popularized in books, movies, and television in *Silence of the Lambs*, "Profiler," and "The X Files," involves criminal behavioral analysis and crime scene assessment. Retired Federal Bureau of Investigation (FBI) profiler Russell Vorpagel describes criminal investigative analysis as a branch of criminology (Vorpagel and Harrington, p. 26), a behavior science and sociological specialty.

Vorpagel says the key to criminal investigative analysis or "profiling" is *patterns*. Patterns, he says, become a mold into which facts from the crime scene are poured to form a casting of information. Incomplete, incorrect, or conflicting information provides a useless picture (Vorpagel and Harrington, p. 26).

While books deal with the infamous cases and movies deal with the sensational, profilers deal with "what is happening every day all over this country" (Vorpagel and Harrington, p. 27). Vorpagel says, "Profiling is not magic, it's art. You paint a picture of what you think the personality of the suspect will be." Sometimes the picture is way off (Vorpagel and Harrington, p. 26).

Criminologists, such as Cesare Lombroso (1835-1909) attempted early on to classify criminals for statistical comparison. In 1876, Lombroso published his book, *The Criminal Man*, in which he compared information about similar offenders based on race, age, sex, physical characteristics, education, and geographic region. Lombrosos developed a criminal anthropology theory of behavioral analysis (Turvey, p. 3).

In 1888 Dr. George B. Phillips, a police surgeon (forensic pathologist) in Great Britain compared wound patterns in the Whitechapel (Jack the Ripper) murders to infer behavioral characteristics of the offender (Turvey, p. 5).

Forensic psychiatrist Dr. James A. Brussel was able to accurately profile the infamous "Mad Bomber" (George Metesky) who terrorized New York City with at least thirty-seven bombs in the 1940's and the 1950's. Profiling was also used in Boston between 1962 and 1964 to profile the Boston Strangler, but the killings suddenly stopped before they were solved. Albert De Salvo, who fit the profile Dr. Brussel gave, confessed in 1964 (Turvey, p. 7-8).

In the 1960's, Howard Teten began to develop his theory of criminal profiling while with the San Leandro Police Department in California. He initiated a criminal-profiling program in 1970 while with the Federal Bureau of Investigation. Teten had studied at the University of California's School of Criminology under the renowned criminalist Dr. Paul Kirk, San Francisco Medical Examiner Dr. Breyfocal, and psychiatrist Dr. Douglas Kelly, who was noted for his work in the Nuremberg War Trials. Teten was also influenced by Austrian magistrate Dr. Hans Gross (Turvey, pp. 8-9).

In 1972, Teten and Pat Mullany, also with the Federal Bureau of Investigation (FBI), applied the profiling theories to hostage negotiation. They were joined by Con Hassel and Tom Strenz. That same year Jack Kirsch established the FBI's Behavioral Science Unit (BSU). Teten was later joined by Dick Ault (1975) and Jim Reese (1978). John Phaff, Roger DePue (1978), and John Douglas later headed the BSU (Turvey, p. 9-10).

By the 1990's, the BSU was reorganized and now operates under the National Center for the Analysis of Violent Crime (NCAVC) (Turvey, p. 10). The NCAVC produced the *Crime Classification Manual* (CCM) by John E. Douglas, Ann W. Burgess, Allen G. Burgess, and Robert K. Ressler. The CCM is the profiling equivalent to the DSM-IV (Diagnostic and Statistical Manual of Mental Disorders, Fourth Edition), used by mental health professionals. Thus, the CCM is, thus, the "Bible" of criminal profiling.

Many major law enforcement agencies today, such as the New York and Chicago police departments, have criminal profilers who were trained in a year-long Fellowship at the Federal Bureau of Investigation (FBI) Academy. Many of these Fellowship graduates and former FBI profilers still profile for law enforcement, while others have marketed themselves via books and seminars. Still others have formed the International Criminal Investigative Analysis Fellowship to "corner the market" on profiling certification. This group and self-proclaimed profilers from the private-sector and academic community are often critical of each other and at odds.

Unfortunately, rather than being of mutual benefit, these separate interests seem to be in competition. This situation gives "profiling" the appearance of a subculture with various sects. Many dedicated profilers exist, however, who have impressive credentials that include both academic achievements and practical law enforcement experience.

ORGANIZED AND DISORGANIZED CRIMINAL BEHAVIOR

Brent Turvey suggests that there are two categories of reasoning behind the criminal profiling process: **inductive** and **deductive**.

Inductive reasoning refers to a "comparative, correlational and/or statistical process reliant upon subjective expertise that is most like the development of psychological syndromes (Turvey, p. 14).

Deductive reasoning refers to "a forensic-evidence-based, process-oriented, method of investigative reasoning about the behavior patterns of a particular offender" (Turvey, p. 14).

The Organized/Disorganized theory of profiling states that there are two types of crime scenes: *Organized* and *Disorganized*. Subtitles of these are **altered** and **unaltered**. (Vorpagel and Harrington, p. 33).

The *Crime Classification Manual* (CCM) says, "The amount of organization or disorganization at the crime scene will tell much about the offender's level of criminal sophistication." It goes on to note that it demonstrates how well the offender was able to control the victim and how much premeditation was involved with the crime. The authors note, however, that crime scenes are rarely "completely organized or disorganized" (Douglas, Burgess, Burgess, and Ressler, p. 9)

Turvey, however, considers the Organized/Disorganized theory to be a "false dichotomy," saying this theory is the "epitome of **inductive** profiling" (emphasis added) (Turvey, p. 146).

Turvey says this is a simplistic theory:

- A crime scene that is messy, with a lot of physical evidence suggests a **disorganized, psychotic** offender.
- A crime scene with very little evidence and that appears less chaotic suggests an **organized, psychopathic** offender.

(Turvey, p. 146)

Turvey's criticisms include:

a) The majority of crime scenes fall somewhere on a continuum, not one or the other.

b) Only competent forensic analysis can give insight into how and why a crime scene presents the way it does.

c) Disorganized characteristics can be created by non-psychotic and on-mentally-illness-oriented events.

d) Organized characteristics do not automatically suggest a psychopathic offender and a psychopathic personality disorder is not evidenced merely by a lack of psychotic behavior.

e) Labeling an offender may not account for an offender's development over time (e.g. more skilled, competent, or taking precautionary acts).

f) The organized/disorganized theory relies on offender classification based on *modus operandi* considerations, rather than considering *why* it occurred.

g) There are ethical dangers in speaking clinically on issues of courtroom relevance.

(Turvey, pp. 148-149)

ORGANIZED

Robert K. Ressler, however, suggests this theory draws a distinction between offenders who display "a certain logic in what they had done" and those whose mental processes were…not apparently logical" (Ressler and Shachtman, p. 3). He characterizes **organized** offenders as methodical and taking care to avoid leaving clues versus **disorganized** offenders who have "a full-blown and serious mental illness" (Ressler and Shachtman, p. 4).

Russell Vorpagel says the *organized* crime scene does not imply that the crime itself has been concealed, but that there is a sense of organization aimed at deterring detection. He writes, "The offender takes precautions against discovery of himself. Few, if any, weapons or fingerprints are found. The crime appears to be deliberated, calculated, and preplanned. Investigators find little evidence…" (Vorpagel and Harrington, p. 33).

DISORGANIZED

The *disorganized* crime scene gives the impression that the crime was committed suddenly and without attempting to deter detection. There is great disarray and disorganization. Vorpagel observes. "The weapon is often present at the scene. No attempt has been made to conceal the body. There is usually a great deal of evidence to use in the investigation." (Vorpagel and Harrington, pp. 33-34).

Dr. Ronald M. Holmes of the University of Louisville disagrees with Turvey, saying the theory of the **Disorganized Asocial** and **Organized Nonsocial** is "particularly useful" to profilers (Holmes, p. 43).

The *disorganized asocial typology* is disorganized in most daily activities, including their home or apartment, employment (if employed at all), their car or truck, clothing, demeanor, general appearance, lifestyle, and psychological state. (Holmes cautions that this has not been empirically validated) (Holmes, p. 43).

The disorganized offender is likely to be of below average or of low birth order. The offender may have had a harsh disciplinary upbringing. The father's work history is often unstable, as is the offender's. The offender is often "preoccupied with recurring obsessional and/or primitive thoughts and is in a confused and distressed frame of mind at the time of the crime." (Ressler, Burgess, and Douglas, p. 130).

The disorganized offender is socially inadequate, often having never married and living alone or with parents. They frequently live close to the crime scene. They may be fearful of people and have a "well-defined delusional system." They often act impulsively under stress and find their victims within their geographic area (Ressler, Burgess, and Douglas, p. 130).

Disorganized offenders are often sexually incompetent, often never experiencing intimacy with a peer, may be ignorant of sex, and may have sexual aversions (Ressler, Burgess, and Douglas, p. 130).

The *organized nonsocial typology* has a organized personality which is reflected in their lifestyle. They insist upon organization and this is reflected in their home or apartment, automobile, and personal appearance. This typology will have an anal personality type. They are nonsocial by choice and are usually a loner "because there is no one good enough for him." (Holmes, pp. 46-47).

Organized offenders are typified as having average intelligence, perhaps even doing well in school, and socially competent. They have sex partners, perhaps being married, and most are intimate with someone. They tend to be from middle-class families and of high birth order. Their father frequently held a stable job, but provided inconsistent discipline (Holmes, p. 48).

This typology is more comfortable venturing away from home, is able to work, and easily makes superficial personal relationships. They have masculine personalities, dress in a flashy manner, and drive cars that reflect their personality (Holmes, p. 48).

Precipitating situational stress may precede the crime, such as financial, marital, relational, or employment problems. The organized offender is usually socially adept and frequently lives with a partner (Ressler, Burgess, and Douglas, p. 121).

The organized typology is likely to have a car in good condition. They may take souvenirs or collect news clippings of the crime. Alcohol may be used prior to the crime and offenders may report being angry or depressed at the time of the offense (Ressler, Burgess, and Douglas, p. 122).

Charles Manson and his "family" are examples of organized killers and, although they took measures to make their murders appear as if a disorganized personality had committed them, they were typical organized offenders (Ressler and Shachtman, p. 38).

Characteristic attributes of organized and disorganized offenders are "*generally* applicable" and not an absolute. Ressler notes that, "Some crime scenes, and some murders, display organized as well as disorganized characteristics…" called a **mixed** typology (Ressler and Shachtman, p. 114).

Roy Hazelwood describes the **organized** offender as a classic *psychopath*—indifferent to his fellow humans, irresponsible, and self-centered. While he is like "a crafty wolf," the **disorganized** offender is "more like a wild dog." (Michaud, p. 66).

MIXED

The **mixed** typology involves the exceptions to the rule, such as Ted Kaczynski (the Unabomber) who was highly *organized* yet socially isolated, unkept, and lacking social skills. He was diagnosed as a paranoid schizophrenic. Another exception is the *disorganized* offender who creates havoc, while dropping hints of who he is and where he's been (Michaud, p. 66).

Tables of Typology Characteristics are included in **Appendix B** for reference.

UNDOING, STAGING, PERSONATION, AND SIGNATURE
UNDOING

Undoing involves "…rituals for the purpose of undoing the crime in a sad attempt at restitution," says Robert K. Ressler (Ressler and Shachtman, 1997, p. 6).

This is a term the investigator and profiler must be familiar with. An understanding of the concept of symbolic reversal of a crime is important to grasp.

Turvey writes that, "This can include washing or bathing the victim, placing a pillow under the victim's head, covering the victim with a blanket, sitting the victim upright in a vehicle, or otherwise returning the victim to a natural looking state." (Turvey, p. 450).

STAGING

Staging refers to a conscious criminal action by an offender to thwart an investigation, but does not include *undoing* (Turvey, p. 142). *Staging* is "the purposeful alteration of a crime scene." (Douglas, Burgess, Burgess, and Ressler, p. 10).

Organized offenders may stage a crime scene with the intent of confusing the authorities. This takes some planning and is indicative of a logical and rational mind. **Disorganized** offenders, Ressler says, are not capable of staging (Ressler and Shachtman, pp. 118-119).

Staging is indicative of "criminal or precautionary intent," says Turvey (Turvey, p. 142). **Disorganized** violent criminals do not bother to deliberately mislead the police (Ressler and Shachtman, p. 157).

The **three manifestations of criminal behavior** at a crime scene are 1.) *modus operandi* (MO), 2.) *personation* (the signature), and 3.) *staging* (Douglas, Burgess, Burgess, and Ressler, p. 249). Two of these, staging and personation/signature, are described in this section. The other, modus operandi, is covered in the following section.

Staging indicates that the responsible person (offender) is not someone who happened upon the victim, but someone who had some kind of association or relationship with the victim. The offender attempts to steer the investigation away from him/her by his/her conduct. Overly cooperative or distraught behavior should not be the basis for eliminating a suspect (Douglas, Burgess, Burgess, and Ressler, p. 252).

Protective staging involves a desire to protect the victim from a degrading position by covering them or changing their position (Douglas, Burgess, Burgess, and Ressler, p. 252). This is not for the purpose of misleading the police.

Investigators should also not be misled into believing a crime scene is **disorganized** based on **staging** intended to give that impression. This could, in fact, be the planned staging of an **organized** offender.

PERSONATION

Unusual behavior by an offender, beyond what is necessary to carry out the crime, is known as **personation** (Douglas, Burgess, Burgess, and Ressler, p. 251).

This is a simple, but important concept (like staging) to understand. *Undoing* (described above) is a form of *personation*, but has a more obvious meaning. Undoing frequently occurs when there is a close association between the offender and the victim or the victim has significance to the offender (Douglas, Burgess, Burgess, and Ressler, p. 251).

When a serial offender demonstrates "repetitive ritualistic behavior from crime to crime," this **repetitive personation** is referred to as a **signature** (Douglas, Burgess, Burgess, and Ressler, p. 251).

SIGNATURE

Again, a **signature** is a *repetitive personation*. Violent, repetitive offenders often exhibit a *signature* or "calling card" involving conduct that goes beyond the actions necessary to perpetrate the crime. It is a unique but integral part of the offender's behavior while committing the offense (Douglas, Burgess, Burgess, and Ressler, p. 261).

This **signature** can be thought of as acting out the expression of violent fantasies. The offender introduces an aspect of his personality to the crime through this ritualistic act. A **verbal signature** may involve vulgar and/or abusive language or **scripting** (Douglas, Burgess, Burgess, and Ressler, p. 261).

Scripting refers to the language used by an offender during a crime and/or language they command the victim to use (Turvey, p. 135). The offender's *modus operandi* may change, but, while the *signature* may evolve, the core of the ritual never changes (Douglas, Burgess, Burgess, and Ressler, p. 261).

MODUS OPERANDI, MOTIVATIONAL TYPOLOGIES, AND OFFENDER CHARACTERISTICS
MODUS OPERANDI

The **Modus Operandi** (method of operation, simply, M.O.) is significant when investigators attempt to link cases. Crime analysis and correlation includes connecting cases due to similarities in M.O. M.O. is a learned behavior and the offender's actions during the perpetration of a crime form the M.O. The offender develops and uses an M.O. over time because it works. M.O., however, evolves and an offender modifies M.O. with experience (Douglas, Burgess, Burgess, and Ressler, p. 260).

MOTIVATIONAL TYPOLOGIES

Typology refers to "any systematic grouping of offenders, crime scenes, victims, or behaviors by virtue of one or more shared characteristics," according to Turvey. He says this "in essence, any classification system" (Turvey, p. 169).

Turvey defines a **motivational typology** as "any classification system based on the general emotional, psychological, or material need that impels, and is satisfied by, a behavior." (Turvey, p. 443).

Turvey identifies the following **behavior—motivational typologies:**

1. Power reassurance (compensatory);
2. Power assertive (entitlement);
3. Anger retaliatory (anger is displaced);
4. Anger excitation (sadistic); and
5. Opportunistic (profit) (Turvey, pp. 170-179).

OFFENDER CHARACTERISTICS

As previously stated, Turvey identifies profiling methods as either **inductive** or **deductive** (Turvey, p. 14). The *deductive* method, he says, bases its inferences on the behavioral evidence in a particular case or series of related cases. This, he says, is behavioral evidence analysis (Turvey, p. 183).

As part of this *deductive* behavioral evidence analysis, Turvey divides **offender characteristics** into two categories: hard characteristics and soft characteristics (Turvey, p. 184).

Hard characteristics are offender attributes that are verifiable and uninterpreted facts. These include age, sex, DNA, blood type, secretor status, fingerprints, race, marital status, residence history, formal education history, employment history, incarceration history, medical history, mental health history, military history, vehicle ownership history, and property ownership history (Turvey, p. 184).

Soft characteristics are offender characteristics that are a matter of opinion. They require interpretation to define them and are subject to national or intentional change (Turvey, p. 184).

These characteristics include relationship history, physical characteristics, grooming habits, skill levels, vehicle type or color, personality habits, hobbies, self-esteem, empathy, deceitfulness, criminal versatility, acceptance of responsibility for actions, glibness or superficial charm, impulsivity, remorse or guilt, behavioral controls, aggressiveness, and motive/fantasy aspects (Turvey p. 185).

Deducing offender characteristics, Turvey says, is "about asking the right question of the offender's behavior." This involves defining the characteristic and agreeing upon what type of behavior evidences that characteristic. "If the crime reconstruction includes those behaviors," Turvey says, "then the criminal profiler has a good argument for that characteristic." (Turvey, p. 185).

CRIME CLASSIFICATION WORKSHEET

Russell Vorpagel recommends each profile contain the following disclaimer:

It should be noted that the attached analysis is not a substitute for a through and well-planned investigation and should not be considered all-inclusive. The information provided is based upon reviewing, analyzing, and researching criminal cases similar to the case submitted by the requesting agency. The final analysis is based upon the probabilities, noting, however, that no two criminal acts or criminal personalities are exactly alike, and therefore the offender at times may not always fit the profile in every category. (Vorpagel and Harrington, p. 62).

The *Crime Classification Manual* (CCM) provides a sample worksheet outlining each category of the defining characteristics of the **Crime Classification Worksheet.** The outline includes the following:

Crime Classification Worksheet

A. **Victimology**
    Why did this person become the victim of a violent crime?
    1. **The Victim**
        a. Life-style
        b. Employment
        c. Personality
        d. Friends (type, number)
        e. Income (amount, source)
        f. Family
        g. Alcohol/drug use or abuse
        h. Normal dress
        i. Handicaps
        j. Transportation used
        k. Reputation, habits, fears
        l. Marital status
        m. Dating habits
        n. Leisure activities
        o. Criminal history
        p   Assertiveness
        q. Likes and dislikes
        r. Significant events prior to the crime
        s. Activities prior to the crime
    2. **Sexual Assault: verbal interaction**
        a. Excessively vulgar or abusive
        b. Scripting
        c. Apologetic

     3.   Arson: targeted property
          a.   Residential
          b.   Commercial
          c.   Educational
          d.   Mobile, vehicle
          e.   Forest, fields

B.   Crime Scene
     1.   How many?
     2.   Environment, time, place
     3.   How many offenders?
     4.   Organized or Disorganized
     5.   Physical evidence
     6.   Weapon
     7.   Body disposition
     8.   Items left/missing
     9.   Other (witnesses, escape plan, wounded victims, etc.)

C.   Staging
     1.   National death
     2.   Accidental
     3.   Suicide
     4.   Criminal activity (e.g. robbery, rape/homicide)

D.   Forensic Findings
     1.   **Forensic Analysis**
          a.   Hair/fibers
          b.   Blood
          c.   Semen
          d.   Saliva
          e.   Other
     2.   **Autopsy Results**
          a.   Cause of death
          b.   Trauma (type, extent, location on body)
          c.   Overkill
          d.   Torture
          e.   Facial battery (depersonalization)
          f.   Bite marks
          g.   Mutilation

h.   Sexual assault (when, sequence, where, insertion, insertional necrophilia)

i.   Toxicological results

E. **Investigative Considerations**
  1.   **Search warrants**
      a.   Home
      b.   Work
      c.   Car
      d.   Other
  2.   **Locating and Interviewing Witnesses**
(Douglas, Burgess, Burgess, and Ressler, pp. 12-14)

The *Crime Classification Manual* (CCM) provides three-digit codes for a Crime Classification Numbering System. There are three major categories identified by this three-digit code system: **homicide** (codes 100-199), **arson** (codes 200-299), and **sexual assault** (codes 300-399). The second and third digits represent subclassifications (Douglas, Burgess, Burgess, and Ressler, p. 14).

HOMICIDE
CRIMINAL ENTERPRISE HOMICIDE

A. *Criminal Enterprise Homicide* involves murder committed for material gain, including money, goods, territory, or favors (Douglas, Burgess, Burgess, and Ressler, p.23).
  1. **Contract (Third Party) Killing** involves murder by surprise or secret assault and is usually committed by one having no personal, family, or business relationship to the victim.

  Victimology: The victim is usually viewed as an obstruction or hindrance to a goal (personal or financial).

  Crime Scene: The offender typically spends as little time as possible at the scene and kills quickly. The level of professionalism may be indexed by the sophistication of weapon (suppressors, customized weapons, etc.). Other factors may include effective staging, elaborate disposal, a systematic, orderly approach, and the absence of physical evidence. **Arson may** be uses to conceal the murder (See **Murder Arson**)

  Staging: **If** staging is absent, **secondary** criminal activity may be indicative of a youthful or amateur offender or lower intelligence. **If** staging is present, **secondary** criminal activity may be intended to confuse the primary motive.

Forensic Findings: The weapon may be difficult to trace and a blitz or ambush attack is common. There will likely be few wounds, usually to vital areas such as the head, and overkill is uncommon.

Investigation: Most often there is evidence of premeditation and the killer may have stalked the victim. The contractor (individual who engaged the killer) usually has personal or business conflicts with the victim, but often demonstrates an apparent improvement in this relationship prior to the murder. The contractor often demonstrates selective recall but has an unusually detailed alibi.

(Douglas, Burgess, Burgess, and Ressler, pp. 23-25).

2. **Gang Motivated Murder** involves both street gangs and subculture biker groups.

Victimology: The victims are usually members or associates of a gang, although innocent bystanders are also peripheral victims. Extortion of local businessmen may be involved, but is usually associated with Asian gangs.

Crime Scene: The scene is usually an open, public place and is often in front of or near the victim's residence, such as drive-by killings.

Staging: Staging is usually not present.

Forensic Findings: Multiple wounds from handguns, shotguns, assault rifles and full-auto weapons (optimum lethality) are characteristic. Knife attacks are not. Ritualistic attacks may methodically target the arms, knees, groin, and legs **first**, then the chest and head.

Investigation: Intelligence on organized criminals will be useful.

(Douglas, Burgess, Burgess, and Ressler, pp. 28-30).

3. **Criminal Competition Homicide** is a result of *Organized crime* conflict over territory.

Victimology: Intergroup and intragroup conflicts between organized crime figures characterize this typology.

Crime Scene: Characterized by well-planned, expedient killing. May appear to be high-risk, but safeguards (e.g. an escape plan) makes the risk lower. Indications reflect experience with the weapon of choice and body disposal may be at either end of the spectrum.

Staging: Usually not present.

Forensic Findings: Evidence of bombing or small-caliber, untraceable weapons are most common.

Investigation: Use of organized crime intelligence is useful.
(Douglas, Burgess, Burgess, and Ressler, pp. 32-33).

4. **Kidnap Murder** involves taking a person by force or fraud against their will.

Victimology: The risk level is greater due to offender perception and resistance and control considerations are factors affecting the risk.

Crime Scene: Crime Scenes may include the abduction location, the death scene, and the body disposal site. There may be evidence of a struggle or interruption of activities. A ransom note may be present and future communication is possible.

Staging: Not present.

Forensic Findings: Evidence may include a ransom note, recordings, victim communication, background noise, document examination, and gunshot wounds.

Investigation: Phone traps and traces, financial records, and threat assessment should be considered.

(Douglas, Burgess, Burgess, and Ressler, pp. 36-37).

5. **Product Tampering Homicide** results from contact with a commercial product that has been sabotaged, usually for financial gain.

Victimology: Victims may be random or specific.

Crime Scene: Crime Scenes may include the location where the product was altered, where it was procured by the victim, where it was used or consumed, and the death scene.

Staging: Staging may be present if the motive is a litigation strategy or if it is intended to look like an accident.

Forensic Findings: Examination of the product, toxicological and chemical analysis, the presence or lack of fingerprints, repackaging, etc. are all evidentiary considerations.

Investigation: Threat assessment, financial checks of litigants, preoffense and postoffense behavior should be considered.

(Douglas, Burgess, Burgess, and Ressler, pp. 41-43).

6. **Drug Murder** involves the motive of removing an obstacle or facilitating illegal drug operations.

Victimology: Five motives are characteristic-discipline, informant, robbery, territory disputes, and anti-drug advocates.

Crime Scenes: Often occurs in a public place to provide a message. Evidence may be removed, along with drugs and proceeds. The weapon of choice is usually brought to the scene and taken away.

Staging: Usually not present.

Forensic Finding: Overkill or drug overdoses may be present.

Investigation: Intelligence and informants may reveal known associates in the drug trade.

(Douglas, Burgess, Burgess, and Ressler, pp. 26-48).

7. **Insurance/Inheritance—Related Death** involves the *subcategories* **individual profit murder** and **commercial profit murder.**

   a. **Individual Profit Murder**

   Victimology: The victim will have a relationship (family, business, live-in partners etc.) with the offender.

   Crime Scene: The body is usually not concealed but left where it will be discovered. Where the scene falls within the Organized–Disorganized continuum depends upon the amount of planning.

   Staging: Staging is frequently encountered in this typology and its complexity is reflected by offender capabilities, resources, and premeditation.

   Forensic Findings: Asphyxial and/or chemical modalities are common and toxicological analysis of blood, liver, hair, etc, may be useful.

   Investigation: Beneficiary provisions and the mechanisms of financial transfers should be checked. Precipitating events and multiple motives should be considered.

   b. **Commercial Profit Murder:**

   Victimology: Likely to involve a partner/professional, family, or personal relationship.

   Crime Scene: (Same as for **individual profit murder**).

   Staging: (same as for **individual profit murder**).

   Forensic Findings: Range from violent death to accidental to natural causes.

   Investigation: Financial and business relationship structures should be examined.

   (Douglas, Burgess, Burgess, and Ressler, pp. 52-61).

8. **Felony Murder** occurs during the commission of a property crime or crime of violence where murder was a secondary motivation. There are two types: **indiscriminate felony murder** and **situational felony murder.**

a. **Indiscriminate Felony Murder** is planned in advance of committing the felony but without a specific victim in mind.

Victimology: Often a potential witness to a crime. No apparent threat to the offender or resistance. Environmental factors and attitude may contribute (occupation, location, time of day, etc.).

Crime Scene: The location is usually a source of cash, the weapon is brought to and removed from the scene, and there is little or no effort to conceal the body.

Staging: If staging occurs, arson may be used to conceal the murder.

Forensic Findings: Use of firearms and/or blunt-force trauma may be present. Signs of restraints (handcuffs, gags, blindfolds, etc.) may be present.

Investigation: Focus on the **robbery** rather than the murder (robbery suspects).

b. **Situational Felony Murder** is unplanned and committed out of panic, confusion, or impulse.

Victimology: Victim of opportunity that is perceived as a **threat** or impediment to a successful **robbery**.

Crime Scene: Less indication of interaction and often a blitz-style attack. May be indicative of **paradoxical** elements (e.g. meticulous entry and hasty retreat).

Staging: Arson *may* be used to conceal the murder.

Forensic Findings: Nonspecific traumatic modalities ranging from blunt trauma to edged weapons to near-contact firearms wounds.

Investigation: Often mid-career criminals, alcohol or drug abuser(s), possibly triggered by something (e.g. alarm, screams, etc.).

(Douglas, Burgess, Burgess, and Ressler, p. 64-70).

PERSONAL CAUSE HOMICIDE

Personal Cause Homicide is an act involving interpersonal aggression resulting in death to person(s) who may not know each other resulting from and underlying emotional conflict.

1. **Erotomania—Motivated Killing** is motivated by an offender-victim relationship based on the offender's fixation. Fantasy is sometimes expressed as **fusion** (the offender blends his/her personality into the victim's) or **erotomania** (fantasy based on idealized romantic love or spiritual union). The killing may result from being rebuffed, conflicts involving *fusion*, or similar motives.

Victimology: These victims are usually targeted as a result of their notoriety. They may also include superiors at work or even strangers, often perceived as having higher status.

Crime Scene: The greater the distance, the more planning and less spontaneity is indicated. Most of these murders are close range and confrontational. The offender may even remain at the scene and witnesses are likely.

Staging: Usually not present.

Forensic Findings: Firearms are the most common weapons and ballistics and trajectory evidence will be critical.

Investigation: Preoffense behavior, such as surveys and stalking, should be examined. Interviews may reveal the offender's preoccupation and/or fantasy

(Douglas, Burgess, Burgess, and Ressler, pp. 72-74).

2. **Domestic Homicide** occurs when a family or household member kills another member of the household, including common-law relationships. **Subcategories** include *spontaneous domestic homicide* and *staged domestic homicide*.

    a. **Spontaneous Domestic Homicide** is typically triggered by a stressful event or a cumulative buildup of stress.

        Victimology: The relationship may have a history of abuse or conflict.

        Crime Scene: The scene often reflects disorder and perhaps an escalation of violence. **Undoing** is common as a way of expressing remorse rather than for concealment.

        Staging: Staging will not be present, although **personation** in the form of **undoing** (moving, positioning, or covering) is possible.

        Forensic Findings: Alcohol or drugs may be involved.

        Depersonalization, indicated by facial battery, overkill, blunt-force trauma, and/or focused area(s) of injury, may be present. Strangulation and gunshot wounds are common.

        Investigation: Residential murder should be considered for domestic murder. Financial, vocational, and alcohol/drug conflicts should be considered.

    b. **Staged Domestic Homicide** is planned due to stressful event(s).

        Victimology: (same as domestic homicide).

        Crime Scene: The scene reflects a more controlled, organized crime, often with evidence removed.

Staging: Staging is frequently encountered in a planned murder and may be intended to look accidental, due to a secondary crime (e.g. rape or robbery), or a suicide.

Forensic Findings: If the suspect includes himself/herself in the crime scene, he/she receives only superficial wounds while the victim of lesser threat is killed.

Investigation: Preoffense behavior and post offense interviews should be considered.

(Douglas, Burgess, Burgess, and Ressler, pp. 76-81).

3. **Argument/Conflict Murder** results from a dispute between persons other than family or household members.

Victimology: The *victim* often has a history of assaultive behavior and of using violence to resolve his problems. The *exception* is the victim who encounters a volatile, impulsive offender who is predisposed to violence.

Crime Scene: The scene may be spread out and show signs of a struggle. The weapon may be brought to the scene due to the offender's predisposition **or** one of opportunity due to impulsiveness.

Staging: Not present.

Forensic Findings: Alcohol and drugs may be involved and the mode of death is usually based upon weapon availability.

Investigation: Precipitating events (argument or conflict) should be determined. The suspect may live in the vicinity of the attack and/or the victim.

    a. **Argument Murder** results from a verbal dispute.

    b. **Conflict Murder** results from personal conflict between the victim and the offender.

(Douglas, Burgess, Burgess, and Ressler, pp. 86-88).

4. **Authority Killing** involves the killing of person(s) that have an authority relationship or symbolic authority relationship by which the killer perceives he/she has been wronged.

Victimology: **Primary** targets are those perceived as doing wrong to the offender (based on psychotic or paranoid delusions). **Secondary** victim(s) become random targets.

Crime Scene: Because the offender is mission oriented, he/she has little or no intention to abort his/her plan and escape the scene or responsibility for the act. On the contrary, the offender may desire to die at the scene by suicide or confrontation with police. The act may result in a **mass** or **spree** murder.

Staging: Not usually present.

Forensic Findings: Often numerous shell casings are found. Multiple wounds on a victim may be indicative of the **primary** target. If the primary target is not taken, the offender may commit suicide or surrender when he/she runs out of ammunition.

Investigation: The offender is likely to have a history of paranoid behavior and open dissatisfaction with general or specific circumstances in life.

(Douglas, Burgess, Burgess, and Ressler, pp. 91-92).

5. **Revenge Killing** involves murder in retaliation for a perceived wrong.

Victimology: The victim may be known or unknown, multiple persons, and is likely to have had some interaction or significant event with the offender.

Crime Scene: Though less spontaneous, often reflecting a well-organized crime scene, the mission oriented offender may not be experienced at criminal activity. The crime scene may reflect this inexperience and indicate a **shift from organized to disorganized behavior** (e.g. well planned, skillful approach leaving no evidence, followed by a blitz style attack and rapid exit leaving a great deal of evidence). The weapon may be left at the scene, although it was brought to the scene. There may be no escape plan.

Staging: Usually not present.

Forensic Findings: The weapon is usually one of choice, often a firearm or knife, and used at close range. Contact wounds are prevalent and defensive wounds are possible.

Investigation: Preoffense behavior often verbalizes the perceived wrong (motive). The offender may have sought a weapon. There may be witnesses.

(Douglas, Burgess, Burgess, and Ressler, pp. 96-97).

6. **Non specific—Motive Killing** involves a homicide that appears irrational and is committed for a reason known only to the offender. It may be defined and categorized after extensive investigation.

Victimology: Random, with no apparent relationship.

Crime Scene; **Disorganized,** with no attempt to conceal victim(s). Nothing missing. Usually a public place which poses a high risk to the offender. Often multiple weapons intended to kill as many people as possible, often becoming a **massacre**.

Staging: Not present.

Forensic Findings: Usually a great deal of physical evidence, including weapons, shell casings, prints, etc. Wounds concentrate on vital areas.

Investigation: Public places intended for high death tolls result in witnesses. The offender is not concerned with being identified, has no escape plan, and may intend to commit suicide or be shot by police. Preoffense characteristics include disheveled appearance and withdrawn, isolated, and erratic behavior.

(Douglas, Burgess, Burgess, and Ressler, pp. 99-100).

7. **Extremist Homicide** is committed on behalf of a political, religious, economic or social ideology. The group, however, does not sanction the offender's actions. There are three *typologies:*

  a. **Political extremist homicide** is motivated by doctrines or philosophies in opposition to a current position of a government or its representatives (e.g. the Robert Kennedy assassination).

  b. **Religious extremist homicide** is motivated by a fervent devotion to a cause, principle, or system of beliefs based on supernatural or supernormal agencies.

  c. **Socioeconomic extremist homicide** is motivated by an intense hostility and aversion toward another individual or group that represents a certain ethnic, social, or religious group.

    Victimology: **Primary** targets usually represent the antithesis of the offender's belief system, although there may be **secondary** targets.

    Crime Scene: Often a public place indicative of the motive. Less organized than a group effort. A blitz style attack or long-range attack (e.g. sniper) is common.

    Staging: Usually not present.

    Forensic Findings: Multiple wounds, often from a firearm or knife.

    Investigation: Preoffense behavior may include generalized derogatory comments and stalking. Post offense conversation may reflect an interest in the homicide. Communiqués claiming responsibility should undergo threat assessment to determine authenticity.

    (Douglas, Burgess, Burgess and Ressler, pp. 104-106).

8. **Mercy/Hero Homicide** is usually perpetrated on the critically ill. The **mercy** offender believes he/she is relieving suffering. The **hero** offender is unsuccessful in attempts to save the victim's life.

a. **Mercy Homicides** are motivated by a sense of power and control and are often **serial murders.**

Victimology: Elderly and/or ill, usually in a hospital, nursing home, etc. in a client/caregiver relationship. The victim is rarely random, but usually known to the offender.

Crime Scene: Instrument of death is one of opportunity, often common to institutional settings (e.g. drugs, syringes, toxic substances, etc.). Signs of struggle are minimal or absent.

Staging: The body is arranged to represent a peaceful, natural death or sometimes an accident or suicide.

Forensic Findings: Toxicology for poisoning, signs of broken ribs or suspicious death, liver biopsy, blood and urine screens, and hair analysis (arsenic and drugs) should be completed. Asphyxiation should be checked for petechial hemorrhage.

Investigation: Inspection of suspect's employment history is important.

b. **Hero Homicide** occurs when the offender creates a life-threatening condition for the victim and then unsuccessfully attempts to rescue/resuscitate the victim to appear as a hero.

Victimology: Victims may include the critically ill, infants and, in institutional settings, victims of opportunity.

Crime Scene: Drug inducement, syringes, medicine vials, etc. or fire with evidence of arson may be present.

Staging: Staging is intended to stage a life-threatening crisis or scenario staring the offender as the hero, including natural calamities, accidents, or criminal activity.

Forensic Findings: Look for drugs and toxic substances.

Investigation: Interviews with co-workers may be revealing.

(Douglas, Burgess, Burgess, and Ressler, pp. 111-116).

9. **Hostage Murder** takes place during a hostage situation. This category is for classification and definition only and does not include offender identification characteristics in the CCM. (Douglas, Burgess, Burgess, and Ressler, pp. 122-123).

SEXUAL HOMICIDE

Sexual homicide involves sexual activity as the basis for the sequence of acts leading to death. These acts may range from rape (before or after death) to a symbolic sexual assault (Douglas, Burgess, Burgess, and Ressler, p. 123).

1. **Organized Sexual Homicide** describes a sexual offender based on the criminal act, analysis of victim(s) and crime scene(s) (including staging), and evaluation of forensic reports. An **organized offender** appears to plan his/her murders, to target victims, and to display control at crime scenes, reflecting an orderly, methodical approach.

   Victimology: The victim of a sexual homicide by an organized offender is ften female, although male adolescents are also targeted. A single, employed person, living alone, is common. The victim is usually not known but is often chosen because he/she meets certain criteria.

   Crime Scene: Crime scenes involving organized sexual murder may include the point of contact/assault, the death scene, and the body disposal site. Weapons are brought to and taken from the scene. It reflects a methodical approach and evidence may be removed. Time permitting, the body will be concealed.

   Staging: The offender may stage the scene to appear careless and disorganized to distract and mislead the police. Secondary criminal activity may also be staged.

   Investigation: The offender is usually socially adept with verbal skills and often dresses neatly. The offender may impersonate a police officer or security guard to gain confidence. The offender's methodical approach is incorporated into victim selection (Douglas, Burgess, Burgess, and Ressler, pp. 123-125).

2. **Disorganized Sexual Homicide** refers to a sexual homicide based upon victim and crime analysis, forensic evaluation, and assessment of the act. It is unplanned and spontaneous, as reflected in each of these factors. *Disorganization* may be the result of youthfulness, lack of criminal sophistication, drug and/or alcohol abuse, and/or mental deficiency.

   Victimology: The victim may be known as the offender selects victims of opportunity near his/her residence or employment. The offender acts impulsively under stress and has confidence in familiar surroundings. The victim's age, sex, and other characteristics will vary to a greater extent due to their random selection.

   Crime Scene: The scene reflects the spontaneous and sometimes symbolic nature of the killing. It is random, sloppy, and in greater disarray. The death scene and crime scene are often the same. **Depersonalization** may be present as evidenced by the victim's face being covered or the body turned over. There is no plan to deter detection or conceal the body or evidence. The weapon is one of opportunity, obtained and left at the scene.

Staging: Secondary criminal activity does not necessarily indicate staging. Positioning may have more to do with sexual fantasies than staging. **Personation** may also be present.

Forensic Findings: The **disorganized** offender is often socially inept and feels inadequate, compelling an ambush or blitz attack. **Depersonalization** may involve mutilation of the face and **overkill** to the face, genitals, and breasts. Body parts may even be missing. Insertion of foreign objects into body orifices (*insertional necrophilia*) and mutilation may be involved with sexual acts.

Investigation: the disorganized offender usually lives alone or with a parental figure. He lives or works in proximity to the crime scene. He has a history of inconsistent or poor work performance. Preoffense circumstances may involve minimal stress and life-style change. The offender is usually sloppy, disheveled, and has nocturnal habits. Postoffense behavior may include a change in eating and drinking (alcohol) habits and nervousness.

(Douglas, Burgess, Burgess, and Ressler, pp. 128-130)

3. **Mixed Sexual Homicide** crime scenes may reflect *both* **organized** and **disorganized** characteristics for the following reasons:
   a. More than one offender.
   b. The attack may begin as a well-ordered, planned assault but may deteriorate as unanticipated events occur, such as losing control of the victim.
   c. The primary motive may be rape, but victim resistance or the offender's emotional state may result in escalation (particularly with the **hostile/retaliatory rapist**).
   d. Inconsistencies in offender behavior, the youthfulness of the offender, and/or alcohol or drug use.
   e. External stressors may alter offender behavior, perhaps leading to an explosive, impetuous assault.
   (Douglas, Burgess, Burgess, and Ressler, p. 134).

4. **Sadistic Murder** involves sexual gratification from excessive mental or physical torture and the victim's response to torture. Fantasies are associated with domination, degradation, and violence.
   Victimology: Men, women, and children sometimes indicating a resemblance to someone of significance in the offender's life. The victims are selected through systematic stalking and surveillance and may be approached via a ruse or pretext.

Crime Scene: There are often multiple crime scenes: the initial encounter, the torture/death scene, and/or the body disposal site. Sadism requires a solitary location for prolonged periods for the torture (hours to weeks). Restraints, gloves, customized torture equipment, soundproofing, etc. may be present.

Staging: Overkill and/or depersonalization may be indicated (i.e. to conceal the victim's identity, etc.). Secondary criminal activity (e.g. rape, murder, robbery, etc.) may be indicated to conceal the motive of sadistic murder.

Forensic Findings: The offender engages in sex with the victim prior to the victims death, particularly anal rape, fallatio, vagina rape, and foreign object penetration, *respectively.* The majority of offenders force their victims to engage in **all** of these. The primary motive is the victim's pain rather than the sex act. Battery is focused on the sex organs, genitals, and breasts and may include biting or overkill. Evidence of sexual fluid will usually be found and may be indicative of partners. Offenders may also urinate on victims, even forcing them to drink or eat feces. Death is slow and deliberate, often by asphyxial modality, but not exclusively.

Investigation: The perpetrators are predominantly white, males, sometimes with a male or female partner. Research indicates that 43 percent are married and 50 percent have children. The offender may have an occupation that brings them into contact with the public. Antisocial behavior may be indicated in arrest records and a history of drug abuse. The offender may be a police buff who collects paraphernalia, literature, and weapons. The offender is likely to have a well-maintained vehicle. He may **return** to the scene to determine discovery or progress in the investigation (Douglas, Burgess, Burgess, and Ressler, pp. 136-138).

GROUP CAUSE HOMICIDE

Group Cause Homicide involves two or more people with a common ideology that sanctions an act, committed by one or more of its members, that results in death (Douglas, Burgess, Burgess, and Ressler, p. 144).

1. **Cult Murder** involves a murder committed by two or more members of a *cult.* A **cult** is a group with excessive devotion or dedication to ideas, objects, or persons, is regarded as unorthodox or spurious, and whose primary objectives involve sex, power, and/or money but are unknown to the general membership.

Victimology: Victims may be random but are usually a member or fringe member of the cult. **Multiple** victims are common.

Crime Scene: The scene may contain symbolic artifacts or imagery. Mass grave sites, evidence of multiple offenders or victims, etc. may indicate a **mass** or **spree** killing.

Staging: Usually not present.

Forensic Findings: Multiple weapons may be involved and most often include firearms, blunt-force trauma, and sharp, pointed objects. Mutilation of the body may be present.

Investigation: Cult leaders may have criminal histories and are often involved in scams, unless the cult is a sect or splinter group of a mainstream, conventional religion. There may be a message, following the killing, intended for the public. Cult literature, clothing, artifacts, candles, etc. may be found during searches.

(Douglas, Burgess, Burgess, and Ressler, pp. 145-146).

2. **Extremist Murder** is motivated by ideas of a particular political, economic, religious, or social system.

> *Typologies:* Group causes are rarely isolated to a single typology, often blending one or more motivations. Classification is based on the predominant motive.

>> a. **Political** type homicides are motivated by doctrines or philosophies that oppose a current position of government and/or its representatives.

>> b. **Religious** type homicides are prompted by a fervent devotion or belief system based on "orthodox religious conventions," but does **not** include cult or occult murder.

>> c. **Socioeconomic** murder is a result of intense hostility and aversion toward another individual or group for ethnic, social, economic, or religious reasons.

> *Subclassifications:*

>> d. **Paramilitary Extremist Murder** involves extremist groups with paramilitary organizational structures and methods of operation. These are characterized by uniforms, training compounds, hierachial ranks, internal codes of discipline and conduct, etc.

>> e. **Hostage Extremist Murder** involves a murder during a hostage or kidnapping situation perpetrated by an extremist group.

> *Victimology:* The victim represents the antithesis of the offenders' belief systems. The victim may be a random victim of opportunity or

one targeted to die in a premeditated, well-planned attack. Victims may have come into conflict with the group, such as informants, or be associated with a targeted group.

Crime Scene: Multiple sites may include the confrontation site, the death scene, and the body disposal/burial locale. The "calling card" of the group (symbols, communiqués, etc.) may be left at the scene. The **organized** use of military tactics and MO are common to the Paramilitary Extremist Murder.

Staging: Staging to mislead investigators is **not** present because the murder has an intended message.

Forensic Findings: Physical evidence from multiple offenders may include fibers, hairs, prints, and impressions. A combination and variety of weapons may be indicated. Forensics may indicate the "calling card" or **signature** of the group. Paramilitary attacks do not usually demonstrate overkill.

Investigation: Preoffense behavior is indicative of planning, surveillance, and victim selection. Post offense analysis of the group's "calling card" is important to verify authenticity. Group protection conspiracy is common. Booby traps should be expected (Douglas, Burgess, Burgess, and Ressler, pp. 150-156).

3. **Group—Excitement Murder** involves two or more persons who cause a death that is **structured** or **unstructured** and has a contagious and spontaneous component.

Victimology: The victim may be initially targeted but, as chaos and excitement escalate, random victims may be involved. The group may also select a victim randomly and may involve multiple victims. Survivors of the attack are possible.

Crime Scene: Witnesses are common, but may be reluctant, as attacks are ally in open, public places. Weapons of opportunity, particularly personal weapons (hands and feet) are common and the scene is typically **disorganized** with no cover up or concealment. Signs of multiple offenders (fingerprints, footprints, fibers, semen, etc.) are common.

Staging: Not present.

Forensic Findings: Overkill from bludgeoning and generalized blunt-force trauma is common. Multiple wounds and sexual assault or insertion may be present.

Investigation: Drugs and alcohol are typically involved. The attack is of short duration and involves a loosely structured group with no primary leader.

(Douglas, Burgess, Burgess, and Ressler, pp. 158-159).

ARSON

Arson is the willful and malicious burning of property.

Vandalism—Motivated Arson

Vandalism—motivated arson is a result of malicious and mischievous motivation that results in destruction and damage. Categories include **willful and malicious mischief, peer/group pressure,** and **other.**

1. **Willful and Malicious Mischief**
2. **Peer/Group Pressure**
3. **Other**

(Douglas, Burgess, Burgess, and Ressler, p. 167).

> *Victimology:* Targeted property, such as educational facilities, residential areas, and vegetation, which is selected for vandalism.
>
> *Crime Scene:* Often indicative of multiple offenders who act spontaneously and impulsively. One person tends to be the leader or instigator. The scene typically represents a **disorganized** crime with materials at the scene being used and physical evidence left.
>
> *Forensic Findings:* Flammable liquids are commonly found and, sometimes, fireworks or firecrackers will be present.
>
> *Investigation:* The typical offender is a male juvenile with 7-9 years of education and a poor record of school performance. He does not work, is single, lives with one or both parents, and may be known to the police and/or have an arrest record. The offender may also be known to school authorities as being disruptive and having a problem dealing with authority. Most live less than one mile from scene, flee immediately from the scene and do not return. If they do view the fire, it is from a safe distance. (Douglas, Burgess, Burgess, and Ressler, pp. 167-168).

Excitement—Motivated Arson

Excitement—motivated arson is prompted by a craving for excitement that is satisfied by firesetting. The offender rarely intends to harm anyone. This category includes the subcategories:

1. **Thrill Seeker**
2. **Attention Seeker**
3. **Recognition (Hero)**

4. **Sexual Perversion**
5. **Other**

> *Victimology:* Targeted property type helps ascertain the motive. This offender may choose to observe the fire suppression and investigation from a safe location. Volunteer firefighters and fire buffs should not be ruled out as suspects, alone or with multiple offenders. A small percentage of these type of offenders are motivated by sexual perversion, but may be indicated by ejaculate, fecal deposits, and/or pornographic material.
>
> *Forensic Findings:* Vehicle and bicycle tracks, incendiary devices or components, etc., may be present. Indicators of sexual perversion may also be present.
>
> *Crime Scene:* Offenders usually use materials on hand and incendiary devices usually have a time-delay mechanism. Offenders who are 18-30 years of age are more likely to use accelerants. Matches and cigarettes are often used to ignite vegetation fires.
>
> *Investigation:* Excitement arsonists are typically juveniles or young adult males with ten or more years of formal education. They are generally unemployed, single, and living with one or both parents. His family tends to be from the middle to lower-middle-class. He is socially inadequate, particularly in heterosexual relationships. A history of nuisance offenses is likely and the older the offender, the longer the record. Target and cluster analysis helps determine the distance of the offender and if he is mobile. Many mingle at the scene with a crowd and/or return to the scene. Many are **serial** arsonists (Douglas, Burgess, Burgess, and Ressler, pp. 170-171).

Revenge—Motivated Arson

Revenge—motivated arson occurs in retaliation for some perceived injustice. This may be a one-time, well-planned event **or** committed by a serial arsonist taking revenge against society with little or no pre-planning. This category includes:

1. **Personal Retaliation**
2. **Societal Retaliation**
3. **Institutional Retaliation**
4. **Group Retaliation**
5. **Intimidation**
6. **Other**

Victimology: The victim (targeted property) often has a history of inter-personal or professional conflict with the offender. Targeted property often varies with the sex of the offender and female offenders typically target something significant to the victim. Ex-lover revenge arsonists often burn clothing, bedding, and/or personal effects.

Crime Scene: While females typically burn areas of personal signifi-cance, males may start there but extend the range of damage. Males may use excessive accelerants or Molotov cocktails.

Forensic Findings: Females tend to use what is available, such as lighter fluid, while males are inclined toward excessive accelerants, such as gasoline. Cloth fibers, fingerprints, residue, etc. may be present.

Investigation: The revenge fire is usually an adult male with ten or more years of formal education. If employed, he is usually a blue-col-lar worker of lower socioeconomic status. He typically rents, tends not to be a loner, and has close but not stable or long-term relation-ships. The *exception* is the revenge-motivated **serial** arsonist who is often a loner. The offender often has prior offenses, such as burglary, theft, or vandalism. Use of drugs and, especially, alcohol during the crime is typical. The offender is rarely accompanied to the scene and rarely returns. He frequently uses a vehicle and wants to distance him-self from the fire to establish an alibi. Precipitating events may have occurred months or years prior and escalate (Douglas, Burgess, Burgess, and Ressler, pp. 173-174).

Crime Concealment—Motivated Arson

Crime concealment—motivated arson involves arson as a secondary or collateral criminal activity to cover up the primary criminal activity. This category includes:

1. **Murder**
2. **Suicide**
3. **Breaking and Entering** (burglary)
4. **Embezzlement**
5. **Larceny** (theft)
6. **Destroying Records**
7. **Other**

Victimology: Targeted property depends on the nature of the conceal-ment (primary crime) and may include a business, residence, or vehicle.

Crime Scene:

Murder concealment attempts to conceal the fact a murder has been committed, destroys evidence, and/or attempts to conceal the victims identity. The **origin** is usually on or near the victim. The offender tends to be **disorganized.** An attack that appears personalized is indicative of a lone offender. The "DNA torch" uses fire to conceal *genetic markers* of sexual homicide.

Burglary concealment is reflected by inexperienced or unsophisticated burglars using available materials to conceal the presence of multiple offenders.

Auto Theft concealment involves arson to eliminate prints after use or stripping a vehicle, often by multiple offenders.

Destruction of Records involves arson-for-profit and usually the point of origin starts with the records.

> *Forensic Findings:* Determine if the victim alive when the fire started and why he/she did not escape.
>
> *Investigation:* The offender is most likely a young adult who lives within the surrounding community and is highly mobile. The offender who conceals **burglary** or **auto theft** is often accompanied by co-offenders, who leave the scene immediately and does not return. **Murder** concealment is usually a one-time event and does not involve serial arson. With an arson to **destroy records**, determine who benefits from such concealment (Douglas, Burgess, Burgess, and Ressler, pp. 176-177).

Profit-Motivated Arson

Profit-Motivated Arson involves fire for the purpose of achieving material gain (directly or indirectly). *Arson for profit* is a commercial crime exhibiting the least passion. Categories include:

1. **Fraud**
   a. Insurance
   b. Liquidating property
   c. Dissolving business
   d. Inventory
2. **Employment**
3. **Parcel Clearance**
4. **Competition**
5. **Other**

> *Victimology:* Targeted property includes residential, business, and transportation property.

Crime Scenes: This type of arson reflects a well-planned and methodical approach and **organized** style containing less physical evidence. Large business arsons may involve multiple offenders' excessive use of accelerants. Multiple sets are also typical, including accelerant trails. A lack of forced entry, elaborate timers, remnants of devices, etc. are common. Items of value, especially in residences, are frequently removed and sometimes replaced with cheaper items before the fire. Personal items, such as photos, may be removed. *Count the clothes hangers* for an indicator.

Forensic Findings: Accelerants, mixtures, component devices, etc. may be present.

Investigation: The **offender** is typically an adult male with 10 or more years of formal education. The **secondary offender** is the "torch for hire" who is usually a male, twenty-five to forty years of age, and often unemployed. The average **primary offender** may have no criminal record, while the **secondary offender** often has prior arrests for burglary, assault, public intoxication, and possibly prior arson arrests. The offender usually lives more than a mile from the scene, may be accompanied to the scene, and most leave without returning. (Douglas, Burgess, Burgess, and Ressler, pp. 180-181).

Extremist—Motivated Arson

Extremist—Motivated Arson is committed to further a social, political, or religious cause. These include:

1. **Terrorism**
2. **Discrimination**
3. **Riots/Civil Disturbances**
4. **Other**

Victimology: Targeted property depends on the motive and usually represents the antithesis of the offender's beliefs.

Crime Scene: The scene reflects an **organized** and focused attack, often by multiple offenders. Incendiary devices, symbolic messages, communiqués, and "overkill" are also typical. Be **cautious** for unexploded devices.

Forensic Findings: Arson evidence and incendiary devices may be indicated.

Investigation: Extremist offenders may be identifiable via their group or cause and may have an arrest record (Douglas, Burgess, Burgess, and Ressler, p. 184-185).

Serial, Spree, and Mass Arson

1. **Serial Arson** involves three or more separate fire settings with a characteristic cooling-off period between fires. It may appear random and unpredictable in nature. *Serial* arsonists may also commit *spree* arsons. It is **not** a separate motive, but a **pattern** of *revenge -, excitement-, or extremist-, motivated arsons.*

2. **Spree Arson** involves three or more separate locations with no emotional cooling-off period between them.

3. **Mass Arson** involves one offender who sets three or more fires at the same location during a limited period of time, e.g. a multi-story building.

    Victimology: Targeted property usually includes vulnerable targets such as unoccupied or abandoned property during the night and may be random.

    Crime Scene: Typically **disorganized**, physical evidence is often present. Materials found at the scene are often used while the source of ignition is brought by the offender, who is usually alone.

    Forensic Findings: Dependent upon motive.

    Investigation: The offender is usually male and younger than the single-event arsonist. He tends to be a loner, although a secondary party may have knowledge of his activities. He is likely an underachiever with minimal education. He has poor interpersonal skills and is socially inadequate. He is often unemployed or has an erratic, unskilled work history. This offender walks to the scene and typically lives within one mile. The tighter the cluster, the closer he lives.

    The **exception** is the **extremist serial arsonist** who may be well educated and have above average intelligence. He is highly mobile, focuses his attack on specific targets, uses sophisticated incendiary devices, and leaves little or no physical evidence. This is an **organized** type offender (Douglas, Burgess, Burgess, and Ressler, pp. 186-188).

RAPE AND SEXUAL ASSAULT

Criminal Enterprise Rape

Criminal Enterprise Rape or sexual assault involves sexual coercion, abuse, or assault committed for material gain (Douglas, Burgess, Burgess, and Ressler, p. 199).

1. **Felony Rape** involves sexual assault committed during the commission of a felony, whether the rape was the primary or secondary intent (Douglas, Burgess, Burgess, and Ressler, p. 199).

    a. **Primary Felony Rape** is a nonsexual felony (robbery, burglary, etc.) in which the victim is at the scene and sexually assaulted as a second offense.

    Victimology: Usually an adult female.

    Crime Scene: Evidence of primary felony (robbery, burglary, etc.).

    Forensic Findings: Forensic evidence of sexual assault.

    Investigation: Look for similar felonies in the area, including MO and similar stolen items (Douglas, Burgess, Burgess, and Ressler, pp. 199-200).

    b. **Secondary Felony Rape** involves a sexual assault accompanied by a second planned felony (robbery, burglary, etc.). The nonsexual secondary felony would occur if the victim was not present.

    Victimology: Usually an adult female.

    Crime Scene: Evidence of burglary or robbery.

    Forensic Findings: Sexual assault evidence and indications that the offender knew the victim would be present.

    Investigation: The offender is likely to have been in the area before and probably has a history of robbery and rape in the area. The sexual offense is preferentially motivated.

(Douglas, Burgess, Burgess, and Ressler, p. 201)

Personal Cause Sexual Assault

Personal cause Sexual Assault results from interpersonal aggression and sexual victimization to person(s) who may or may not be known to the offender. The assault is motivated by an "underlying emotional conflict or psychological issue" (Douglas, Burgess, Burgess, and Ressler, pp. 202-203).

1. Nuisance Offenses

Nuisance Offenses include:

a. **Isolated/Opportunistic Offenses** in which the offender takes an opportunity or something that presents itself (e.g. wrong-number obscene phone calls).

b. **Preferential Offenses** involving preferential sexual acts characterized by rigid, ritualistic patterns of behavior (peeping, exposing, repeated obscene phone calls, etc.).

c. **Transition Offenses**, such as peeping, may be a result of exploring arousal patterns, building confidence, improving the ability to commit the offense, etc. as an early step in criminal sexual development.

d. **Preliminary Offenses** are nuisance offenses which are a preliminary component of a contact sexual offense, e.g. a fetish burglar who cases a home prior to returning to commit a rape. This is a prelude to even more serious sex offenses.

(Douglas, Burgess, Burgess, and Ressler, pp. 203-204)

2. **Domestic Sexual Assault** involves a family, household, or former household member who sexually assaults another member, including common-law relationships. The assault may be spontaneous, situational, and triggered by a real or imagined stressful event perceived by the offender as an injustice.

a. **Adult Domestic Sexual Assault** involves assault to a spouse or common-law relationship and usually is characterized by a history of prior abuse or conflict.

Victimology: Familial or common-law relationship.

Crime Scene: Usually one scene reflecting **disorder**, impetuousness, and/or the escalation of violence.

Forensic Findings: Alcohol or drugs may be involved. The sexual assault is preceded by violence, including trauma to the face and body.

Investigation: Look for a history of conflict due to external sources, e.g. financial, vocational, alcohol, etc.

b. **Child Domestic Sexual Abuse** includes sexual assault on any household member under the age of majority.

Victimology: Familial or common-law relationship, usually associated with prior abuse or conflict.

Crime Scene: Usually the victim's and/or offender's residence.

Forensic Findings: Vaginal or anal scarring. Lack of medical corroboration does **not** preclude victimization.

Investigation: Look for prior reports.

(Douglas, Burgess, Burgess, and Ressler, pp. 205-207)

3. **Entitlement Rape** involves the offender forcing the victim into sexual activity. Issues of power and control are underlying psychological conflicts.

a. **Social Acquaintance Rape** involves prior knowledge or a relationship between the victim and offender, e.g. "date rape," student/teacher, or athlete/coach relationships. With children it might involve a neighbor or family friend. Subcategories include:

i.) Adult

ii.) Adolescent

iii.) Child

b. **Subordinate Rape** involves a status imbalance in which one person has power over another by employment, education, or age. Subcategories include:

    i.)   Adult

    ii.)   Adolescent

    iii.)   Child

c. **Power—Reassurance Rape** involves the goal of developing a relationship with an adolescent, with sexual activities being secondary to the interpersonal intent. The victim is seen as an appropriate social and sexual companion and the offender perceives it as mutually satisfying. This is usually **not** violent in nature. Subcategories include:

    i.)   Adult

    ii.)   Adolescent

    iii.)   Child

d. **Exploitative Rape** or *opportunistic rape* is an expression of low aggression, not exceeding the force necessary to gain compliance. Callous indifference to the victim is evident. Subcategories include:

    i.)   Adult

    ii.)   Adolescent

    iii.)   Child

(Douglas, Burgess, Burgess, and Ressler, pp. 209-217)

4. **Anger Rape** is characterized by highly expressive, unprovoked physical and verbal aggression or force in excess of that necessary to gain victim compliance. Rage is evident and may be manifested by **sadistic** sexual assault motivated by punishment rather than sexual gratification. Subcategories include:

a. **Anger Rape, Gender (Women Hating)** which is intended to hurt, demean, humiliate, or punish the victim.

b. **Anger Rape, Age** which is motivated by expressing anger toward a specific age group (usually the young or elderly). Sub-subcategories include:

    i.)   **Anger Rape, Elderly Victim** and

    ii.)   **Anger Rape, Child Victim.**

c. **Anger Rape, Racial** is racially motivated and victims are usually of a different race than the offender.

d. **Anger Rape, Global** involves an offender who is angry at the world and expresses high aggression. They also have a history of fighting men. This offender is impulsive, exhibits behavior

problems, and begins his encounters with the law at an early age. Offenses are usually not planned.
(Douglas, Burgess, Burgess, and Ressler, pp. 219-225)

5. **Sadistic Rape** involves the offender's sexual arousal as a result of the victim's pain, fear or discomfort. Behavioral evidence may include whipping, bondage, violence against erogenous parts of the victim's body, insertion of foreign objects, intercourse after the victim is unconscious, and the use of urine and/or feces. Subcategories include:
    a.   **Sadistic Rape, Adult**
    b.   **Sadistic Rape, Adolescent**
    c.   **Sadistic Rape, Child**
(Douglas, Burgess, Burgess, and Ressler, pp. 227-229)

6. **Child/Adolescent Pornography** involves collectors who collect, maintain, and prize child pornography. They are classified as:
    a.   **Closet Collectors** who keep secret their interest in pornography and deny involvement with children.
    b.   **Isolated Collectors** choose sexual activity with one child at a time and may be involved with their own child, children of neighbors, nephews, nieces, friends' children, or children under their care, such as students. They may also seek out children, not known to them, by traveling.
    c.   **Cottage Collectors** are pedophiles who sexually exploit children in a group. The intent is to create relationships with other pedophile collectors and as a method of communications.
(Douglas, Burgess, Burgess, and Ressler, pp. 230-231)

7. **Historical Child/Adolescent Sex Rings** use children to create obscene materials, i.e. photos, movies, and videos for private and commercial uses.
    a.   **Solo Child Sex Rings** involve several children in sexual activities with an adult (usually male) who recruits them.
    b.   **Transitional Child Sex Rings** involve multiple offenders and victims. The offenders are known to each other and collect and share victims.
    c.   **Syndicated Child Sex Rings** are well-structured organizations involved in the recruitment of children, the production of pornography, the delivery of sexual services, and the establishment of an extensive network of customers.
(Douglas, Burgess, Burgess, and Ressler, pp. 232-237)

8. **Multidimensional Sex Rings** involve multiple young offenders, multiple offenders, fear as a control tactic, and bizarre or ritualistic activity (Douglas, Burgess, Burgess, and Ressler, pp. 240-241).

    a.   **Adult Survivor Sex Rings** (almost always *women*) of almost any age in therapy and often diagnosed with *multiple personality disorder*. Adult survivors reveal childhood victimization that includes multiple victims and offenders, fear as a control tactic, and bizarre and/or ritualistic activities. Offenders are described as members of **satanic** or **cult groups** with civic leaders, **police** officers, or persons wearing police **uniforms** present during the exploitation. The offenders may still harass or threaten the victims and in several cases women claim to have had babies taken for human sacrifice. Therapists often fear for their own safety after learning their patient's secret. (Douglas, Burgess, Burgess, and Ressler, p. 241)

    b.   **Day-Care Sex Rings** involve multiple victims and offenders, fear, and bizarre or ritualistic activity. Descriptions of strange games, of killing animals, of photographing activities, and of wearing costumes are common. (Douglas, Burgess, Burgess, and Ressler, p. 241).

    c.   **Family/Isolated Neighborhood Sex Rings** are described by children in which their victimization is within their family or extended family. The group is often defined by geographic boundaries (e.g. cul-de-sac, apartment buildings, isolated rural areas, etc.). Offenders are usually male and victims tend to be more than six years of age. Custody or visitation disputes are often involved. (Douglas, Burgess, Burgess, and Ressler, p. 241).

    d.   **Custody/Visitation Dispute Sex Rings** involves the same dynamics as other multidimensional sex rings but also involves the taking of the child victim into hiding by a parent during a custody or visitation dispute.

(Douglas, Burgess, Burgess, and Ressler, p. 242).

9.   **Abduction Rape** involves forcibly removing a person from one location to another and committing a sexual assault at a second location. Subcategories include:

    a.   Adult

    b.   Adolescent

c. Child
(Douglas, Burgess, Burgess, and Ressler, p. 242).

10. Group Cause Sexual Assault

Group Cause Sexual Assault involves multiple (three or more) offenders. **Group dynamics** (contagion effects, defusing of responsibility, etc.) and **social dynamics** (e.g. developed gang cultures) foster gang rape, yet motivations may vary (Douglas, Burgess, and Burgess, p. 244).

a. **Formal Gang Sexual Assault** is characterized by some internal, organizational   structure and a gang with a name and identifying features (e.g. colors, insignias, dress patterns, etc.). The gang must have a mission or purpose other than the assault. Subcategories include:
i) Single Victim and
ii) Multiple Victim
(Douglas, Burgess, Burgess, and Ressler, p. 244)
b. **Informal Gang Sexual Assault** involves a loosely structured group that congregates, perhaps on the spur of the moment, for antisocial purposes. There is no formal organizational structure or evidence that the group constitutes a formal gang. Subcategories include:
i) Single Victim and
ii) Multiple Victims
(Douglas, Burgess, Burgess, and Ressler, p. 245)

The CCM describes taxonomic descriptions of rapists based on sexual and aggressive motivations. These include:

1. **The Power—Reassurance Rapist**, who expresses his rape fantasies.
2. **The Exploitive Rapist**, who expresses impulsive predatory sexual behavior.
3. **The Anger Rapist**, who expresses sexual behavior as anger and rage.
4. **The Sadistic Rapist**, who expresses sexual behavior through sexually aggressive sadistic fantasies.
(Douglas, Burgess, Burgess, and Ressler, pp. 194-195)

For clarification and elaboration on the classification of crimes and typologies, the *Crime Classification Manual* (CCM) by John E. Douglas, Ann W. Burgess, Allen G. Burgess, and Robert K. Ressler should be consulted. This standardized classification system and study is the criminologists' equivalent to the *DSM-IV* and should be considered a required reference source for the investigator and criminologist.

Stephen Michaud and Roy Hazelwood divide rapists into six groups:

1. **The Power Reassurance Rapist,** who tries to reassure himself of his own masculinity by exercising physical control over women (Michaud and Hazelwood, p. 71).
2. **The Power Assertive Rapist,** who assaults to assert his masculinity and his macho self-image (Michaud and Hazelwood, pp. 72-73).
3. **The Anger Retaliatory Rapist,** who is angry at women for real or imagined wrongs. His is impulsive, spends little time with victims, often experiencing sexual dysfunction, and uses excessive force (Michaud and Hazelwood, p. 73).
4. **The Anger Excitation Rapist,** who is the **most dangerous** and is a sexual *sadist* who is stimulated by his victim's suffering (Michaud and Hazelwood, p. 74).
5. **The Opportunistic Rapist,** who is the **only** type who commits sexual assault for sexual desire, usually while committing another crime (e.g. robbery, kidnapping, etc.) (Michaud and Hazelwood, p. 76).
6. **The Gang Rapist,** who participates in pathological group behavior in which the victim is almost always seriously injured. "There is always a leader and a reluctant participant, who often makes himself known to the victim." (Michaud and Hazelwood, p. 76).

INTERVIEWING

Data for the following section were compiled from official records (psychiatric and criminal records, pretrial records, court transcripts, interviews with correctional staff, and/or prison records) and interviews with offenders. For some variables, data were not available due to incomplete records, conflicting responses, and offender unwilling to respond to certain questions. Those who refused to be interviewed did so on advise of their attorney or due to their psychotic condition (Ressler, Burgess, and Douglas, p. xi).

One of the **goals** of *psychological profiling* is to provide interviewing suggestions and strategies to investigators. The profile packet should contain information regarding personality characteristics and strategies for soliciting information from diverse groups of offenders (Holmes, p.12).

For example, the psychopaths mature at a slower rate than most people and do not reach maturity until they near their thirties. The **psychodynamic** approach suggests that feelings and behavior are overtly symbolic of a wide variety of unconscious conflicts. These conflicts result from a continual battle between the **id**, the **ego**, and the **superego** (Holmes, p. 29).

The **id** represents the biological drives of personality. The **superego** is the social response component. The **ego** is the personality component, which controls the impulses of the *id*. The *id's* impulses center on sex and aggression and the *ego* controls and minimizes the conflict between the *id* and the *superego* (Holmes, pp. 29-30).

Russell Vorpagel describes this, saying, "The **superego** or conscience dictates to you what is good or what is bad. The **id** tells you to do things for your won pleasure and not regard basic norms." He goes on to say, "When the *superego* is overcome by the *id*, the person can perform aberrations or antisocial behavior. When the *superego* 'recover,' it cannot tolerate believing that it would have done a normally prohibitive act." (Harrington and Vorpagel, p. 148).

Vorpagel continues "In order to assuage this guilt feeling, subconscious acts are fed to the *superego*, showing acts of restitution or forgetting what really happened." This is a way of lying to your conscious (Harrington and Vorpagel, p. 148).

The interview strategy not only assists in corroborating the facts of a case, but also can provide the information needed for case linkage, motive assessment, and the development of further investigative strategy (Turvey, p. 288).

CONCLUSION

Brent Turvey describes two types of criminal profiling—**inductive** and **deductive**. While mainstream profilers (criminal investigative analysts) utilize the **organized** and **disorganized** model, Turvey says this is a false dichotomy (Turvey, pp. 13, 25, and 145).

Turvey identifies motivational typologies and offender characteristics as major components of profiling (Turvey, pp. 169 and 183).

The *Crime Classification Manual* (CCM) by John E. Douglas, Ann W. Burgess, Allen G. Burgess, and Robert K. Ressler is the "Bible" of profiling and analogous to the *DSM-IV.* The *CCM* outlines classifications for Homicide, Arson, and Rape and Sexual Assault typologies.

The **Organized** and **Disorganized** characteristics are identified in the following reference table.

REFERENCES—CHAPTER 6

Douglas, John, Ann W. Burgess, Allen G. Burgess, and Robert K. Ressler. **Crime Classification Manual: A Standard System for Investigating and Classifying Violent Crimes.** New York, NY: Lexington Books, 1992.

Holmes, Ronald M. **Profiling Violent Crimes: An Investigative Tool.** Newbury Park, CA: Sage Publications, 1989.

Michaud, Stephen. **The Evil That Men Do: FBI Profiler Roy Hazelwood's Journey Into the Minds of Sexual Predators.** New York, NY: St. Martin's Press, 1998.

Ressler, Robert K., Ann W. Burgess, and John E. Douglas. **Sexual Homicide: Patterns and Motives,** New York, NY: Lexington Books, 1988.

Ressler, Robert K., and Tom Shachtman. **I Have Lived in the Monster: A Report from the Abyss.** New York, NY: St. Martin's Press, 1997.

Ressler, Robert K., and Tom Shachtman. **Whoever Fights Monsters: My Twenty Years Hunting Serial Killers for the FBI.** New York, NY: St. Martin's Press, 1992.

Turvey, Brent. **Criminal Profiling: An Introduction to Behavioral Evidence Analysis,** San Diego, CA: Academic Press, 1999.

Vorpagel, Russell, and Joseph Harrington. **Profiles in Murder: An FBI Legend Dissects Killers and Their Crimes,** New York, NY: Plenum Press, 1998.

Chapter Seven
MASS, SERIAL, AND SPREE CRIMES

Thou shalt not kill. Exodus 20: 13 (The Bible, KJV)

You shall not murder. Exodus 20:13 (The Bible, NAS)

You shall not murder. Exodus 20: 13 (The Bible, NKJ)

You must not murder. Exodus 20: 13 (The Bible, TLB)

Thou shalt not kill. Exodus 20: 13 (The Bible, NAS)

NOTE: These scriptural references are not intended to serve as a theological discussion, but are for literary reference just as other literary quotes in this text are. While the various translations are referenced to demonstrate the significance of the translated versions of the words "kill" and "murder," the author of this text does not intend to imply any expertise in either theology or Biblical languages. These quotes are for literary reference only.

INTRODUCTION

When *mass crimes* are discussed most people think of mass murder. *Mass murder,* says Lt. Vernon Geberth (NYPD. Ret.), is a "homicide involving the killing of four or more victims during a single event at one location" (Geberth, p. 849). This is the commonly accepted definition among homicide investigators and criminal profilers.

The *Classic* mass murder, according to Geberth, involves a single individual who kills more than four persons at one location during a period of time (minutes, hours, or days) (Geberth, p. 849).

Family-member murder involves more than *three* family members who are killed *and* the perpetrator takes his own life in a mass murder/suicide (Geberth, p. 849).

A *Family Killing* involves *four* or more family members killed by a family member who does *not* commit suicide (Geberth, p. 849).

Other crimes may also be classified as *mass* crimes. The *Crime Classification Manual* (CCM) identifies **mass arson** as arson involving one offender who sets *three* or more fires at the same location during a limited period of time, e.g. each floor of a multi-story building (Douglas, Burgess, Burgess, and Ressler, p. 189).

When one thinks of *serial crimes*, we commonly associate this with serial murder or serial homicide.

Serial murder, notes Geberth, involves two or more separate murders "where an individual, acting alone or with another, commits two or more homicides over a period of time, with time breaks between each murder event." this, Geberth says, is a homicide detective's perception of serial murder (Geberth, p. 856).

Again, *serial crimes* may also be associated with other offenses, such as arson, rape, and even robbery or burglary.

The *CCM* identifies arsonists who repeatedly set fires as *serial firesetters*. The serial arsonist is "involved in three or more separate firesetting episodes, with a characteristic emotional cooling-off period between fires" (Douglas, Burgess, Burgess, and Ressler, pp. 186-187).

Serial rapists may engage in a series of sexual assaults, *sometimes* involving repeated acts of *sexual ritual.* Such rituals may involve sexual needs based on physical characteristics, age, gender, the particular sequence of acts, the bringing or taking of specific objects, the use of certain words or phrases, etc. (Douglas, Burgess, Burgess, and Ressler. p. 195).

Spree crimes are also commonly associated with murder. Geberth identifies *spree murder* as the "murder of more than one person at two or more locations during a single event without any cooling-off period" (Geberth, p. 857).

The *CCM* identifies a spree arsonist as one who "sets fires at three or more separate locations with no emotional cooling-off period between them" (Douglas, Burgess, Burgess, and Ressler, p. 189).

Geberth's *Practical Homicide Investigation* is considered to be the "Bible" of homicide investigation. The *Crime Classification Manual* (CCM) is the primary reference and academic study for criminal profilers. These two landmark works are a must for anyone studying crime, homicide, and the criminal mind.

Mass crimes, we see involve:

1. Four or more victims (three or more fires),
2. during a single event, at one location,
3. with no emotional cooling-off period between them.

Serial crimes involve:

1. Two or more separate murders (three or more separate firesetting pisodes),
2. over a period of time with breaks between each murder event (or fire),
3. with a characteristic cooling-off period between,
4. often characterized by premeditation, planning, and/or fantasy.

Spree crimes involve:

1. The murder of more than one person (or fires),
2. at two or more locations (three or more separate locations for fires),
3. during a single event without any cooling-off period between.

Although mass, serial, and spree crimes may characterize murder, arson, rape, robbery, and burglary, most research has concentrated on murder and, to a lesser extent rape (sex crimes) and arson. Thus, I will deal primarily with murder.

MASS MURDER

To many the popular image of the mass murderer is typified by Alfred Hitchcock's *Psycho* in which the character Norman Bates depicts a "warped sense of reverence" for his deceased mother. The 1957 Waushara County, Wisconsin, case of Edward Gein, inspired this cinematic portrayal (Levin and Fox, pp. 3-6).

Gein was not only implicated in multiple murders, but also admitted to having "robbed" corpse and body parts from several graves. He used the limbs and organs to make ornaments, such as a belt of nipples, a hanging human head, chairs upholstered with human skin, and bedposts crowned with skulls (Levin and Fox, p. 4).

Gein's bizarre and macabre collection included a shoebox containing nine vulvas. On "moonlit evenings he would prance around his farm wearing a real female mask, a vest of skin complete with female breasts, and woman's panties filled with vaginas" reportedly to "recreate the form and presence of his dead mother" (Levin and Fox, p. 4).

In their book, *Mass Murder: America's Growing Menace*, Jack Levin and James Allan Fox incorrectly characterized serial and spree murders generically as "mass murder." They give examples of serial killers, such as Edward Gein (1957), Theodore Robert (Ted) Bundy (1974-1978), John Norman Collins in the Ann Arbor-Ypsilanti murder series (1967-1969), David Berkowitz (the "Son of Sam" .44 caliber killer) (1975-1977), John Wayne Gacy (suburban Chicago), Wayne Williams (Atlanta), Ken Bianchi (the "Hillside Strangler"), etc.

Levin and Fox identify one infamous mass murder as the 1929 "St. Valentine's Day Massacre," in which members of Al Capone's gang double-crossed members of the George "Bugs" Moran gang in an ambush. Having arranged a bootleg liquor deal, Capone's men masqueraded as police officers, lined up six of Moran's gangsters against a wall, and machine-gunned them to death in the infamous Chicago slaughter (Levin and Fox, p. 43).

Another infamous Valentine's Day mass murder occurred in New Rochelle, New York, in 1977. Frederick W. Cowan, a 33-year old, 250-pound weightlifter and Nazi cultist, killed six and wounded four while attempting to exterminate his Jewish boss (Levin and Fox, p. 43).

In July, 1966, Richard Franklin Speck (AKA Benjamin) approached a Chicago townhouse shared by nine nursing students of the South Chicago Community Hospital. Twenty-three year old Corazon Amurao answered the door thinking it was one of her roommates. A somewhat intoxicated Richard Speck said he only wanted money to get to New Orleans and threatened her with a knife and pistol (Levin and Fox, p. 10).

Speck tore up bed sheets to tie and gag Corazon and her friends who he had forced into the back bedroom. The roommates complied to avoid angering the intruder into a violent rage. One-by-one Speck led his victims away to die (Levin and Fox, p. 10).

Corazon managed to hide beneath a bed, hoping Speck had not counted his victims and would not find her. Each time Speck led away another victim, she would plead with her friends to ambush and overtake Speck, but they were all so afraid that they awaited their turn to die (Levin and Fox, p. 10).

After more than six hours, Corazon emerged from her hiding place to find the mass murder of her eight friends. The massacre scene was full of Speck's bloody fingerprints and he was arrested two days later in a nearby flophouse (Levin and Fox, pp. 10-11).

Levin and Fox say that Speck remained a public curiosity for at least two weeks following the "wholesale murder," until another killer made bigger headlines for "the crime of the century" (Levin and Fox, p. 11).

Levin and Fox note that war produces acts that would normally never be considered in peacetime. The March 16, 1968, My Lai Massacre in which Lt. William Laws Calley, Jr. allegedly committed mass murder at the direction of his superiors is the classic example. In this infamous episode, Lt. Calley ordered his platoon to slaughter *hundreds* of South Vietnamese civilians—unarmed women, children, and elders (Levin and Fox, p. 74).

Still another bizarre and infamous example of mass murder occurred on November 19, 1978, in Jonestown, Guyana, when a cultist dictator, James Jones, orchestrated the murder of 913 men, women, and children. Removed from outside influences and under the total control of the cult's dictator, the 913 members of the People's Temple were subjected to a mass poisoning (Levin and Fox, p. 72).

Using fatal doses of cyanide-laced Kool-Aid, the infants were the first to have *volunteers* squirt the flavored cyanide into their open mouths. The older children went next. Armed guards stood by to force compliance as the public address system blared "We're going to meet again in another place." As the adults lined up, some accepted with enthusiasm while others were forced to comply. Most were dead within five minutes (Levin and Fox, p. 72).

Mass murder is often associated with the street term "going postal." Indeed, the U.S. Postal Inspection Service, the law enforcement agency of the U.S. Postal Service, has had experience in this unfortunate phenomenon. Incidents in which postal employees have committed mass murders and/or postal facilities have been targeted have given rise to the expression "going postal."

With the assistance of U.S. Postal Inspector Paul Hartman of the USPS Cleveland office, I have compiled a list of recent incidents. The perpetrators, dates, and locations include:

- Stephen W. Brownlee—March 6, 1985, Atlanta, GA
- Patrick H. Sherriff—August 20, 1986, Edmond, OK
- John M. Taylor—August 10, 1989, Escondido, CA
- Joseph M. Harris—October 10, 1991, Ridgewood, NJ
- Tom McIlvane—November 14, 1991, Royal Oak, CA
- Mark Hilbun—May 6, 1993, Dana Point, CA
- Bruce W. Clark—July 9, 1995, Industry, CA

Just as a large number of works have been written on both *mass murder* and *violence in the workplace*, a related and equally horrific phenomenon is now emerging in the United States. This *youth violence* and *school shootings*.

Here, again, examples are abundant. Again, a partial list includes:

- February, 1997, Bethel, Alaska, high school principle and a student are shot to death and two other students are wounded by Evan Ramsey (16). He is sentenced to 210 years in prison.
- October 1, 1997, Pearl, Mississippi, Luke Woodem (16) kills his ex-girl-friend and another girl at their high school after slitting his mother's throat (spree murder). He is serving two life sentences.
- December 1, 1997, West Paducah, Kentucky—three students are killed and five are wounded at a high school prayer meeting. Michael Carneel (14), the shooter, is eligible for parole in twenty-five years.
- March 24, 1998, Jonesboro, Arkansas—Andrew Golden (11) and Mitchell Johnson (13) open fire from the woods behind Westside Middle School, killing four students and a teacher. They will be released from juvenile homes at age 21.
- April 25, 1998, Edinboro, Pennsylvania—Andrew Wurst (14), kills a teacher and wounds two 14 year-old boys at a dance. He is tried as an adult.
- May 19, 1998, Fayetteville, Tennessee—Jacob Davis (18) is charged with murder for killing an 18 year-old classmate.
- May 21, 1998, Springfield, Oregon—two students are killed and twenty-two others are wounded by Kip Kankel (15), who also killed his parents at home the night before. (spree murder).
- June 15, 1998, Richmond, Virginia—Quinshaw Booker (14) shoots a teacher and a school volunteer. He was sentenced to probation and com-munity service.
- April 20, 1999, Littleton, Colorado, Eric Harris and Dylan Klebold killed fifteen students, a teacher, and themselves. Twenty-three others were also wounded.

(Source: CNN News and Fox News Channel, April 20 and 21, 1999)

Levin and Fox say there are three types of mass murder: family slayings, mur-der for profit or expediency, and killing for the sake of sex or sadism (Levin and Fox, p. 89). This latter category more appropriately or specifically falls under *serial murder.*

Levin and Fox insightfully write, "Some mass murderers kill so obtrusively that their crimes are featured in the news across the country; others hardly disturb the night as they massacre their entire sleeping families and so are renowned only in their own communities" (Levin and Fox, p. 11).

Bizarre and frightening ritualistic homicides and human sacrifices are described in detail and abundance throughout the United States, according to Larry Kahaner, author of Cults That Kill: Probing the Underworld of Occult Crime (Kahaner, p. vii). Cult and ritualistic crime, workplace and school violence, domestic homicide, and all categories of mass murder are a macabre homicidal phenomenon.

SERIAL MURDER

The original definition of *serial murder* used by the FBI was "the killing of three or more separate victims with emotional time breaks between the killings." They have since adopted Vernon Geberth's definition from his text *Practical Homicide Investigation*. That is "two or more separate murders where an individual, acting alone or with another, commits multiple homicides over a period of time, with breaks between each murder event" (Geberth, p. 438).

In 1961, William F. Kessler, MD, and Deputy Inspector Paul B. Weston (NYPD) wrote, "Sometimes a murderer will commit more than one murder and will establish a definite pattern." They observed, "In such cases each murder is recognized as the work of the person who committed the previous murders." They go on to add, "It was the pattern of the crimes that revealed the type of individual who would commit it" (Kessler and Weston, p. 79).

Geberth wrote thirty-five years later, "Serial killers have been described as intelligent, charismatic, streetwise, charming, and generally good looking. They are mobile individuals capable of traveling any number of miles in search of the 'right' victim" (Geberth, p. 439).

Geberth goes on to describe serial killers as manipulative, often able to talk their victims into their "comfort zone," and at times using a ruse to gain access to their victims. Many are interested in police procedures. Some have even worked as police officers, reserve officers, or security guards and use this experience to avoid detection (Geberth, pp. 440-441).

Joel Norris reiterates Kessler's and Weston's comments, saying, "A serial killer's addiction to his crime is also an addiction to a specific pattern of violence that becomes the killer's way of life." Each serial killer, he says, incorporates the act of killing into a ritual of "psychological survival." This ritual is the identifier of the serial murderer and "sets him apart from his traditional counterparts" (Norris, p. 23).

Norris says there are seven key phases of the serial murder ritual:

1. **The Aura Phase**—a form of withdrawal from reality into primal fantasies.
2. **The Trolling Phase**—a compulsive stage in which the killer searches for or stalks his next victim. Trolling does not consist of random or accidental patterns, but is an unconscious compulsion that becomes a deliberate form of "cruising for the likeliest prey."
3. **The Wooing Phase**—serial killers disarm their suspects by winning their confidence and luring them into a trap. Homicide investigators have noted that victims of serial murderers rarely seem to struggle with their killers.
4. **Capture Phase**—an event that can be sudden (e.g. locking a car door, a break-in through a window, a blow that renders the victim helpless, etc.) or a gradual and terrifying ordeal.
5. **The Murder Phase**—the victim plays a role in "the killer's private vision of his own hell."
6. **The Totem Phase**—the serial killer's "triumphant vision of truth fades rapidly after the victim is finally dead." As the murderer's fantasy fades, he quickly moves into depression. Some serial killers try to preserve the intensity of the murder and prolong the feelings of power and triumph by trying to preserve the body through ritualistic dismemberment of the dead victim. This totem phase symbolizes what the murderer had hoped would be an emotional triumph. The victim has been transformed into a symbolic trophy in hopes of preserving the feelings of power and glory.
8. **The Depression Phase**—the serial killer is left with feelings of emptiness and hopelessness.

(Norris, pp. 23-34).

In 1989, there were approximately 21,500 murders in the U.S. with 2,546 unsolved. By 1990 there were 23,600. Predictions of a turn-of-the-century peak for 2000, however, do not seem to be supported. (Refer to the appropriate Federal Bureau of Investigation Uniform Crime Reports for these periods).

While *most* of these murders were committed by below average intelligence, 18-24 year old, male (70%), blacks, from a lower socioeconomic class, serial murderers are likely to be of average to bright intelligence, organized and well-planned, white perpetrators. They tend to become better criminals with practice and 81% of them start as window peekers (James, p. 1).

While a friend, acquaintance, or other known perpetrator commits 54% of murders, serial murders are usually committed by strangers (James, p. 2).

Because the organized serial killer strives for perfection, he leaves few clues or little physical evidence. Other problems with serial murder investigations involve:

- task force organization,
- dealing with tips,
- investigation, surveillance, and undercover operations,
- the arrest of the murderer,
- the recovery of incriminating evidence,
- the interrogation of the killer,
- conducting photo shows ups (arrays), and
- preparation of the case for trial.

(James, p. 3).

This involves close coordination between the police, crime lab, coroner (medical examiner), and prosecutor.

Similarly, Robert D. Keppel of the Washington Attorney General's Office observes that serial murder has become one of the central concerns in homicide both because of the increasing frequency of occurrence and the unique problems associated with such investigations (Keppel, p. 3).

The usual "reactive response" is inadequate when investigating serial murder cases. Because the investigation of serial murders is uncommon to most agencies, the existing resources and "routine investigative techniques are ineffective" (Keppel, p. 3).

Keppel identifies five "**solvability factors** and common **appellate issues** affecting such investigations:

1. The quality of **interviews** of witnesses,
2. The circumstances leading to the **initial stop** of the suspect,
3. The **probable cause** to search and seize physical evidence,
4. The quality of **crime scene** investigations, and
5. The quality of the **scientific analysis of physical evidence** seized from the murderer and/or his property and its comparison to evidence recovered from the victims and scenes.
   (Keppel, p. 4).

James also identifies problems specifically relating to the trial. **Trial Problems:**

- insuring that evidence is present for the trial,
- assisting with jury selection,
- protecting the suspect during the trial,

- handling evidence throughout the appeal process,
- storage of evidence after it has been returned by the courts,
- storing other evidence from other serial murder cases where the defendant was *not* charged and brought to trial on *both* cases,
- returning personal possessions owned by the victims to their families, and
- providing an opportunity to the families to tell the police how they feel about the way the case(s) was/were handled and clearing up misunderstandings.

(James, p. 3)

In his text, *Serial Murder: Future Implications for Police Investigations*, Robert D. Keppel describes the investigations and cases of five serial killers: Larry Eyler, Wayne Williams, John Gacy, Ted Bundy, and Juan Corona. He specifically briefs each case and identifies issues of judicial appeal in each to underscore investigative errors or considerations.

These cases are cited below:

- *People v. Eyler, 87 Ill. Dec. 648, 132Ill. App. 3d 792, 477, N.E. 2d 774 (1985)*
- *People v. Gacy, 103 Ill. 2d 1, 82 Ill. Dec. 391, 468 N.E. 2d.1171 (1984)*
- *Bundy v. State, So. 2d 330 (Fla.1984)*
- *Williams v. State, 251 Ga. 749,312 S.E. 2d 40 (1983)*
- *People v. Corona, 80 Cal. 3d 684, 145 Cal. Rptr.894 (1978)*

Of these five murderers, each offender was convicted of at least one murder but suspected of twenty or more. Their "stats" follow:

Offender	Convictions	Suspected Murders
Larry Eyler	1	20
Wayne Williams	2	28
John W. Gacy	33	33
Juan Corona	25	25
Ted Bundy	3	36

(Keppel, p. 62)

In these five cases, there were two types of investigations: 1) task force investigations a.) to review continuing murder cases and b) to coordinate multiple investigations of known perpetrators and 2) task forces formed a) after the murderer was identified with b) multiple bodies recovered at a central location (Keppel, p. 61).

In addition to the suggestions given above, Keppel identifies **difficulties involving unsolved serial murder investigations:**

- numerous victims,
- hundreds or thousands of suspects,
- hundreds of acquaintances of victims,
- little or no physical evidence directly leading to a suspect,
- cross-jurisdictional offenses,
- thousands of telephone contacts,
- "pride of authorship" problems between individual detectives and administrators within one department,
- lack of experienced personnel to investigate and supervise the cases,
- inadequate experience in establishing a priority system for lead follow-up,
- improper press relations, and
- ill-conceived filing procedures for case information.

(Keppel, p. 61)

Each of the problems may result in leads that are not followed up. Task forces formed by several agencies have been effective in alleviating these problems (Keppel, p. 61).

Keppel also identifies the unique **problems of task forces** created to investigate serial murders:

- they are usually a new and untried experience for the affected departments,
- the need for safeguards to assure proper lines of communication,
- the proper commitment of resources and personnel,
- the establishment of mutual goals and investigative priorities, and
- hidden agendas of individual departments the attitudes of members.

(Keppel, p. 62)

Earl James' book, *Catching Serial Killers: Learning from Post Serial Murder Investigations*, reviews the individual murders of six serial killers. The case of **John Collins** (The Michigan Murders) analyzes nine murders. The case of **Johann Scharaditsch** and **Harold Sassak** (Vienna, Austria; early 1970's) involved the collective study of fifty-five incidents. **Christopher Bernard Wilder** ("The Beauty Queen Killer") (Florida, 1984) and **Kenneth Erskine** (London, England, 1986) also provide collective examples of multiple murders (James, pp. 7-161).

The fifth case study in James' book involves the individual analysis of fourteen murders (one attempted) by **Albert Frank DeSalvo** ("The Boston Strangler;"

1962-1964). Finally, the murders (two attempted) by **Theodore Robert Bundy** provide twenty-one individual case studies of serial murder (James, pp. 162-250).

James says of serial killers, "These criminals and their crimes are different from other types of crimes and the criminal investigation into them must, therefore, follow a dissimilar approach…" He suggests that we learn how serial murders differ from other investigations (James, p. 301). These differences are:

Most serial killers, who use some kind of ruse, are above average in intelligence. They use cons and are smarter than most other criminals. They may be more intelligent than their police pursuers (James, p. 301).

In many regular crimes, the police are able to find trace evidence at the scene of the crime that can be used to track down the perpetrator. Most serial killers take the time to conceal or remove physical evidence. Some even study police procedures. The more "esoteric forms of evidence" tends to "trip them up" (James, p. 301).

In a serial murder case the method of operation (modus operandi) cannot be relied upon to render an opinion as to whether the crimes have been committed by the same criminal (James, p. 302).

While many homicide investigations are handled by one or two officers, serial murder investigations may involve over 100 officers working on the killings. Some detectives work better alone while others do well as a part of team effort (James, pp. 302-303).

Only a few crimes warrant the formation of a task force (James, p. 303).

A task force may have access to funds that are not available in other investigations. The resources, amount of attention, and public support may be exceptional (James p. 303).

Media attention may be higher than normal (James, p. 304).

While the media are sparingly used in most criminal investigations, *the media are commonly used to help solve serial murder cases* (James, p. 305).

In serial murder cases, if a confession is received at all, *the logical interrogation approach is more apt to be effective.* While the emotional approach may work in other cases, it is unlikely to be effective with serial killers (James, p. 308).

Tipping off the murderer prematurely that he is a suspect affords the opportunity to dispose of incriminating evidence (James, p. 310).

Thirty-six (36) percent of the perpetrators had kept items of evidence in their houses, apartments, or cars (James, p. 311).

Keppel says that, in most cases, the murderer's initial approach to their potential victims was unalarming and even charismatic. In most cases the victims were approached while sleeping, looking for a job, meeting people in a tavern, soliciting for prostitution, walking on a college campus, or hitchhiking (Keppel, p. 63).

Rather than asking witnesses what they saw that was out of place, Keppel suggests asking what they saw that was *usual and normal* for that particular area.

Most witnesses will observe the murderers in victim contact areas, apparently doing nothing out of the ordinary and not drawing attention to themselves (Keppel, p. 63).

While James reveals that his study demonstrates that thirty-one (31) percent of serial murderers are arrested as a direct result of police investigative work (James, p. 318), uniformed police patrols play an important role in the apprehensions because they patrol the areas and at times when the killer doesn't expect them. Therefore, patrol briefings should regularly be conducted by investigative personnel. Eight (8) percent of serial killers in James' study were apprehended through patrol work (James, p. 323).

SPREE MURDER

> Michael Newton has authored an *Encyclopedia of Serial Killers.* He writes, "The face of modern homicide is changing. We are caught up in the midst of what one expert calls an 'epidemic of homicidal mania,' victimized by a new breed of 'recreational killers' who slaughter their victims at random for the sheer sport of killing." (Newton, p. 1)

Joel Norris says, "These killers belong to a newly identified class of criminals called serial murderers, motiveless killers, recreational killers, spree killers, or lust murderers whose numbers are increasing at an alarming rate every year" (Norris, p. 15).

A classic example of a spree killer or spree murderer was Charles Whitman, the "Texas Tower Killer."

On August 1, 1966, Whitman climbed to the top of the 307-foot tower at the University of Texas in Austin. From behind the tower's huge clock he opened fire. Ninety-one minutes later fourteen people were dead or dying and thirty more were injured in the sixteen-block casualty area (Levin and Fox, p. 14).

Another victim of Whitman's carnage was the stillborn fetus of an eight-month pregnant woman (Levin and Fox, p. 14).

These casualties alone would have warranted the designation of a *mass murder.* However, the night before Whitman had killed his mother and his wife (Levin and Fox, p. 14). This changes the designation to a *spree murder:* the murder of *more than one person* at **two or more locations** during a *single event* **without any cooling-off period** (Geberth, p. 857).

INVESTIGATIVE PROCEDURES

Dr. Robert D. Keppel, Chief Criminal Investigator for the Washington Attorney General's Office, provides an outline of procedures for investigators. These steps are summarized here.

Investigative Technique

1. *Initial Report*—The initial report may be a missing person report or a report of the discovery of unidentified remains. It is essential to determine if the disappearance or homicide is related to others in a series as soon as possible. A unified, coordinated effort is imperative.
2. *Interviewing Techniques*—The highest investigative priority is to isolate the dates and times victims were last seen and to identify their activity patterns up to their disappearance. This information must be thoroughly corroborated. A **strategic interviewing plan** must include the proper questions to ask all persons interviewed. The **documentation** of all interviews is essential.
3. *Crime Scene Investigation*—CSI includes, but is not limited to, the documentation, photography, diagramming and collection of all pertinent physical evidence. Scenes may include the body recovery site, the murder site, the victim contact area, and the suspect's body, residence and vehicle.
4. *Scientific Analysis of Physical Evidence*—involves the procedures for collecting, logging, cross-referencing, and laboratory analysis of evidence.
5. *Search and Seizure*—considerations include periodic briefings of patrol officers of important aspects relevant to potential stops of suspects. **Investigators must keep a continuing search warrant affidavit containing all pertinent facts as the investigation progresses.**
6. *Advise on Constitutional Rights*—a clear waiver must be obtained at the point of a custodial interrogation, following the advice of rights.
7. *Investigation of Suspects*—The establishment of a priority system for past and incoming suspects and their elimination is essential. Caution should be used when using elimination criteria unless it is conclusive.

(Keppel, p. 73-76)

Preparation for Trial

- All Police **reports and** original officer **notes** must be complete and able to withstand the scrutiny of defense attorneys.

- All **evidence** must be cataloged, cross-referenced and the chain of custody maintained.
- The current addresses and telephone numbers for all **witnesses** must be updated.

(Keppel, p. 76).

Testimony at Trial

- A **criminal profiler** can assist prosecutors during defendant testimony for determining questions for cross-examination.
- Investigators should be **prepared** for lengthy testimony without appearing monotonous.
- Investigators should be able to readily identify each exhibit that is to be introduced through his/her testimony.
- Constant and active coordination when legal issues arise during the course of the investigation reduces problems at pretrial hearings and trials.

(Keppel, pp. 76-77)

Legal Issues Raised on Appeal

The general categories of issues raised on appeal of cases include:
- Police conduct in interviewing witnesses.
- The initial confrontation of the suspect by police.
- The search of the suspect's property.

(Keppel, p. 77-82).

CONCLUSION

Earl James, First Lieutenant (Retired), Michigan State Police, writes, "During this past twenty years, there has 'apparently' been a dramatic increase in **serial, mass,** and **spree murders** within the United States" (James, p. 324) (emphasis added).

Keppel says that when the police are hampered by "traditional approaches to homicide investigation, limited resources, and jurisdictional boundaries," and the "very nature of the serial killer" they frequently find themselves several steps behind (Keppel, p. 82).

By understanding the nature of serial, mass, and spree murders and crimes, identifying difficulties and problems, and outlining a planned, coordinated, investigative strategy and procedure the success at solving these crimes may be increased dramatically.

REFERENCES–CHAPTER 7

Douglas, John E., Ann W. Burgess, Allen G. Burgess, and Robert K. Ressler. **Crime Classification Manual: A Standard System for Investigating and Classifying Violent Crimes.** New York, NY: Lexington Books, 1992.

Geberth, Vernon. **Practical Homicide Investigation: Tactics, Procedures, and Forensic Techniques** (Third Edition). Boca Raton, FL: CRC Press, 1996.

Kahaner, Larry. **Cults That Kill: Probing the Underworld of Occult Crime.** New York, NY: Warner Books, Inc., 1988.

Keppel, Robert D. **Serial Murder: Future Implications for Police Investigations.** Cincinnati, Ohio: Anderson Publishing Co., 1989.

Kessler, William F. (M.D.), and Paul B. Weston. **The Detection of Murder: A Handbook for Police Officers, Detectives, Coroners, Judges, and Attorneys.** New York, NY: Arco Publishing Co., Inc., 1961.

Levin, Jack, and James Alan Fox. **Mass Murder: America's Growing Menace.** New York, NY: Berkley Books, 1991.

Newton, Michael. **Hunting Humans: The Encyclopedia of Serial Killers, Volume I.** New York, NY: Avon Books, 1990.

Norris, Joel. **Serial Killers.** New York, NY: Anchor Books (Doubleday), 1988.

James, Earl ((J.D., Ph.D.). **Catching Serial Killers: Learning from Past Serial Murder Investigations.** Lansing, MI: International Forensic Services, Inc., 1991.

Chapter Eight

CULTS AND RITUALISTIC CRIMES

Whoever fights monsters should see to it that in the process
he does not become a monster.
And when you look into the abyss, the abyss also
looks into you.

- Frederick Nietzsche -

INTRODUCTION

Participation in cults and the occult are generally considered Constitutionally guaranteed freedoms (freedom of religion), although the argument could be made that these are counter religions. While participation is protected, associated ritualistic crimes are not. To study cults and ritualistic crime it is important to start with a few definitions.

John Collins writes that religion represents "...an attempt on the part of most members to transform themselves to some kind of higher level of existence, to gain enlightenment or salvation." He says that religions assume that a more powerful or authentic reality exists and "offers ways to bring the individual into contact with it, or at least to have some sort of relations with that reality" (Collins, p. 3).

Collins differentiates *sects* as representing smaller religious associations, which are often started as "protest movements" within established churches or religions. *Cults*, Collins says, are based at least in part on aspects of a cult individuals wish to emphasize. This emphasis may involve structure or function (Collins, p. 5).

Cults based on structure will emphasize authority and organization. Cults based on function will stress what the cults hope to accomplish (agenda) or what may be seen as their effects (Collins, p. 5).

Cult crime and ritualistic abuse has involved organized religious groups, such as Jim Jones' *The People's Church*, alleged Satanic cult practices in day care centers, student involvement in the occult, and murder by "isolated individuals" (MacHovec, p. 3).

Frank J. MacHovec writes that "...some law enforcement officers suspect there may be organized hard-core criminal cults operating nationwide involved in drug dealing, prostitution, child pornography, kidnapping, and ritual murder." He goes on to note, "Other law enforcement experts report that they have expended a great deal of time and effort to search for criminal cults and have discovered no convincing evidence" (MacHovec, p. 3).

Whether prolific or not, cult and ritualistic crimes are serious offenses. It is this criminal activity that is of interest to law enforcement.

THE NATURE OF CULTS

Not all cults or occult groups actively engage in regular criminal conduct, although the nature of most ritualistic occult practices does seem to promote criminal activity. An example of this is the belief that the *theft* of a copy of the *satanic bible* makes it more powerful than a purchased copy.

The headlines dominated the front pages of the afternoon papers, became the big news on radio and TV. The bizarre nature of the crime, the number of victims and their prominence—a beautiful movie star, the heiress to a coffee fortune, her jet-set playboy paramour, an internationally known hair stylist—would combine to make this probably the most publicized murder case in history, excepting only the assassination of President John F. Kennedy (Bugliosi, p. 28).

This quotation from *Helter Skelter*, the story of the Charles Manson cult murders, typifies what most people think of when they hear "cult crimes." This is one of the more extreme examples and, although there are a number of ritualistic or cult murders, ritualistic or cult crimes encompass much more. Less dramatic are the thefts, burglaries, arsons, and related crimes. More bizarre are the sex crimes, kidnappings, and public welfare and health violations.

Frank MacHovec says that "religious, psychotherapy, or personal growth cults deviate from traditional approaches in their theory and practice" (MacHovec, p. 10). John J. Collins cites the Church of Scientology (L. Ron Hubbard and *Dianetics*), Hare Krsna (A.C. Bhaktive-danta Swami Prabhupada), and the Divine Light Mission (Guru Maharaj Ji) as classic examples of typical American cults (Collins, pp. 11, 15, and 19).

ATTRIBUTES

Cults share four major attributes:

1. an authoritarian structure,
2. the regimentation of followers (dress, talk, and thought),
3. the renunciation of the world (secular society), and
4. a belief that only members of the cult are gifted with the truth
(Collins, p. 6).

ATTITUDES

Cult attitudes involve an attitude of moral superiority in that what members do is right or correct under any circumstances. They involve rigidity of thought or an unwillingness or inability to think in "non-cult terms" which is often ascribed to brain washing. Finally, they may involve a diminution of regard for the individual to promote the cults' goals beyond any individual (Collins, p. 7).

CHARACTERISTICS

Cult **characteristics** include:

1. a sharp break with society,
2. a dominant leader with great force or charisma,
3. a lack of organizational structure (more like sects than churches),
4. heavy involvement in a search for mystical experiences (more like sects than churches),
5. a tendency to be small, short lived, and local, and
6. a main concern with problems of the individual rather than those of society at large (i.e. converts seek their own salvation, enlightenment, or answers to their own problems)

(Collins, p. 7-8).

WHAT ARE CULTS?

Cults represent "unorthodox or spurious" religious groups which differ significantly from the "normative expression of religion in our total culture." This is a subjective definition requiring a value judgment (Larsen, p. 14).

Bob Larsen writes that cultic philosophy is diverse and ranges from "the rigidly ascetic to the sexually permissive." It is characterized by an allegiance to the founder's ideals which are absolute (Larsen, p. 15).

Larsen observes that those targeted by cult propaganda fit a composite psychological profile: conventional solutions and institutions are unfulfilling, an affirming community is sought, a single idealistic principle for life to revolve around is appealing, lost or discovered truths are thought to have been restored, etc. (Larsen, p. 15).

Larsen also notes that loneliness, indecision, despair, and disappointment are the emotional characteristics exploited by cult recruiters. They utilize feeling over doctrine to create a sense of meaningful belonging that will encourage acceptance of any teachings (Larsen, p. 15).

MacHovec identifies what cults are by classifying them by type:

> **Satanism** is one of the most infamous types of cult or occult group. *Witchcraft* is a form of Satanism but the range of Satanic worship includes solitary obsession, temporary experimentation by small groups of *"dabblers,"* formally organized "churches" or "temples" of Satan, etc. (MacHovec, p. 21).

Secret societies attempt to keep their rituals from public view, but is sometimes used to describe not-so-secret groups, such as the Masons. MacHovec suggests a better definition might be "A select group of persons who join together to share in a system of beliefs or values using oaths, rituals, signs, or passwords not made known publicly and who do not publicly describe, promote, or represent themselves as members of the secret society" (MacHovec, p. 28).

Mysticism is the practice of "uniting one's self with the Deity or other unifying principle of life," usually in a religious setting or a non-rational belief (MacHovec, p. 29).

A **sect** is an "organized, identified, distinctive subgroup of a larger organization" or a group which has separated from its organization due to deviations or refinements of belief or practice (MacHovec, p. 31).

WHY ARE THERE CULTS?

Larsen identifies the origin of cults as false teachings twisted into a "diabolical error" (Larsen, p. 60). From a more sociological or psychological perspective MacHovec says, "People who feel lost or inadequate, who see little or no purpose to life, who are depressed and insecure, are susceptible to a cult or secret society which claims to know the secret of the life or some special truth (MacHovec, p. 29).

MacHovec goes on to note that if these secrets or truths are not readily obvious, hidden and requiring a "special search or unique approach" available only to and practiced by the chosen and initiated, the group can further be described as **occult** (MacHovec, p. 29).

The reasons why cults thrive are based in three basic human needs:

1. the desire for community,
2. a desire for engagement—to feel we can deal directly with social problems (e.g. poverty, racism, world peace, etc.), and
3. a desire for dependence (other people to help in guiding or lives)
(Collins, pp. 23-24).

HOW ARE CULTS FORMED?

Cults offer an ideology through systematic indoctrination in the form of repetitive lectures, rituals, and group behavior and norms. Myths, superstitions, magic or mysticism, symbols and unprovable abstract ideas "weaken critical judgment and increase suggestibility" (MacHovec, p. 31).

Recruitment techniques and methods have already been mentioned. Cult leadership tends to emerge from psychopathic and sociopathic personality problems (MacHovec, p. 67) and may be associated with antisocial personality disorder.

Authors Josh McDowell and Don Stewart write that it is "wrong to classify all occultists as either sick or on the fringe of society" (McDowell and Stewart, pp. 15-16). They observe that practitioners of the occult may fall into one or more of three categories of characteristics:

- Many are *escapists* who find it difficult to face moral responsibilities:
- Many are *superstitious* and assume that demonic influences are directly responsible for all sickness, depression, anger, or unusual or unexplained behavior; and
- All are *victims* of immeasurable powers

(McDowell and Stewart, pp. 15-16).

Such persons may be curious, conformists, dissatisfied, sad, rebellious, inclined to develop suspected latent psychic powers, the conditioned offspring of practicing occultists, and the credulous (McDowell and Stewart, p. 16). These are characteristics of occult practitioners. The characteristics of targets for cult recruitment have been previously identified. These, however, may overlap based upon the level of entry.

McDowell and Stewart note that only seven percent of those surveyed in a Gallup Pool denied believing in some form of paranormal phenomena. They observe that belief in the devil rose from 39% in 1978 to 55% in 1990 and belief in ghosts went from 11% in 1978 to 25% in 1990. Belief in witches rose only slightly from 10% to 14% during the same periods (McDowell and Stewart, p. 17).

The proliferation of occult involvement is also evidenced by the fact that more than 3,000 publishers of occult books and magazines have a combined revenue in excess of one billion dollars annually. Further, the University of California (Berkeley) and other institutions offer courses in magic, witchcraft and parapsychology (McDowell and Stewart, pp. 18 and 19).

Occult involvement is propagated by a curious interest in seemingly harmless practices such as horoscopes and Ouija boards (McDowell and Stewart, p. 20). The thought processes are continually influenced by advertising, television, movies, music, magazines, newspapers, books, conversations, speeches, sermons, etc. (McDowell and Stewart, p. 23).

INVESTIGATING CULT AND RITUALISTIC CRIMES

Until recently, occult investigators read books on religion, witchcraft, and Satanism and sought out clergy, professors, and occult practitioners for their only source of information on the occult. Soon they began exchanging support, information, notes, lectures, and techniques. Eventually they developed law enforcement manuals and a legitimate area of law enforcement study (Kahaner, p. 15).

Soon most occult investigators shared at least one basic belief: "Bizarre crimes, related to ancient occult teachings, actually were taking place in the twentieth century" (Kahaner, p. 15). Some allegations of illegal drugs, guns, and kidnapping were substantiated that involved groups like the Moonies, the Rastafarians, the Hare Krishnas, etc. (Kahaner, p. 16).

One difficulty encountered by many investigators is skepticism within their own departments. Many officials choose to deny that cult activity exists in their community. Others believe that investigating any cult is a violation of religious freedom, despite the presence of criminal activity (Kahaner, pp. 25-26).

One reason for a reluctance to investigate cult crimes is active participation in cults by some police command personnel. Another is that some communities find it embarrassing and feel that the bad publicity outweighs the need to investigate. Still another reason is a lack of understanding by police administrators and a jealousy over subordinates working cases that their superiors do not understand (Kahaner, p. 39). It is important to keep the bosses informed and to never stop learning.

Because ritualistic crimes may add a new dimension not commonly encountered in other investigations, the information and evidence collected may be unique. When searching for physical evidence investigators should:

- Check for basements, closets, and hidden entrances.
- Check graveyards and funeral homes for burglary, theft, or vandalism.
- Watch for artifacts such as candles, chalices, robes, knives, crosses, pins, dolls, alters, books, animals, bodies and body parts, cages, ceremonial items, fire pits and ashes, photographs, computer and video equipment, laboratory equipment, etc.

Investigators should not assume a case is ritualistic without elements of evidence, but should not overlook the possibility either. Artifacts, including those listed above, should be included in search warrant applications.

When encountering ritualistic scenes in progress, investigators may be confronted. They should be aware of threats, offer protection to potential victims, separate victims from the group (particularly children), and attempt to preserve evidence.

While it is important to continually learn and exchange information, it is also important to have a basic understanding of the dominant cults, particularly those that exist in one's jurisdiction.

MAJOR CULT TYPES
WICCA AND WITCHCRAFT

Witchcraft and Satanism are not synonymous but are often confused. *Wicca* came from the writings of Gerald Gardner and Alex Sanders in Great Britain and is the name often used for the practice of modern witchcraft (Kahaner, pp. 97-98).

Witchcraft is known as the "old religion" and dates back to Biblical times as the performance of magic forbidden by God for non-biblical purposes. The word witchcraft is related to the old English word *wiccian*, which means "the practice of magical arts" (McDowell and Stewart, p. 199).

Christians (and Satanists) believe in Satan while Wiccans do not believe in Satan as an entity or anything else. They believe in "mischievous spirits" or "darkside entities" (Kahamer, p. 100).

While witches and satanists are often confused, they have quite different views and do not get along well. Satanists worship the devil while witches are interested in magic and worship the divinity of nature (McDowell and Stewart, p. 199).

The "strongest, most stable group in Witchcraft is the local coven, grove, or clan." Each is autonomous and able to establish their own systems and practices but have the commonality of worshipping nature and natural phenomena and the use of rituals (Kahaner, p. 97).

Each coven is headed by a high priestess and a high priest. While the high priestess must be present for a ritual to take place, the priest is not required. Membership is by couples and limited to the number of people who can fit within a nine-foot circle (Kahaner, pp. 98-99).

Gardnerian Wiccans hold rituals skyclad and the priest and priestess signify their ranks by bracelets. The witch queen wears a crown and garter (Kahaner, p. 99). The goddess is represented by the moon and the god by the sun, each ruling six months out of the year (Kahaner, p. 100).

While Wiccans or *pagans* are a cult and a form of the occult, they are not commonly associated with criminal activity as a group.

SATANISM

Magick is the use of incantations and techniques to produce a desired effect, versus *magic* (without the "K") which refers to sleight-of-hand tricks or elusions (Kahaner, p. 47). The term *pagan* refers to people who are neither Christians nor Jews (Kahaner, p. 49).

Satanism is of more interest to law enforcement. McDowell and Stewart write, "Satanism is a branch of the occult that involves some of the most sinister rituals imaginable." They go on to say, "Black magic, the black mass, facets of the drug culture, blood sacrifice, sexual and physical abuse rituals, all have connections with Satanism" (McDowell and Stewart, p. 187).

Kahaner, however, says that The Church of Satan, Temple of Set, etc., are bona fide religious groups that are protected by law. He says that while there is no evidence linking them with illegal activity, individuals and subgroups may pose law enforcement concerns (Kahaner, p. 63).

Satanic groups include three types. First is the *traditional* or *orthodox* which are highly organized and have a spiritual base. These worship Satan in a particular form, including that of the Temple of Set, which refers to Satan as *set*, the ancient Egyptian god of the dead (Kahaner, p. 63).

These groups, such as the Church of Satan, the Temple of Set, and the Process Church of the Final Judgment, are highly structured, even generational. Others exist, but some are unknown because they are not made public (Kahaner, p. 64).

Anton Szandor LaVey, founder and head of the church of Satan, joined the Clyde Beatty Circus at age seventeen and a carnival at age eighteen. He later attended the City College of San Francisco and became a photographer for the San Francisco Police Department (Kahaner, pp. 65-66).

On April 30, 1966, the occult holiday of Walpurgisnacht, LaVey proclaimed the age of Satan. He has been referred to as the Black Pope. In 1967, he baptized his daughter Zeena into the Church of Satan. LaVey was also an advisor for the movie *Rosemary's Baby* (Kahaner, p. 66). (See *The Nine Satanic Statements*, LaVey, p. 25)

Many senior members of the Church of Satan believed LaVey's ego was becoming more important than the church's mission and that the church was becoming corrupt. Michael Aquino, a lieutenant in the cavalry squadron of the 82nd Airborne Division who served for nine months in Vietnam, decided to start his own Satanic cult (Kahaner, pp. 72-73).

A group known as The Order of the Trapezoid was an off shoot within the Church of Satan. It had surfaced during the Second and Third Reichs in Germany and was the basis for the Nazis' obsession with "the Black Arts" (Kahaner, pp. 73-74).

Aquino outlined his tenets in *The Book of Coming Forth by Night*, the antithesis for the Egyptian *Book of the Dean*, known as *The Book of Coming Forth by Day*. Aquino asserts that LaVey's work is done and a new Aeon has begun (Kahaner, p. 74).

Aquino was a Lieutenant Colonel in the U.S. Army in "resource management." He was a graduate of the National Defense University, received a Master of Public Administration from George Washington University, and a Ph.D. in Political science from the University of California. He was also an adjunct professor at Golden Gate University (Kahaner, pp. 77-78).

The second category of Satanists are known as *dabblers* or fringe people who are individuals or meet in small unattached groups. They are self-styled and make their ideology and philosophy from a variety of sources (Kahaner, p. 86).

Finally, the third group of Satanists are the *experimenters*, who are often confused adolescents seeking power to overcome youthful anxiety. Their role models are often heavy metal rock stars who portray occult trappings (Kahaner, p. 90).

SANTERIA AND PALO MAYOMBE

Though witchcraft is commonly associated with European pagan cults, the most practiced occult religion is Santeria. Practitioners of Santeria, Spanish for "worship of the saints," are called **Santeros** (Kahaner, p. 111).

Santeria has its origin in African tribal religions found among the Yoruba people of southwestern Nigeria. When the Yoruba were brought to the Americas as slaves, they brought this religion with them. Because the slave owners insisted that they give up their religion in favor of Christianity, the slaves made it seem that they were praying to Catholic saints when they were actually praying to their own gods (Kahaner, p. 111).

This evolutionary combination of tribal and Catholic religions involved the worship of a variety of deities which are individually responsible for different aspects of life. *Each god has its own colors, numbers, special powers, and personalities.* While there are hundreds of gods, only seven particular ones, known as **Orishas**, are the most revered (Kahaner, p. 111)

Santeros sacrifice animals, offer fruits, flowers, or a god's favorite items to win the favor or get the attention of their gods. The larger the sacrifice, the larger the favor or solution to a problem (Kahaner, p. 111).

Variations of Santeria are found throughout the Caribbean and Americas and their rituals are closed to outsiders. In Haiti, Catholicism and the practices of the Fon people from Dahomey combine to form **Voodoo**. In Brazil, variations are known as **Candomble, Umbanda,** and **Macumba**. In Cuba, sects are known as **Abaqua** and **Palo Mayombe** (Kahaner, p. 112).

While criminal activity is not associated with the majority of Santeros, animal and human sacrifices, drug trafficking, and other felonies are often associated with Santeria. This is particularly true of the **Marielitos** (Cuban refugee) sects (Kahaner, p. 112).

The darkest side of Santeria is *Palo Mayombe*. While Santeria witches are usually called **Brujas**, those practicing Palo Mayombe are called **Palo Mayomberos** and do "curses and spells" (Kahaner, p. 112).

The Marielitos, thought to have been isolated to particular regions, have been found to be active across the Americas, including Northwest Ohio. They have been found to have infiltrated the Mexicanos migrant groups in Ohio (Kahaner, p. 113).

RITUALS AND SYMBOLS

Rituals and symbols are important to most religions and cults and the occult are no exception. To understand and investigate ritualistic and cult crimes, it is incumbent to understand the rituals and symbols of these cults.

Occult rituals have the objective of summoning supernatural power. Rituals and ceremonies practiced by occult groups are similar but may differ from one group to another or among individuals of the same group (Kahamer, p. 133).

Satanic rituals often follow those practices found in *the satanic bible* or those found in ancient books (Kahaner, p. 135). Satanic rituals usually try to be an antithesis of Christianity, particularly Catholicism. Symbols are often Satanic symbols found in the Bible, such as "666." While gold is for God, silver is for Satan when used for jewelry, candleholders, or other artifacts.

(Note: Because most satanic rituals are opposites or paradoxes of Christian practices, *the satanic bible* is usually cited without capitalization, opposite that of *The Holy Bible*).

Other examples of symbols and significant artifacts are attached. Their importance as crime scene artifacts, clues, and evidence cannot be over emphasized.

While these symbols are critical, Larry Kahaner writes, "The most commonly found evidence is mutilated animals, ritual sites, and robbed graves" (Kahaner, p. 145).

SYMBOLS AND ARTIFACTS

The importance of symbols and artifacts as crime scene clues and physical evidence cannot be overemphasized. Investigators and profilers should become familiar with such symbols and artifacts and maintain references for others.

Graffiti and tattooing symbols, often found on the webbing of the left hand, of satanic cults include:

- various forms of 666, the sign of "The Beast;"
- FFF—the alphabetical equivalent to 666; the mark of the Beast;
- *NATAS*—"Satan" spelled backwards;
- the Swastika and other Nazi symbols;
- the inverted pentagram;
- the lightning bolt;
- variations of an inverted cross, and
- other tattooed, hand-drawn, spraypainted, or graffiti symbols.

THE NINE SATANIC STATEMENTS

1. Satan represents indulgence instead of abstinence!
2. Satan represents vital existence instead of spiritual pipe dreams!
3. Satan represents undefiled wisdom instead of hypocritical self-deceit!
4. Satan represents kindness to those who deserve it instead of love wasted on ingrates!
5. Satan represents vengeance instead of turning the other cheek!
6. Satan represents responsibility to the responsible instead of concern for psychic vampires!
7. Satan represents man as just another animal–sometimes better, more often worse, than those that walk on all-fours–who, because of his "divine spiritual and intellectual development," has become the most vicious animal of all!
8. Satan represents all of the so-called sins, as they all lead to physical, mental, or emotional gratifications!
9. Satan has been the best friend the Church has ever had, as he has kept it in business all these years!

(LaVey, p. 25)

ARTIFACTS TO LOOK FOR AT CULT AND RITUALISTIC CRIME SCENES

- **Athame**–ceremonial knife.
- **Black Beans**–used in various rituals.
- **Bones**–human and/or animal.
- **Book of Shadows**–list of personal rituals or spells.
- **Brass Bell**–used to start occult rituals.
- **Candles**–used in rituals; colors are significant.
- **Chalice or Witches Cup**–ceremonial.
- **Compass**–used to determine true directions that are critical in certain rituals.
- **Hour Glass Timer**–certain spells call for specific time limits.
- **Incense**–burned during ritualistic ceremonies.
- **Incense Burners**–holds incense.
- **Lotus Pod**–symbolic of the lotus flower which represents the spiritual, emotional, and intellectual centers in the human body.
- **Mortar and Pestle**–used to mix ritual herbs.
- **Pentacles**–the secret seal of Solomon.
- **Pine Cone Tails**–used in various rituals.
- **Modeling Wax**–used to mold and sculpt small items.
- **Quija Boards**–occult artifact.
- **Robes**–often stolen from churches and used in ceremonies.
- **Wood Rose**–believed to contain supernatural powers.

THE SIGNIFICANCE OF COLORS TO SATANISM AND WITCHCRAFT

Color:	Meaning or Significance:
Black	Darkness, night, sorrow, evil, the devil.
Blue	Vigilance, tears, water, sadness, pornography.
Green	Vegetation, nature, soothing, restful.
Red	Blood, physical life, energy.
White	Cleanliness, purity, innocence.
Yellow	Perfection, wealth, glory, power.

Note: This information was gathered from intelligence sources, the observations shared by fellow law enforcement officers, training received by the author, and the personal experiences as a law enforcement investigator of the author. Each of these has been confirmed by hundreds of law enforcement sources at actual crime scenes and other locations involving cult rituals.

CONCLUSION

Cults, the occult, and ritualistic crime are not a daily occurrence in every community, but the bizarre nature of these covert crimes makes understanding them and dealing with them vital to both law enforcement and mental health professionals. While the practice of diverse religions is Constitutionally protected, the practice of criminal rituals and the crimes associated with cults and the occult are not.

While some see occult activity as merely extremist movements, others in law enforcement see these groups evolving into organized criminal rings analogous to street gangs. While cults and criminal rituals are becoming more secretive, more and more incidents of occult crime are being reported to the police (Kahaner, p. 245).

Cult groups, witchcraft, satanism, Hispanic occult groups and other ritualistic criminal organizations are a social problem for law enforcement. Murder, sexual and child abuse, narcotics violations, and other crimes are of primary concern to police. The psychological effects on victims, survivors, and participants are of concern to the mental health professions. But this is also a community and national problem of importance to parents and leaders which must be understood.

REFERENCES—CHAPTER 8

Bugliosi, Vincent. **Helter Skelter**. New York, NY: Bantam Books, 1974.

Collins, John H. **The Cult Experience: An Overview of Cults, Their Traditions and Why People Join Them**. Springfield, IL: Charles C. Thomas Publishers, 1991.

Kahaner, Larry. **Cults That Kill: Probing the Underworld of Occult Crime**, New York, NY: Warner Books, 1998.

Larson, Bob. **Larson's New Book of Cults**, Wheaton, IL: Tyndale House Publishers, Inc., 1982

LaVey, Anton Szandor. **the satanic bible**. New York, NY: Avon Books, 1969.

MacHovec, Frank J. **Cults and Personality.**, Springfield, IL: Charles C. Thomas Publisher1989.

McDowell, Josh, and Don Stewart. **The Occult: The Authority of the Believer Over the Powers of Darkness**, San Bernadino, CA: Here's Life Publishers, 1992.

Chapter Nine

SCHOOL, WORKPLACE, AND DOMESTIC VIOLENCE

INTRODUCTION

Criminologists believe that there have been more than 35,000 murderers in American prisons, including 1,500 on death row. Many more who have murdered are still on the streets and experts believe thirty-five to forty serial killers may be responsible for as many as 5,000 murders per year in the 1980s (Linedecker, p. xii).

While serial, spree, mass, and ritualistic murders are both sensational and horrific, mass murders in our schools, the workplace, and by children and parents are posing an even more specific horror.

Headlines are increasingly filled with school shootings, murders, and bomb threats, workplace shootings, murders, and bombings, school-aged children and teens committing mass murders, and parents murdering their own children.

In 1998-1999 news reports were full of reports of school massacres, such as in Columbine, Colorado. Our children were not only the killers, but also the victims. Parents, too, committed inconceivable acts, such as injecting infants with the HIV virus, suffocating and poisoning their children, and other forms of murder. Many experts have expressed suspicions of the parents in Colorado's investigation of the murder of child beauty queen Jon Bone Ramsey.

SCHOOL VIOLENCE: KIDS THAT KILL

In the 1980s the number of adults who committed murder began to decline while the number of teenagers who committed murder began to rise. Approximately one-fifth, nearly 20 percent, of all murders are committed by persons under the age of eighteen (Kelleher, 1998, p. 3). In 1999 a twelve-year-old in Fort Wayne, Indiana, was arrested for murder after chasing down and repeatedly shooting his robbery victim.

While the age of murderers has declined (age thirteen to eighteen), the number of unknown victims has steadily risen (Kelleher, 1998, p. 4). Adolescent rage can result in self-directed and self-destructive behavior, even extraordinary violence that is incomprehensible to those who know the adolescent.

Home rage, school rage, road rage, work place rage—all buzz words of violence in the 1990s—are not the only form of adolescent violence. Premeditated murder and violence for retribution are also significant aspects of violence by adolescents. Other phenomena have also been documented.

Thrill Killings are another form of teen violence. In 1994 a thirteen-year-old neighbor in Whitehead, Nova Scotia, killed his neighbor and wounded his wife.

The teen rang the couple's doorbell then attacked them with a shotgun. The teen-aged killer had no history of violence. He "casually explained that he was angry because his father had refused to buy him some chewing tobacco." He decided to shoot the first person that answered their door so he would know what it was like to take a life (Kelleher, 1998, p. 86).

In 1997, Bellevue, Washington, experienced the mass murder of a family of four. The seventeen-year-old killer had arranged to meet one of the family's daughters the night of the murder. He later confessed that he arranged and planned the murder because he was in a **rut** (Kelleher, 1998, pp. 90-91).

In this same case a second perpetrator was identified. The two teenagers had prepared a list of potential murder victims and conspired together to commit these murders. Again the motive was *thrill killing* (Kelleher, 1998, p. 92).

Adolescent violence is not removed or unrelated to **cult murders** and ritualis-tic crime. Parents are becoming more aware of and concerned about the increas-ing number of cults our children are joining and the number of children joining them. This awareness is partly a result of publicized accounts of illegal or violent activities associated with bizarre and aggressive cult groups. Some of these cults are highly organized (Kelleher, 1998, p. 107).

Murders of **obsession** and **stalking** are not unknown in adolescent violence. When a murder is precipitated by a sexual or romantic obsession, the crime can be particularly brutal. It may also claim the lives of those associated with or in proximity to the target of the murderer's obsession. (Kelleher, 1998, p. 111).

WORKPLACE VIOLENCE

Workplace violence and lethal employees are a disturbing phenomena in which the murderer represents an unpredicted or unforeseen threat which cannot yet be accurately quantified or completely understood. Many incidents of occu-pational homicides are also mass murders (Kelleher, 1997, pp. 1-2).

The U.S. Postal Inspectors Service has made a study of mass murder and work-place violence. Examples of such incidents committed by USPS employees include:

- Stephen W. Brownlee, March 6, 1985, Atlanta, GA,
- Patrick H. Sherrill, August 20, 1986, Edmond, OK,
- John M. Taylor, August 10, 1989, Escondido, CA,
- Joseph M. Harris, October 10, 1991, Ridgewood, NJ,
- Mark Hilbun, May 6, 1993, Dana Point, CA,
- Bruce W. Clark, July 9, 1995, Industry, CA, and
- Tom McIlvane, November 14, 1991, Royal Oak, CA.

From 1980 to 1989, the National Institute for Occupational Safety and Health (NIOSH, U.S. Department of Health and Human Services) conducted a study of workplace fatalities. They found that workplace homicide was the third leading cause of workplace death at 14 percent. Even more shocking was the revelation that the leading cause of workplace fatalities for women was homicide, at 41 percent of all female worker fatalities (Kelleher, 1997, p. 3).

Characteristics of workplace murderers and victims include:

- The average age of workplace murderer is 38.2 years, while the average for other murders is under age 30.
- Of all workplace murderers, 97 percent were male.
  Of the perpetrators, 41 percent were current employees, 46 percent former employees, and the remaining 13 percent were either domestic partners of employees or clients of organization.
- Of these organizations, 38 percent were governmental agencies, particularly federal, with the U.S. Postal Service being the most dominant.
- The average number of victims for each incident was 2.5 with at least one murder in 39 percent of the cases studied.

(Kelleher, 1997, p. 5)

While all workplace murderers may not fit the typical profile, lethal employees tend to have certain commonalities and patterns of behavior:

- The potentially lethal employee is usually **male** (80 to 97 percent).
- Ethnicity is usually **white** (about 70 percent).
- The typical ages are between **30 and 60 years of age**.
- They are typically socially isolated and may have lived alone for years, changed job locations, or have undergone a separation or divorce.
- They will have experienced one or more **triggering events** prior to acting out violently and at least one of these events will be directly linked to the violent actions.

(Kelleher, 1997, pp. 9-11)

There is a **90 percent probability** that a potentially lethal employee will exhibit **at least one** behavioral warning sign and a **50 percent probability** that they will exhibit two or more. Warning signs include:

- A history of violent behavior (very common).
- Evidence of psychosis or a similar psychological disorder (i.e. loss of contact with reality or loss of the ability to process experience appropriately).

- Obsessive or delusional disorders resulting in behavior targeting another individual (e.g. stalking).
- Alcohol or chemical dependence.
- Severe or chronic depression.
- Pathological blaming of others or the organization.
- Impaired neurological functioning.
- Elevated frustration which is chronic or severe.
- A weapons fetish, preoccupation with weapons or paramilitary subjects, or a fascination with known cases of multiple workplace homicides.
- A personality disorder that can result in violent or antisocial behavior.
- Vocalized or acted out violent intentions prior to committing a violent act.
- Exhibited behavior over a sustained period of time that is interpreted as strange, bizarre, threatening, or uncomfortable to multiple coworkers.

(Kelleher, 1997, pp. 12-22)

Profiles designed to predict rare events tend to overpredict. Although there are few lethal employees, those who are usually commit multiple murders in an apparently indiscriminate manner. It is nearly impossible to predict if or when an employee might become lethal. Attempts at such predictions involves "the analysis of complex modalities of behavior and an understanding of personal motivations." The results are often not much more than an educated guess (Kelleher, 1997, pp. 23).

DOMESTIC VIOLENCE: PARENTS THAT KILL

The U.S. Department of Justice estimates that three hundred to four hundred infants are murdered at birth each year by being discarded or slain by their mothers (Kelleher, 1998, p. 13). As shocking as this is, headlines are full of cases such as the high school girl that discarded her just born baby in the bathroom at her high school prom, then returned to her date.

The same year that Susan Smith drove her children, seatbelted in the back seat of her car into a lake (1999), a father was charged with infecting his infant son with the HIV virus he had stolen form a medical facility where he was employed. This "father" was hoping to avoid child support payments. Smith's motive was to win a boy friend that did not want children.

An Indianapolis woman was charged in 1999 with suffocating her baby by placing plastic over it's face. In the same week, an elderly woman in Pennsylvania confessed that her eight children who were all listed as SIDS (Sudden Infant

Death Syndrome) deaths were murdered in a similar manner at her hand. Examples of these murders go on and on.

Michael D. Kelleher writes, "Many of these infants were still born at birth and were discarded in a moment of panic or indifference by their mothers. However, many others died from exposure after being abandoned while still alive and viable" (Kelleher, 1998, p. 13).

In 1970, forensic psychologist Dr. Phillip J. Resnick at University Hospital of Cleveland defined the term **neonaticide** as the killing of an infant within twenty-four hours of birth (Kelleher, 1998, p. 13). Commonly associated with unwed mothers from lower socioeconomic backgrounds, *neonaticide* and other child murders are found at all class levels.

This is not a new or recent phenomenon. In 1986, a Wisconsin sixteen-year-old gave birth after an eight-month pregnancy. Upon giving birth at home, she killed the baby by multiple stab wounds, wrapped it in a plastic bag and hid it in the garage. Her motive was to hide the pregnancy form her parents and others (Kelleher, 1998, p. 16).

In 1988 a New York fifteen-year-old gave birth to a baby boy. She cleaned the newborn, wrapped him in a towel and placed him in a plastic garbage bag. She then threw the baby down a steep embankment outside the family home, causing death from massive head injuries (Kelleher, 1998, pp. 16-17).

Examples of this abound. The motives range from fear of making the pregnancy known, poverty, and ignorance to the personal and financial, such as the Susan Smith and HIV cases mentioned above.

One theory offered by Dr. Charles D. Katz, a pediatric psychologist at Monmouth Medical Center, suggests that adolescents that have murdered their newborns may experience a severe **dissociative disorder**. This may be a result of fear and anxiety which results in an *emotional detachment* from such gruesome actions. This theory suggests a commonality in several cases of neonaticide (Kelleher, 1998, p. 39).

Dissociative disorders fall into three major categories: 1. multiple personality disorder, 2. psychogenic fugue (dissociative fugue), and 3. psychogenic amnesia (dissociative amnesia) (Kelleher, 1998, p.39).

Domestic violence also includes spousal battery and murder, which are also not new social problems. Though these crimes have similarities to the murders of children by parents and child abuse, they are also unique.

CONCLUSION

Any form of violence is disturbing and forms of bizarre or extreme violence cause special concerns to parents, communities, employers, and law enforcement. It is ultimately impossible to consistently predict domestic, school, or workplace violence or ensure complete protection.

Understanding the causes and etiology of such violence and the statistical norms and characteristics, can help with predicting and preventing such violence. These social problems are of primary concern to those in mental health and law enforcement charged with preventing, interdicting, or responding to such disasters. Planning and research are essential to deal with such crisis.

REFERENCES—CHAPTER 9

Kelleher, Michael D. **Profiling the Lethal Employee.** Westport, Conn.: Praeger Publishers, 1997.

Kelleher, Michael D. **When Good Kids Kill**. Westport, Conn.: Praeger Publishers, 1998.

Linedecker, Clifford. **Night Stalker**. New York, NY: St. Martin's Paperbacks, 1991.

Chapter Ten

Applied Research into the Criminal Mind

INTRODUCTION

My interests in *criminal profiling and behavioral analysis* or *criminal investigative analysis* (also referred to as psychological profiling) started when I was a detective assigned to the Robbery-Homicide Squad of the Fort Wayne Police Department. Later I would become the supervisor for that elite section, which investigates not only homicides, but bank robberies and all other armed and strong arm robberies in the second largest city in Indiana (99th in the United States according to the 1990 U. S. Census).

When I started looking at what new research I could contribute, I noticed that one area of violent crime had not been included in the *Crime Classification Manual* or much of the literature on the subject–Armed Robbery. One of my doctoral Committee consultants, mentor and friend, Detective Raymond Pierce (NYPD Retired) encouraged me to research a specialized area, such as this. Ray had not only served as a homicide detective, but as the New York Police Department's criminal profiler.

I also had a more personal interest in violent crimes in general and, more specifically, armed robberies. The years 1993–1994 were unique in my life and career. On July 6, 1993, I was working in uniform (although I was a detective at the time) at a part-time job at the Allen County Public Library. I had just met my, soon-to-be wife (Mimi) for dinner in the library parking lot. She left just before 8:00 p.m. (2000 hours).

I was in the parking lot talking with the owner of a bed-and-breakfast from across the street when I heard what sounded like an alarm from one of the nearby buildings. As I turned around, I saw a police car and two officers who were making a traffic stop. Although I could not see who they were at the time, I told my visitor that I was going to walk over to "check on them." As I started for the sidewalk, nearing the crosswalk, I saw the driver of the truck, which had been stopped, push a .44 magnum handgun out of the driver's side window and shoot one of the officers down in the street.

The officer fell into the street and, as the truck pulled away toward my position, the officer's partner and I returned fire on the assailant. The truck and driver swerved to the left and struck the side steps of a church, went airborne, and crashed atop a statue on the next corner.

The officer's partner immediately called out an "Officer Down" code and rendered first aid to his critically injured partner. As he called out the direction of flight of the assailant, I realized that he did not see the assailant crash a block away. As I tried calling out the crash, the dispatcher did not realize that I was trying to tell everyone else that the *perpetrator* had crashed. The dispatcher paid little attention to my transmissions, as he thought the officer's assailant was fleeing.

Finally, the shift commander, a Captain (now Chief of Police at the time of this writing) arrived and asked where the perpetrator had fled. I advised the Captain that he was still in the truck and I did not know if he was dead or alive.

We opened the passenger door of the truck, which was now on its side, and the Captain removed the gun from the perpetrator's still hand. As I continued to cover the Captain, he checked the perpetrator and found him to be dead. The officer who was shot survived and retired two years later.

The following month my fiancee, Mimi, suffered a cerebral hemorrhage and had to undergo life-threatening brain surgery. We had started dating on September 19, just four years earlier, and had planned to be married in September. So, on September 19, 1994, we were married in the Chapel of Parkview Hospital. The following February, 1995, we would have our church wedding on Valentine's Day weekend. But before that I would experience more violence.

ENCOUNTERS WITH VIOLENCE

I have investigated a number of violent crimes in my career, as well as police action shootings (officers were shot or shot someone who was attempting to shoot them). I have had many unique experiences. At least they are unique to most people, but perhaps not many police officers or robbery-homicide detectives.

I had been a reserve military officer for several years, including the years of Grenada, Panama, and the Gulf War, but I had never experienced combat like many of my peers had. I have had many violent encounters as a police officer, but most of these have not involved full-bore lethal combat.

Most police officers never discharge their weapons in violent encounters in their careers, although most experience the potential need many times over. Once an officer does experience a "shoot-out," there is often the tendency to assume that your turn is over or that "lightning doesn't strike twice."

On January 27, 1995, my partner, Detective John Moreno, and I arrived for work on the day shift in the Detective Bureau (D.B.). We had spent the night before at an excellent local Japanese steakhouse celebrating my birthday with our wives. We had just left breakfast together and were going to pick something up for John.

As we took the shortcut through a shopping plaza, the police scanner aired a hold-up alarm at a bank on the very road we were on. As we checked the numerical address we were passing, we realized that the alarm was across the parking lot from us. It was an extremely icy January morning and the nearest District Car was quite a distance away, even in normal weather. I changed my hand-held radio from the

Detective Channel to the North Districts Channel and told the dispatcher that we were already there and would check the bank until a uniformed officer arrived.

We pulled into the bank's parking lot to try to see through the pyramid-style building's windows. When we could finally see inside, we observed what appeared to be an old man dressed like a tramp at a check counter. He seemed to be looking for us also. The man moved toward a corner window and appeared to be listening to something. John and I thought it could be police scanner, which it turned out later to be.

I was driving and told John that I was going to park with another car between the bank and ours "just in case it's the real thing." Most alarms are false alarms and officers may be reluctant to "prone out" customers, especially the elderly (appearing) leaving the bank. As the man in the over coat and another man exited the front doors, we exited the detective car (an unmarked vehicle) to stop the two men.

Although we did not know who they were, they knew exactly who we were by listening to their scanner. I observed that the first man's over coat had an empty sleeve on his right side. Having seen this maneuver in many training films, I automatically assumed that he was about to display a long-gun. Before we could order them to stop, the bearded man in the over coat ordered us to "get the fuck back in your car." He immediately swung an AK-47 assault rifle from under his over coat and started firing at us.

"It's a 53," I radioed. The dispatcher only heard "53" (armed robbery). "Unit advising 53," he said. "154, 154," (officer in trouble) I responded. The dispatcher already had his finger on the alert tone and set it off before I finished. "154, Signal 154, involving a 53 at the NBD Bank branch," the dispatcher aired city-wide, "believe we have shots fired."

As the pair rushed us, still firing, I remembered the FBI's Miami shoot-out and recalled how the perpetrators had fired over the trunk of the agents' cars to shoot them behind their cover. As I backed toward the rear of the car, I drew my weapon and fired three shots over the top of the car to discourage their rush. John dropped to the passenger side and fired one shot, also to interdict the assault. It seemed to work.

The heavily armed robbers, also clad in body armor, moved down the sidewalk toward their getaway car. They continued the barrage of bullets which rocked the car from the impact. The flying bullets, glass, metal, and debris seemed to be everywhere, as if a hornets nest had just been unleashed upon us. As I observed bullets passing through the car, I knew I would soon be hit in the head or torso by a round. I moved in behind the wheel well in hopes of additional protection.

Everything seemed to be in slow motion, but at the same time too fast to be real. This is a paradox that cannot be understood until you experience it. I kept looking for a moment to come up with another shot, but the torrent of bullets did not subside. I had last sensed John next to me beside the car, but did not notice that he had literally slipped off the ice and behind some shrubs at the end of the lot.

Suddenly I felt something hit me in the stomach. It felt like I had been punched or hit with a large hammer in the gut. I could not tell, but I assumed that I had been shot in the stomach and I was unable to ascertain the seriousness of the hit. Another impact to my upper shin, just below the right knee, felt like I had been hit in the shin hard with a piece of angle iron.

The robbers reached their getaway car. John fired another shot, but saw no reaction from his target. They began to drive off and I finally took another opportunity to shoot. The car and occupants seemed to be miles away in the parking lot, although it was perhaps a few hundred feet, maybe yards. I fired two more shots at the passenger compartment, hoping to hit anything inside.

The robbers continued their flight. I turned to John, who was about thirty to forty feet away now, and keyed my radio. "John, I think I'm hit," I said. The dispatcher immediately came up on the air, "Unit advising they're hit?" A long silence followed.

My partner started to come to my aid, then said, "Look out! They're coming back." The perpetrators had fled North, but had now turned around to go South toward their switch car. "That was Girod said he had been hit," another responding detective said.

I moved to the other side of our car and John attempted to take another shot at the robbers as they passed at less than twenty m.p.h. on the icy street. He did not take his coveted shot when traffic passed the perpetrators going the opposite direction. The dispatcher, advising all units to standby, again asked which unit had been hit and the condition.

John tried to transmit to an approaching unit that the perpetrators were coming right at him. He continued to transmit as he watched the two cars pass each other, neither of us realizing that his radio was now dead.

John came to me and helped me limp into the bank where we first checked for civilian injuries. There were none and John helped to check where I was hit. Blood was dripping from my hand, I thought from checking elsewhere for wounds.

Pulling open my shirt revealed a six to eight inch diameter red mark that looked as if I had been shot with table salt. We later theorized that the tire had been hit and exploded into my stomach. Next we found a six-inch bruise and three-inch laceration across the top of my shinbone, where a round had shaved across the top of my shinbone at an angle.

Neither wound was serious and the blood was from small cuts and abrasions from flying glass and debris. While I limped for a few days, the Medics immediate concern was over my triple digit blood pressure (both systolic and diastolic).

During the shoot-out, the robbers dropped their scanner and $105,000. One of my rounds was recovered outside of the switch vehicle a few miles away. It had passed through the rear passenger door and front passenger seat, apparently hitting the bearded perpetrator in the back on his body armor and falling off of his overcoat when they switched cars.

The pair of robbers were apprehended after another in a spree of bank robberies in Evansville. An impact was noted in the back of one of the perpetrator's body armor. Both were career criminals with impressive resumes. One had escaped from a life sentence in Canada and was on the Royal Canadian Mounted Police's (RCMP's) 15-Most Wanted List (according to the FBI).

This experience added to my interest in violent crimes and armed robbery perpetrators who commit acts of violence.

ARMED ROBBERS

I had been a robbery-homicide detective and am now the supervisor of the Robbery-Homicide Squad. In April, 2000, the FBI and FWPD had formed a Bank Robbery Task Force, along with ATF, the New Haven Police Department (a suburb of Fort Wayne), the Allen County Police Department, and the Indiana State Police. We were experiencing a series of "serial robberies" or "spree robberies" at banks in the county, particularly in Fort Wayne.

I had been a police office in Indianapolis ten or more years earlier and had many memorable experiences in Indiana's largest city, state capital, and the thirteenth largest city in the U.S. (according to the 1990 U.S. Census). But, in 1999, Fort Wayne experienced more than half of the "major crimes" bank robberies in the state, as defined by the FBI.

I decided to fashion a survey after the format used for other violent crimes in the *Crime Classification Manual*. I attended a "criminal profiling seminar" at which I talked to CMC co-author Robert Ressler. I asked Ressler, an authority in this field, to be a Consultant on my Doctoral Committee and told him what I wanted to do. He agreed to be a "reading" consultant and provided input into my research.

Detective Raymond Pierce, NYPD (Retired), and Commander Thomas Cronin, Chicago PD, both criminal profilers, also offered insight and input as they too were Consultants and mentors in my program. Not only are these two men experienced investigators and profilers, they are scholars and gentlemen. Ray is an adjunct professor at John Jay College of Criminal Justice (The City University of New York) and Tom is an adjunct professor at Northwestern University.

I drafted the first survey (Version One) which I called the <u>Armed Robbery Data Sheet</u> and <u>Crime Classification Worksheet</u> for Armed Robberies. A Copy of

Version One is included here. After conducting the first fifteen surveys of fifteen local armed robberies (two attempted), all of which were bank robberies except one liquor store robbery, I found several areas that were not applicable or that need modification in my survey.

On 29 March 2000, I decided to modify the survey question to delete redundant and irrelevant items and modify others. While the first fifteen surveys are still included here, surveys that were requested from the FBI and other police departments were requested in the new format (Version Three), which is also included here.

A sample copy of the <u>Armed Robbery Data Sheet</u> and <u>Crime Classification Worksheet</u> for Armed Robberies, Version One, is included here for a reference and demonstration of how the final version changed. This illustrates the evolution of and differences between the robbery format and other violent crimes. The sample which follows is succeeded by an explanation of the changes and the <u>Modified Crime Classification Worksheet</u> for Armed Robberies (Version Three).

Armed Robbery Data Sheet
and
Crime Classification Worksheet
for Armed Robberies
Survey

(Version One)

<u>Armed Robbery Data Sheet</u>

1. Case Number _____ Is this case a: (Circle)

2. Is this a
   - a) Bank Robbery
   - b) Other Business Robbery
   - c) Robbery of Individual
   - d) Car Jacking Robbery
   - e) other (please specify) _____

3. Is this robbery a part of a
   - a) Single Robbery (not apparently associated with another robbery).
   - b) Serial Robbery (3 or more, breaks between events, cooling off period, characterized by premeditation, planning, or fantasy).

c) Spree Robbery (more than one, at 2 or more locations, single event w/o a cooling off period)

d) Mass Robbery (3 or more robberies, single event in one location, with no coiling off period)

e) Cult or Ritualistic Robbery (please specify) _____

4. Is there evidence of:

a) Undoing (attempt at restitution or "undoing" the crime or any part of it). Please specify:_____

b) Staging (alteration of the crime scene or attempting to conceal the commission of a crime).
Please specify:_____

c) Personation (unusual behavior beyond what is necessary to commit the crime or repetitive ritualistic behavior from crime to crime).
Please specify:_____

d) Signature (*repetitive personation* and/or scripting, e.g. language used by the offender during the crime or that they commanded the victim to use).
Please specify:_____

5. Use of Force:

a) Force in Resisting/Fleeing Law Enforcement

b) Victim Injured

c) Shots Fired

d) other force
Please specify:_____

6. Has the perpetrator been arrested or apprehended?

a) Arrested and awaiting trial

b) Convicted

c) Incarcerated: location _____

d) Mental health facility _____

7. Do you know if the suspect has ever been diagnosed as:

a) Psychopath (Asocial)

b) Psychotic (Nonsocial)

c) other _____

d) unknown

8. Did the crime/crime scene have evidence of being
    a) organized
    b) disorganized
    c) mixed
    d) other/unknown _____

Crime Classification Worksheet

I. <u>Victimology</u>
    Why did this victim become the victim of a violent crime?
    A. The Victim
        1. Life-style/hours of business

        _____

        2. Employment/type of institution or business

        _____

        3. Personality

        _____

        4. Friends and Associates in Area

        _____

        5. Income (amount, source, or loss)

        _____

        6. Family involvement

        _____

        7. Alcohol/drug use or abuse by victim

        _____

        8. Normal dress

        _____

        9. Handicaps

        _____

        10. Transportation used

        _____

        11. Reputation, habits, fears

        _____

        12. Marital status

        _____

        13. Dating habits

        _____

        14. Leisure activities

        _____

        15. Criminal history

        _____

16. Assertiveness

_____

17. Likes and dislikes

_____

18. Significant events

_____

19. Activities prior to the crime

_____

20. Other relevant information

_____

B. Verbal Interaction
   1. Excessive vulgar or abusive language

_____

   2. (what did the perp say or require the victim to say or communicate)

_____

   3. Apologetic

_____

C. Targeted Location
   1. Bank
   2. Residential
   3. Commercial
   4. Educational
   5. Mobile, vehicle
   6. Forest, fields

II. <u>Crime Scene</u>
   1. How many locations or crime scenes?

_____

   2. Environment

_____

      time

_____

      place

_____

   3. How many offenders (brief description for each):

_____

4. Organized or Disorganized Crime Scene (i.e. evidence of planning, methodical, professional or impromptu, unplanned, sloppy, e.g. body armor, scanner, etc.)

5. Physical evidence (fingerprints, photos, videos, etc.)

6. Weapon(s) used:

    a) Explosives?

    b) Firearms discharged?

    c) Injuries?

7. Physical restraints:

8. Items left or taken from the scene (e.g. security video tape taken, gloves left behind, etc.)

9. Other (witnesses, escape plan, wounded victims, etc.)

III. <u>Staging</u> (attempts to conceal the crime or alter the crime scene)

IV. <u>Forensic Findings</u>
    1. Forensic Analysis

    2. Video tape or fingerprints

    3. Hair/fibers

    4. Blood, Semen, or saliva

    5. Other

V. <u>Autopsy</u> applicable?

_____
_____
_____

VI. <u>Investigative Considerations</u>:

_____
_____
_____

Submitted by: _____ Agency:

_____

Survey Revisions and Research Modifications

In Version One *Item #2*, "Is this a…" (type of robbery) was eliminated and *I-C Targeted Location* under *Victimology* in the <u>Crime Classification Worksheet</u> was modified to include "*Car Jacking Robbery*" and "*Other.*"

Item #4, "Is there evidence of…" (Undoing, Staging, Personation, Signature) was deleted and consolidated with *I-B Verbal Interaction* under *Victimology* in the <u>Crime Classification Worksheet</u>. This section was renumbered and renamed—*II–Perpetrator Characteristics.*

In the *Victimology* section of the <u>Crime Classification Worksheet</u> *Item #13* (dating habits) was deleted as not applicable. *Items # 3, 4, 6, 7, 8, 10, 11, 12, 14, 15, 16,* and *17* were also found to be inapplicable to the victimology in these cases, but were applicable to the perpetrator. These items were moved to the *Perpetrator Characteristics* section (Section II) and both sections were renumbered.

Items 5, 6, 7, and *8* at the beginning of the survey were renumbered *3, 4, 5,* and *6* to account for the change in questions 2 and 3 (above).

Section II—Perpetrator Characteristics of the <u>Crime Classification Worksheet</u> was renumbered (letters changed to numbers) to be consistent with the format of the rest of the survey.

Part B. Verbal Interaction was placed under Signature/Scripting and renumbered as part of *Section II—Perpetrator Characteristics* of the <u>Crime Classification Worksheet</u>. *Part C. Targeted Location* was moved to the *Victimology* section and the "C" removed.

Part II. Crime Scene was renumbered as Part *III. Crime Scene*. Part *III. Staging* was also eliminated as it was included in *Section II—Perpetrator Characteristics* and, therefore, redundant. The sections following this were again renumbered.

The entire first page (six question items) was moved in a second revision to the end and incorporated into the <u>Crime Classification Worksheet</u> Section *VII*. The resulting modification of the original <u>Crime Classification Worksheet</u> format, adapted from the *Crime Classification Manual* outline, seems to more specifically apply to robbery, armed robbery, and/or bank robbery classification.

Adapting the *Crime Classification Manual* outline for Criminal Enterprise Murder, I have adopted a proposed taxonomy or classification for armed robberies—Criminal Enterprise Robbery.

Criminal Enterprise Robbery involves robberies committed for material gain, including money, goods, territory, or favors. Nearly all robberies fit this category and those that do not may, for the time being, be classified as *Robberies Not Otherwise Classified*.

Subcategories of *Criminal Enterprise Robbery*:
- Contract (third party) robbery.
- Gang motivated robbery.
- Criminal competition (intergroup/intragroup).
- Drug robberies (facilitating drug operations).
- Felony-murder robbery (primary and secondary).
- Erotomania or excitement robbery.
- Peer/group pressure robbery.

Modified Crime Classification Worksheet
for Armed Robberies
(Version Three)

<u>Crime Classification Worksheet</u>

Case Number _____

I. <u>Victimology</u>
    Why did this victim become the victim of a violent crime?
    The Victim
        1. Life-style/hours of business

        2. Employment/type of institution or business

        3. Income (amount, source, or loss)

        4. Handicaps

5. Significant events

6. Activities prior to the crime

7. Other relevant information

Targeted Location
1. Bank
2. Residential
3. Commercial
4. Educational
5. Mobile, vehicle (not car jacking)
6. Car Jacking Robbery
7. Forest, fields
8. other (please specify)

II. <u>Perpetrator Characteristics</u>:
1. Undoing/Apologetic (attempt at restitution or "undoing" the crime or any part of it).

2. Staging (attempts to alter the crime scene or to conceal the crime).

3. Personation (unusual behavior beyond what is necessary to commit the crime or repetitive ritualistic behavior from crime to crime).

4. Signature (*repetitive personation* and/or scripting, e.g. language used by the offender during the crime or that they commanded the victim to use).
   a) Verbal Interaction/Excessive vulgar or abusive language

   b) Scripting (what did the perp say or require the victim to say or communicate)

The Perpetrator
1. Personality

2. Friends and Associates in Area

_____

3. Family involvement

_____

4. Alcohol/drug use

_____

5. Normal dress

_____

6. Transportation used

_____

7. Reputation, habits, fears

_____

8. Marital status

_____

9. Leisure activities

_____

10. Criminal history

_____

11. Assertiveness

_____

12. Likes and dislikes

_____

III. <u>Crime Scene</u>

1. How many locations or crime scenes?

_____

2. Environment

_____

    time

_____

    place

_____

3. How many offenders (brief description for each):

_____

4. Organized or Disorganized Crime Scene (i.e. evidence of planning, methodical, professional or impromptu, unplanned, sloppy, e.g. body armor, scanner, etc.)

_____

5. Physical evidence (fingerprints, photos, videos, etc.)

6. Weapon(s) used:

   a) Explosives?

   b) Firearms discharged?

   c) Injuries?

7. Physical restraints:

8. Items left or taken from the scene (e.g. security video tape taken, gloves left behind, etc.)

9. Other (witnesses, escape plan, wounded victims, etc.)

IV. <u>Forensic Findings</u>
    1. Forensic Analysis

    2. Video tape or fingerprints

    3. Hair/fibers

    4. Blood, Semen, or saliva

    5. Other

V. <u>Autopsy</u> applicable?

VI. <u>Investigative Considerations</u>:

VII. <u>Behavioral Data</u>:
    1. Is this robbery a part of a
        a) Single Robbery (not apparently associated with another robbery).
        b) Serial Robbery (3 or more, breaks between events, cooling off period, characterized by premeditation, planning, or fantasy).
        c) Spree Robbery (more than one, at 2 or more locations, single event w/o a cooling off period)
        d) Mass Robbery (3 or more robberies, single event in one location, with no cooling off period)
        e) Cult or Ritualistic Robbery (please specify)

    _____

    2. Use of Force:
        a) Force in Resisting/Fleeing Law Enforcement
        b) Victim Injured
        c) Shots Fired
        d) other force
        Please specify:

    _____

    3. Has the perpetrator been arrested or apprehended?
        a) Arrested and awaiting trial
        b) Convicted
        c) Incarcerated: location

    _____

        d) Mental health facility

    _____

    4. Do you know if the suspect has ever been diagnosed as:
        a) Psychopath (Asocial)
        b) Psychotic (Nonsocial)
        c) other

    _____

        d) unknown

    5. Did the crime/scrims scene have evidence of being
        a) organized
        b) disorganized
        c) mixed
        d) other/unknown

    _____

Submitted by: _____ Agency:

_____
311

CASE STUDIES IN ARMED ROBBERY

The primary data sources in case studies include files and abridged files containing descriptive information. These files contain witness and police officer statements, follow-up detective investigations, analysis of evidence found at scenes, etc. through which definitive classifications and behavioral traits may be determined. (Sobol, p. 364).

Data from the first fifteen *Case Studies* was gathered on the original <u>Version One</u> <u>Armed Robbery Data Sheet</u> and <u>Crime Classification Worksheet</u> for Armed Robberies. This original sample was used for two purposes: 1) to test the applicability of the survey, which was adapted from a format used for other homicide, sex crimes, and arson, and 2) to utilize data for a preliminary test of the premise that robberies, as violent crimes, could also be profiled in a manner similar to the other crimes against persons and arson crimes.

Of the first fifteen cases, twelve were bank robberies, two were attempts, and one was a liquor store robbery. Ten (two-thirds) appeared to be single robberies (not apparently associated with another robbery), five (one-third) were known serial robberies (three or more with a break between events, a cooling off period, characterized by premeditation, planning, or fantasy).

There were no spree robberies (more than one robbery, at two or more locations, involving a single event without a cooling off period) recorded in this sample. There were also no mass robberies (three or more robberies, involving a single event at one location, and no cooling off period) recorded in this sample. There were no cult or ritualistic robberies recorded in this sample.

While there was no evidence of Undoing (an attempt at restitution or "undoing" the crime or any part of the crime), there was some indication of Staging (Alteration of the crime scene or attempting to conceal the commission of a crime). This may have been present in the form of:

- Using gloves to eliminate fingerprints in the premises and getaway car.
- Using masks and/or disguises to conceal the identity of and/or prevent photos and/or video recording of the perpetrators.
- Changing clothes or turning them inside-out while fleeing to change appearance from the description given by witnesses.

- Use of fake beards and disguises to conceal their identity. Disguises may look less suspicious than masks if they look natural. Witnesses may also give descriptions, which may then be changed quickly by fleeing perpetrators. The use of uniforms (such as security guard uniforms) may also reduce suspicion as perpetrators flee.
- Use of "switch cars" (usually a stolen car which is dumped nearby when the perpetrators finally flee in their own vehicle) to evade detection via license plates and vehicle descriptions.
- Use of police scanners to detect that alarms have been sent, that police are responding, and the location of responding or pursuing police units.

Personation (unusual behavior beyond what is necessary to commit the crime or repetitive ritualistic behavior from crime to crime) was also implied in at least five or more cases. This included perpetrators "vaulting" the counter (in at least four case studies of known serial robbers), pulling out phone lines, turning T-shirts inside out, etc. In one sample the perpetrator demanded a bank employees car for the getaway, but specified that it had to be an "automatic transmission." In another a confirmed schizophrenic became belligerent and made death threats, while armed with a BB gun.

Signature (repetitive personation and/or scripting, i.e. language used by the offender during the crime or that they command the victim to use) was also implied. While the aforementioned "vaulting" of the counter was repetitive, the repetitive use of disguises by one bank robbery earned him the monicher "The Santa Claus Robbery." This character was know for his first of a series of bank robberies in which he wore a Santa Claus outfit. In subsequent robberies he wore the beard, but in one was dressed in a security guard uniform (he was a former security guard) and in another a "Reggae." He also carried a scanner.

Use of force was minimal in these samples. Only one attempted to resist law enforcement by fleeing from the presence of the police. Most, however, never came into contact with the police. This one case attempted to "flee" by slipping away from custody.

The only victim injuries in this sample were bruises in one or two cases, but these required no medical attention. No shots fired were reported. The category of "other force" included:

- Pulling a bank teller/victim off the floor (after being ordered to prone out) and moved by "shoving" a gun in their back.
- Cocking or chambering a round in a gun while pointing it at a teller/victim.
- "Slamming" a teller/victim into a wall.
- Threatening to shoot a teller/victim.

- Grabbing a teller/victim by the hair and collar, placing a gun to their head, literally dragging them to the vault, and placing a knee in their back.
- Removing a security surveillance videotape by threatening to shoot and kill a teller/victim.

Only three perpetrators in this sample have been arrested at the time of this writing on charges for these cases (although the "Santa Claus Robber" may soon be charged and has a recent but unrelated arrest).

In one of the case studies involving multiple offenders, only one of the perpetrators has been arrested. That perpetrator is also a suspect in a homicide and may also be charged with that crime, while his co-perpetrators are the subjects of the Bank Robbery Task Force investigation (at the time of this writing). One of these perpetrators has been arrested for the murder of a Sheriff's Confinement Officer and his co-perpetrators may also be charged with that felony murder.

Only one of these fifteen case studies has a confirmed or known history of mental diagnosis. While his psychiatric and psychological records are not accessible, a confidential source confirms that this perpetrator is *both* a psychopath (borderline/sociopath) and a psychotic (schizophrenic). He is described by one mental health worker as "Disorganized" in his thinking, characterized by "poverty of content" or a lack of logical meaning, yet "Organized" in the sense of being neat, clean, and orderly.

This suspect, mentioned above as becoming belligerent and making death threats with a BB gun, was arrested for attempting to rob a bank. He was served with a warrant for intimidation, resisting law enforcement (he, too, was the one mentioned as having tried to "slip away"), and disorderly conduct.

This subject had been involved in a vehicle pursuit (fleeing the police) just nine months earlier over a traffic offense. He had also been involved in a disturbance after being fired from his job, when he forced his way back into his former place of employment to retrieve his personnel file and job application form.

On the date of his "bank robbery," this subject had climbed into a Pepsi delivery truck, just before the robbery, and refused to get out for some unknown reason. His bank robbery note read:

> *to whom it may concern, you dumb ass*
> *MUTA PHUCKAS to rob this small bank I would have shot*
> *that dumb bitch on the phone last and left the money on the floor.*

While this case may sound a bit humorous, it also illustrates the unpredictability of some mentally ill perpetrators. It also hints at the degree of violence that may be on the minds of some perpetrators or would-be perpetrators.

Of these fifteen case studies, only two were speculated to be Organized and only one was speculated to be Disorganized. Two seemed to be Mixed, while the remaining ten were simply unknown or unable to be categorized from the know variables.

In the Victimology section, as stated earlier, most of the categories did not apply and only a few could be adapted to this study. The *Life-style* was used to portray the hours of business which, in this case, was merely used to reflect the time of the crime. Only the liquor store robbery was as late as 2245 hours (10:45 p.m.). The bank robberies occurred at 0856, 0914, 0930, 1005, 1030, 1050, 1018, 1116, 1124, 1400 (2:00 p.m.), 1452 (2:52 p.m.), and one drive-through bank robbery at 1900 hours (7:00 p.m.).

Only the liquor store robbery had a loss as low $125. The bank and federal credit union losses ranged from low of $2,545.00 to a high of over $250,000. The average ranged from a low of $10, 891.01—$36,000.00 to a high average of $70,000—$130,000.

"*Activities prior to the crime*" included only two remarkable comments. In one case the robbery occurred just before closing. In another the bank branch manager/victim joked to the perpetrator not to bring any weapons into her office in the gym bag he was carrying. He had a gun and a mock bomb with an alleged remote control devise.

Verbal Interaction was the section that had the most reportable data, although it was not always that revealing. At least three cases had obviously "excessive vulgar or abusive language." This is subjective and may have been present in the majority of cases. In the three obvious cases, excessive yelling and screaming was characteristic with a preference for the term "bitch" and "fucking bitch." "Shut the fuck up, bitch" was a favorite expression of these robbers, as was "mother fucker" and other vulgar limitation in vocabulary.

While scripting was not characterized, for the most part, by requiring the victim to say anything, perpetrator comments were included:

- "Hurry up. Give me *your* money." (Demanding large bills only, no small bills, and not to push the alarm).
- Several of the sampled perpetrators ordered a teller/victim to go to the vault and several asked for the "vault key."
- "Who has the vault key" and "I'm *not afraid to shoot you, bitch.*"
- "Get down, get on the floor; open the vault; don't play with me or *I'll kill you*" and "get down so no one gets hurt."
- "Okay, the lady with key to the vault…where's the lady with the key" seemed to indicate some knowledge of employee responsibilities and

could even indicate inside help. This perpetrator also said, "I don't want to hurt anybody. Just fill up the bags."

- One perpetrator, who did not don his mask for several minutes while he feigned a deposit until his partner also entered, said, "Do you have video here?" When a teller/victim said they did not, the robber said, "If your lying to me mother fucker…" and made some threat to kill the teller/victim. (The video was removed and taken, as was the demand note).
- A note used in the drive-through bank robbery read "This is a robbery. Give me *your money or I'll kill you.*"
- The case of the pathological schizophrenic was characterized by his comment, "Next time I go in that bank I really am going to kill everybody."

Fourteen of the Targeted Locations in the survey were banks or federal credit unions, while only one was a liquor store. Most had only one crime scene, but at least two had two crime scenes. Several had scenes where stolen "switch cars" were discovered and processed from fingerprints. In one case study, a license plate was reported by a witness and the plate was traced to the perpetrator's mother's house. A tip revealed this was the perpetrator's hideout and the location of both the robbery gun and money.

Five of these cases studies involved single perpetrators. Seven were identified with *at least two* perpetrators and *at least two involved at least three or more* perpetrators. At least one case was involved in which the number of perpetrators could not accurately be estimated (as many as four).

The Organized and Disorganized categories were determined on the basis of evidence of planning, methodical implementation, or professional characteristics versus an unplanned, impromptu, or "sloppy" attack. The employment of a police scanner/monitor, body armor, or other special equipment was also considered. The cases studies revealed these characteristics:

- Ripped out phone lines and took victims vehicle.
- Stole getaway vehicle before crime and reported their own vehicle, used in the switch, stolen just after the crime.
- Cased bank ahead of time and/or rehearsed the robbery.
- Backed getaway car in to obstruct the plate and/or aid in getaway.
- The use of both a gun and a fake (mock) bomb to keep employees of the bank immobile for six minutes. Threatened remote detonation via a communication device with an alleged partner.
- The use of a police scanner/monitor to listen for alarms and police responses.
- The use of gloves, masks, and/or disguises.

- Disorganized cases were indicated by the impromptu or unplanned nature of the crimes.
- A "Mixed" case study was indicated by the fact that one of the two perpetrators entered the bank without his mask on, wrote the robbery note on a deposit slip, went to the far end of the bank, and feigned a deposit as a ruse before his partner entered. Although this was characterized by a plan, it was implemented with a poor plan.

Physical evidence included one or more of the following items in at least one or more of the case studies:

- Fingerprints,
- Security surveillance video tape or still photos,
- Bait bills, marked bills, and/or bank bands on packaged money,
- Demand notes,
- Shoe impressions, and
- The tape used in a mock bomb.

Weapons in these case studies included revolvers and semi-automatic pistols in almost every case. Of these fifteen robberies, some perpetrators were involved in more than robbery and some robberies involved multiple perpetrators. In a few of these cases weapons were not observed. However, case reports confirm that *at least* three revolvers, nine semi-automatic pistols, and four unspecified handguns were used. In one case a fake bomb was utilized. This was the only reported case in the sample which involved an explosive or alleged explosive. Reported injuries were limited to bruises.

Physical restraints were not commonly used in this sample. In one case the fake (mock) bomb was used to detain or delay occupants of the bank. The perpetrator threatened that if anyone moved before six minutes had elapsed, he would communicate by radio for his alleged partner to detonate the alleged bomb by remote control. Bank employees ushered the bank's occupants into the vault for protection from the alleged bomb.

In one case, the perpetrators attempted to lock the bank's occupants inside the vault. Another teller/victim was restrained with a gun placed to her head. One report said a teller/victim was "forced" to "empty the entire safe" while another was "forced" to remove the security surveillance videotape. These were considered as potential forms of restraint, while binding was not present in these cases.

Items left or taken involved two cases where demand notes and a videotape were taken and a fake or mock bomb was left. Witnesses, aside from the occupants of the crime scenes, were present in *at least* two cases, while an escape plan was evident in *at least* two cases. Again, staging was implied by the use of gloves, masks, disguises, and switch cars in *at least* two or more of the case studies. The security surveillance videotape was taken in one case.

Videotape and/or fingerprints were available as physical evidence in more than a third of the cases. Other cases also involved bait money, marked bills (with teller initials and/or bank markings), money with bank bands, shoe impressions, and the remnants of the fake bomb in one case.

Investigative considerations were many and diverse. The liquor store robbery cases was solved when one of the victim/clerks later spotted the perpetrator, who was arrested for an outstanding *battery warrant involving a shooting*. The suspect used his brother's name when stopped by the police.

In another case, mentioned previously, a witness observed a license plate, which was traced to the suspect's mother's house. A tip also revealed that the perpetrator, his gun, and the bank money were at his hideout in his mother's house. The suspect had just been released from prison for a burglary. His mother said he was "rebellious," had a drug problem, and of the bank robbery said, "he's capable of this."

FOLLOW-UP DATA

Four other robbers were studied as case studies of serial robbers, accounting for thirty-two armed robberies and a variety of other offenses between them.

Graves was a black male, age 26, and was known to have committed at least four armed robberies. In addition to these, he has prior arrests for escape, public intoxication, theft, and an unspecified warrant.

King, a black male, age 19, was a six-foot, 165-pound serial robber with a scar across his neck. He accounted for at least eight armed robbers in a series. He had a handgun permit application pending during some of his other arrests that included armed forgery, "fail to appear," auto theft, forgery, three unrelated thefts, two arrests for possession of a handgun without a license within two days, an unspecified warrant, and an arrest involving a stolen vehicle recovery. He also had an arrest for theft from vehicles.

King's traffic offenses include four speed citations, two driving while suspended arrests, three charges for failure to provide proof of financial responsibility (driving with no insurance), four citations for disregarding an automatic signal (stop light), and one for running two stop signs. He also had citations for improper tail lights and license plate lights, two seat belt violations, an unsafe lane change, an illegal turn, and three driver's license violations.

King was also arrested on a warrant and in an unrelated traffic stop for unspecified charges. He had four arrests or citations for noise violations. His possession upon arrest included a gun, a pager, and a cell phone.

Wilson, a white male, age 18, has blue eyes and a shaved head. In addition to his series of at least six armed robberies, Wilson had six missing child/runaway arrests as a minor and an alias. Other charges in his young career include criminal confinement, two thefts, burglary, battery, and rape. He was also involved in a pursuit by police and a suicide attempt. His possession upon arrest included a police scanner/monitor.

Jones, a black male, age twenty, has a scar on his right wrist and uses an alias with the same name, but a different date of birth, and three other alias names. He accounted for a series of fourteen serial robberies. He has been arrested or cited for unsafe lane changes, no financial responsibility (insurance), and driving while suspended.

Jones other arrests include a robbery/battery, three possessions of marijuana, two possessions of hashish, two possessions of a handgun without a permit, two contributing to the delinquency of a minor, two thefts, two probation violations, two resisting law enforcement charges, and false informing. He also had two pursuit-related arrests, a burglary, an auto theft, and an unspecified warrant.

On May 3, 2000, I received a FBI teletype message alerting police agencies to be aware of a serial bank robber. I made a follow-up telephone call to the agent who sent the message to receive more information before our Bank Robbery Task Force meeting.

The suspect was an atypical bank robber. He operated interstate and, at the time of my notification, had committed twenty two bank robberies in New Jersey, Pennsylvania, and Ohio between September, 1999, and December, 1999. After eighteen bank robberies in NJ in a dozen different counties, a bank surveillance photo was published in a statewide newspaper. The robberies stopped in NJ and started in Pennsylvania and then in Ohio.

The suspect preferred locations with access within a mile of an interstate highway. The robber waits in a teller line, then passes a note warning not to set off an alarms or call the police. The suspect watches the tellers' hands for signs of an alarm. The suspect is described as "well dressed," wearing a shirt and tie. A "profile" is indicative of the day and time pattern of the suspect. This is an example of the type of case in which profiling could be valuable in not only apprehending the suspect, but perhaps in a threat assessment of his violence potential.

Another case study, a case assigned to my detectives, involved an Allen County Sheriff's Confinement Officer who was murdered during a robbery. This case is illustrative of the violence that armed robbers are capable of.

The victim, whose name will not be used, had just finished a shift at the "lockup." He was also the owner of sandwich shop franchise and stopped in to check on his business and employee. When he made a call home to his wife, the employee left him alone in the office.

The employee, returning to her duties, heard the door buzzer signal that someone had entered, but it was not a customer. The suspect was armed with a handgun and asked if anyone else was in the store. The employee said that there was and was ushered into the office where the victim was sitting in the desk chair, still in his Sheriff's uniform.

The suspect told him to hang up the phone. The officer said, "I have to go. Bye," to his wife and hung up the phone. The suspect then fired a shot at him, hesitated, then fired a second shot. One of the two shots hit the wall, but the other hit the officer in the neck, fatally wounding him.

The suspect demanded money and the employee moved toward the cash register. "The safe," demanded the robber, threatening to kill her too. After that he emptied the register, taped the employee's hands behind her back, and prepared to leave. "You better call for help. Call Five-O; he needs it," the suspect taunted as he left with less than $100.

While this investigation awaits trial at this writing, three suspects were identified and information reveals that they had not planned this robbery. It was an impulsive, *disorganized* crime by psychopaths who later joked and celebrated the murder of one that they thought was a police officer. These suspects were revealed to be *serial robbers*–bank robbers.

While there was little evidence that supports the use of profiling in armed robbery cases, it should also be noted that this study was attempted from a single perspective, that of the law enforcement investigator. While this perspective reveals useful information about the nature of the crimes, it reveals only limited information about the offender.

Because of this shortcoming, I attempted on several occasions in the course of this study to elicit the cooperation of the Indiana Department of Corrections (DoC). The DoC could provide a great deal of follow-up information on the psychiatric and psychological diagnosis of convicted armed robbers. After the police have incarcerated these offenders, they are remanded to the custody of the correctional system and are usually unavailable for "analysis." Unfortunately, the DoC was also "unavailable" for analysis.

The mental health profession also could be of valuable assistance in comparing behavioral diagnosis to investigative profiling. Again, however, this system implements confidentiality policies which make such research virtually impossible.

This research merely presents an opportunity, at this point, for a cooperative research effort between law enforcement, corrections, and the mental health communities to conduct comparisons of crime patterns, behavioral characteristics, and clinical diagnosis. Such a comparison could provide insight into the nature of violence associated with armed robberies.

CRIME STATISTICS

While crime statistics are not "criminal profiling," they do provide "crime analysis" data that are indicative of patterns, such as locations, days, and times of specific incidents. Examples of such *crime analysis data* (statistics and crime maps) from the Fort Wayne Police Department's Crime Analysis Unit are included in Appendix A.

Crime statistics from a police department's crime analysis unit or criminal intelligence section can help establish patterns of crime by Modus Operandi, day, date, and time of crimes, location probabilities, etc. Criminal statistics from correctional facilities can help identify offender diagnostic characteristics and demographic profiles by offense classification. Thus, crime statistics can be useful to criminal profilers in making predictions about crime patterns and behavior.

While the police use crime statistics, which are in turn used for the FBI Uniform Crime Reports (UCRs), state correctional agencies (Department of Corrections) also maintain offender statistics for those who are incarcerated. In 1999, for example, the Indiana Department of Corrections maintained statistics on an adult population of 19,197 inmates in twenty-four institutions.

Offenders were classified by level, sex, and ethnicity:

- Minimum   10.9%
- Low medium   54.8%
- High medium   15.2%
- Maximum   19.0%
- Maximum control   0.1%

- Female   6.3%
- Male   93.7%

- White   53.1%
- Black   41.0%
- Hispanic   3.1%
- Unknown   2.4%
- American Indian/Alaskan Native   0.3%
- Asian/Pacific Islander   0.1%

(Internet: http://www.ai.org/indcorrection/statistics.html).

These offenders were also classified by their offenses. Crimes against person accounted for 40.3%, controlled substance offenses were involved in 17.2%, weapons charges were involved in 1.8%, and 0.1% were serving habitual sentences. This does not include the 4,064 men and 341 women on parole or the 1,184 incarcerated juveniles in state facilities (Internet: http://www.ai.org/indcorrection/statistics.html).

Juveniles are classified on a "security level" that includes four categories: violent, serious, less serious, and minor and of these juveniles 29.8% are classified as *violent* (Internet: http://www.ai.org/indcorrection/statistics.html).

While crime statistics and crime maps are not "profiling," Detective Inspector Kim Rossmo, Ph.D., of the Vancouver Police Department in British Columbia, Canada, has conducted research in the art and science of Geographic Profiling. Geographic Profiling is an investigative methodology used to analyze the locations of a connected series of crimes to determine the most likely area of an offender's residence, thereby allowing investigators to more effectively manage information on which to focus their investigations.

I was fortunate enough to meet with Dr. Rossmo, attend his lecture on Geographic Profiling, and discuss the subject with him in person and by e-mail. In his book, Dr. Rossmo explains the *Modus Operandi Matrix*, *Criminal Hunting Typologies*, *Predator Patterns*, etc. based on his research in Geographic Profiling (Rossmo, *Geographic Profiling*). His writings are very informative.

OFFICER SAFETY

Finally, a word on officer safety. Officer deaths resulting from robbery calls have accounted for 11% to 21% of the death toll (from approximately 1976 to 1986). One of the causes of this tragedy is complacency. Because nationally 95% of alarms have proven to be false, officers sometimes automatically assume that they are being sent to yet another false trip. Despite *visible danger cues*, this presumptiveness continues right up to the lethal moment (Remsberg, p. 239).

Another cause of fatalities, when an alarm or robbery is confirmed, is a zealous response that takes the form of charging in with fatalistic commitment. Good tactical planning can eliminate these risks and reduce these fatalities (Remsberg, p. 241). This planning includes "Tactical Thinking, offender style." Remsberg says (in 1986) that three-fourths of bank robbers don't even use disguises, but "their motivation and desperation can be just as dangerously high." He suggests that half are narcotics users and 46% are armed (Remsberg, pp. 243-244). This latter figure may be higher now in the 21st Century.

While it is true that most robberies last less than two minutes, one study related to response time to apprehension rates indicates that even when you take four minutes to arrive at the scene, there is still a 50-50 chance that the robbers will be apprehended. While this suggest a high proportion of police–offender confrontations at the scene, odds are even higher if officers are nearby when they receive the call. Remsberg cautions, "In making your response to *any* robbery call, your safety is best assured if you assume the robbery is still in progress...and you *anticipate an armed confrontation*" (Remsberg, p. 244).

REFERENCES–CHAPTER 10

Rossmo, D. Kim. **Geographic Profiling**. Boca Raton, Florida: CRC Press, 1999.

Remsberg, Charles. **The Tactical Edge: Surviving High-Risk Patrol**. Northbrook, IL: Calibre Press, Inc., 1986.

Internet: http://www.ai.org/indcorrection/statistics.html, 09-15-99, 2:17 p.m.

Sobol, James J. "Behavioral Characteristics and Level of Involvement for Victims of Homicide," Homicide Studies: An Interdisciplinary & International Journal, Volume 1/Number 4, November, 1997.

Chapter Eleven

FUTURE IMPLICATIONS AND RESEARCH

INTRODUCTION

In this study we have examined the foundations, theories and concepts of criminology, the sociology of deviance, abnormal psychology, and forensic psychology. These social and behavioral sciences lay the foundation for understanding the criminal mind. The chapter on forensic science provides a framework for evaluating crimes scenes and what these scenes can identify about the crime and it's perpetrator.

These studies and scientific disciplines are the structures around which criminal profiling and behavioral analysis become a scientific sub-discipline or specialty, now known as criminal investigative analysis. Once the concepts and principles of criminal profiling and behavioral analysis are established, this criminal investigative analysis can also be used to help analyze macabre and bizarre crime scenes and criminal activity that are not commonly encountered.

The analysis of mass, serial, and spree crimes is not commonplace, but criminal investigative analysis can help identify them as such when they might otherwise be assumed to be commonplace or unrelated acts. Likewise, while ritualistic and occult/cult crimes are also not commonplace, when they do occur it is helpful to identify their nature through criminal investigative analysis.

Another sensational but, fortunately, uncommon category of violent phenomena are school, workplace, and domestic or family violence. These often massively fatal occurrences can be better managed with the help of criminal investigative analysis.

There are a variety of categories of crime that can be detected, deterred, or investigated through the help of criminal investigative analysis. Other examples include the detection of assassins and their intentions, predictions and profiles about stalkers, and the criminal investigative analysis of bombers and their crimes.

PROFILING VIOLENT CRIME

While the majority of studies into the field of criminal profiling and behavioral analysis has concentrated on murder, rape or sex crimes, and arson, this study and text has attempted to expand the study of violent crime, particularly armed robbery and the attendant violence that is perpetrated in such robberies. The most violent of armed robberies and increasingly so are take-over bank robberies.

It is this lack of much data in this area, the need for investigative and officer safety tactics, and my own personal experiences with violent armed robbers that prompted me to attempt to expand and adapt this study to this subject area.

The study of armed robbery and take-over bank robbers in the field of criminal investigative analysis is far from complete. I have barely gone beyond identifying the need for such studies in this work, but I have, I believe, identified the methodology and preliminary findings to continue long term studies in this field.

PROFILING THE CRIMINAL MIND

Criminologists, sociologists, psychologists, psychiatrists, and other social and behavioral scientists have long studied the criminal mind. Many theories and practical methodologies have been identified to help understand crime, criminals, the ways crimes are committed, what crime scenes mean, and the peculiarities of the criminal mind. Much has been contributed from these fields on how to prevent, deter, detect, and deal with crimes, once they occur, and criminals.

The fields of criminology and forensic psychology is still breaking new ground and discovering new revelations in such areas as the psychology of *voir dire (jury selection)* (e.g. using body language, linguistics analysis, scientific content analysis [SCAN], etc.) and *hostage negotiations (crisis management)*. Criminology, forensic psychology, and the sub-specialty field of criminal investigative analysis can be beneficial in these areas as well as in the investigation of crimes.

THE FUTURE OF CRIMINAL PROFILING

Criminal profiling and behavioral analysis has evolved into what is known today as criminal investigative analysis. But this evolution has not ended.

Some forensic behaviorists and investigators, even among the "certified" criminal investigative analysts, have debunked the Organized (Nonsocial/Psychopathic) versus Disorganized (Asocial/Psychotic) theory that has been the backbone for the criminal profiling method. Critics argue, as we discussed earlier in this text, that this simplistic theory does not account for criminals who are simply not mentally abnormal, but merely criminal.

The effects of this argument on criminal investigative analysis have yet to be determined. Also to be determined is what theories will dominate this study in light of the proven effectiveness of criminal profiling and behavioral analysis.

New sub-sub-specialties of criminal profiling are also emerging and continue to develop, such as Rossmo's *Geographic Profiling*, Sapir's *Scientific Content Analysis (SCAN)*, and Korem's *The Art of Profiling*, as discussed in earlier chapters of this text.

Still another concern and topic in the art and science of criminal profiling and behavioral analysis involves the actual education, training, and "certification" in criminal investigative analysis. When the Federal Bureau of Investigation ended its pilot criminal profiling and behavioral analysis Fellowship program the void was filled by those who had taken advantage of this program.

This void was filled in a variety of ways, some good and some not so good. One of these ways was the proliferation of books that flooded the market by those who established the FBI's program, those who conducted the program, and those who participated in the program. Several of the authors of these books claimed to be the "father of criminal profiling," while others claimed to have headed the FBI's Behavioral Science Unit and the criminal profiling and behavioral analysis program. Even among former members of these programs such claims have sometimes been disputed.

While many of these books (and even some of these claims) are well grounded and practical, others are merely "hawked" as the latest fad in criminal investigations and forensic behavioral science to further the retirement plan of their peddlers.

These books have also found themselves competing, sometimes bitterly, with similar books (and claims) from the academic sphere. While many of these academics have made viable claims to have validated research in this field, the law enforcement community criticizes them, perhaps with some credibility, for lacking any practical experience in applying these studies. Meanwhile, some of their critics have embarrassed their profession by engaging in shameless territorial disputes.

Then there are the seminar peddlers. I don't mean this as a derision of those who are providing valuable and useful training in this field, however, there are *some* who are merely selling a pretty package to customers (students) who leave with nothing more than a piece of pretty paper. Yes, the art and science of criminal profiling and behavioral analysis has become a big dollar business.

Still another void that has been filled is in the area of "certification" for would-be criminal profilers or criminal investigative analysts. There are a couple of groups which has seemingly attempted to co-opt a monopoly on what seems to regarded as "sacred territory" by devising a very exclusive and preclusive "certification" process.

Again, while there is sometimes money to be made in this field, politics and egos also play a major role in this field. While a valid form of certification must be established to maintain the quality and integrity of most professions, the provision for practical succession is also an important issue that should ethically outweigh the agenda of territorialists.

While criminal profiling and behavioral analysis is a specialty field, there are many specialty fields in both law enforcement and behavioral science that do not carry a certification requirement before one is deemed capable of providing some benefit from practicing specialized techniques.

Still, certification may have some practical benefits if it is not monopolized by profiteers or for anyone's ego agenda. In this sense the future might bring a sort of criminal profiling and behavioral analysis "cult" or subculture if such organizations are not properly directed and influenced by the most selfless of their members.

Having insulted nearly everyone I know and don't know in law enforcement, behavioral science and academics who study, practice, teach, or write on criminal investigative analysis, let me emphatically express that most in this field are dedicated, competent, and ethical professionals. Most have made extensive contributions to their fields, their communities, and to the world. Many of them have contributed greatly to me in my research and to my personal development through their mentorship.

The study and practice of criminal profiling and behavioral analysis may have many interesting, surprising, useful, and useless developments in the future. Because this is an exciting and extremely effective investigative tool, its value should be recognized and nurtured as this field's future continues to evolve.

CONCLUSION

I have shared some of my own experiences in this study of the criminal mind. Like most lawmen (and women), I could share "war stories" all day long and, like some, I enjoy "talking shop." Perhaps this is why, in addition to having served as a reserve military officer, I adopted an additional secondary vocation as a university professor.

Like most peace officers I can recount many incidents involving violence (in academics we call them "case studies" and in the military we called them "scenarios," but they are still "war stories").

Not long after my second shooting incident or "shoot-out," as many pistoleros prefer to refer to them as, I found myself again faced with a potentially lethal armed encounter. (I have repeated these circumstances since then also).

Three times within an hour I became professionally involved in potentially violent disturbances with a mentally unstable individual. This subject had a prior history of perpetrating violence on law enforcement when he took a tire iron to a traffic officer's head. In my three encounters with the subject on this single day, each encounter became increasingly threatening until, in the third and final incident, the subject produced a gun.

While many "Monday-morning quarterbacks" (who are never at the scene and probably wouldn't be even if they were) have questioned why I didn't immediately shoot this subject, there were extenuating circumstances that only I could evaluate at the time. While legally justified in taking the subject's life, tactical and practical factors were also involved. After the subject retreated into and barricaded himself inside his house SWAT officers later arrested him without major injury.

The point of these "case studies" is not to entertain, as I am sure that any of the readers of this work could find more entertaining material to consume. These "scenarios" are intended to help better understand the criminal mind, criminal behavior, and the ways in which we can prevent, deter, detect, and deal with crime.

I hope that in some small way I have contributed to this objective of dealing with crime and criminals. I hope that my both my research and my professional efforts have contributed in some way to making my fellow peace officers safer and more effective and that we have made safer communities in the process.

APPENDIX A

TABLES OF TYPOLOGY CHARACTERSISTICS

Organized/Disorganized
Profiling Characteristics

Organized (Nonsocial/Psychopathic)	*Disorganized (Asocial/Psychotic)*
Average (good) to high intelligence (may have done well in school)	Average to below average intelligence (usually high school dropout)
High birth order status	Low birth order status
Socially adequate (personal, but superficial relationships	Socially inadequate/immature
Charming (makes friends easily)	Poor personal hygiene
Nonsocial by choice (no one is good enough)	
Masculine image	Usually does not date
Sexually competent (some married; most intimate with someone)	Sexually incompetent
Often from middle-class family	
Inconsistent childhood discipline	Harsh childhood discipline
Father's work stable	Father's work unstable
Prefers skilled work	Unskilled work
Occupationally mobile	Poor work history
Geographically mobile (car in good condition)	Lives/works near crime scene (no car)
Situational cause/Precipitating situational stress	Minimal situational stress
Controlled mood during crime	Anxious mood during crime (confused and distressed)
Use of alcohol with crime	Minimal use of alcohol
Follows crime in media	Minimal interest in news media
May change jobs or leave town following crime	
Model prisoner	Significant behavioral / lifestyle change (.e.g. drug/alcohol abuse religiosity, etc.) Secret hiding places
	Nocturnal person
Anal personality type (there is a place for everything and everything must be in its place); insists upon organization. Character disorder – sociopath	Disorganized in daily life: vehicle*, appearance, clothing, home, demeanor, employment**, lifestyle, psychological state, etc. Preoccupied with recurring, obsessional and/or primitive thoughts
	* *If* he or she drives. ** *If* he or she is employed at all.

(Holmes, p. 43-48; Ressler, et.al., p. 122 and 130; Turvey, p. 147).

Crime Scene Characteristics

Organized (Nonsocial/Psychopathic)	Disorganized (Asocial/Psychotic)
Planned offense (preplanned)	Spontaneous offense / event
Targeted stranger	Victim known
Personalizes victim	Depersonalizes victim
Controlled conversation	Minimal conversation
Controlled crime scene	Chaotic crime scene (random and sloppy)
Submissive victim	Sudden violence
Restraints used	Minimal or no restraints
Aggressive acts prior to death	Sexual acts after death
Body moved/hidden	Body not moved/left in view
Weapon taken / evidence absent	Weapon left / evidence often present
Transports victim or body (attack occurs at primary scene; victim dumped).	Body left at death scene (primary scene)

(Holmes, p. 51; Turvey, p. 147).

Post Offense Behavior

Organized (Nonsocial/Psychopathic)

Returns to crime scene

Volunteers information

Anticipates questioning

May move body

May dispose body to advertise crime

Police groupie

Disorganized (Asocial/Psychotic)

Returns to crime scene
May attend funeral/burial
Memoria in media
May keep diary or newsclippings
May turn to religion
May change residence
May change job
May have personality change

Interview Techniques

Direct strategy

Be certain of details

He will only admit what he has to

Empathize with him
Indirectly introduce evidence
Counselor approach
Night time interview

(Homes, p. 44 and 47).

Characteristics of Rapists Typologies

Power Reassurance Rapist	Anger Retaliation Rapist	Power Assertive Rapist	Sadistic Rapist
Single	Married	Serial marriages	Married
Lives with parents	Parents divorced	69% from single-parent families	60% of parents divorced; 60% from single-parent home
Social loner	Socially competent	Image conscious	Middle-class family man
Quiet / passive	20% are adopted	31% were foster children	13% in foster homes
No sex partners	Hates women	Domestic problems	Sexually-deviant home
Nonathletic	Athletic-likes contact sports	Athletic	In his 30s
Menial occupation	Action - oriented occupations	Macho occupation	White-collar occupation
Frequents adult book stores	Frequents bars	Frequents singles' bars	Compulsive personality
Voyeur	Does not assault wife	Dishonorable discharge	
Exhibitionist	56% physically abused	74% were physically abused	63% suffered physical abuse
Transvestite	9th grade education	High school dropout	Same college education
Fetishist		Property crime record	No arrest record
Elements	**Elements**	**Elements**	**Elements**
Neighborhood attack	Neighborhood attack	Attacks from 7:00 p.m. to 1:00 a.m.	Stalks victims
Uses little profanity	Excessive profanity		Degrading language
Asks victim to remove her own clothing	Rips off clothing	Likely to tear clothing	Cuts victim's clothing
Same age group	Victim is same age or older	Victims in same age group	Victim's ages vary
Rapes every 7-15 days	Rapes every 6 to 12 months	Rapes every 20-25 days	Rapes vary according to time
Increasing violence	Aggression increases	Very assaultive	Increase in violence
May be impotent	Possible retarded ejaculation	Retarded ejaculation	Retarded ejaculation
May cover victim's face	Intends to harm victim	Cons or overpowers victim	Uses gags, bonds, handcuffs, blindfolds, etc.
May collect souvenirs	Blitz attack		Has rape kit
May keep a diary of rapes	Little planning	No attempt to hide identity	
Believes victim enjoys the rape		Selfish behavior	
Wants victim to "talk dirty"	Anal and oral sex	Anal *then* oral assault	May exhibit *triolism*
Exposes only body parts essential for rape	May ejaculate into face of victim		Ritualistic rape
Rapes within same race		Rapes within own race	
Travels on foot		Cruises singles' bars	Transports victims
Weapon of opportunity	Weapons of opportunity		
May later contact victims	Situation precipitated	No contact with victim	
Continues until apprehended		Multiple assaults	***Will eventually kill***

(Holmes, p. 104 & 105).   (Holmes, p. 106 & 107).   (Holmes, p. 108 & 109).   (Holmes, p. 111 & 112).

APPENDIX B

CRIME ANALYSIS DATA

(Statistics and Crime Maps)

Courtesy of the Fort Wayne Police Department Crime Analysis Unit

division1_feb.tif (816x1056x256 tiff)

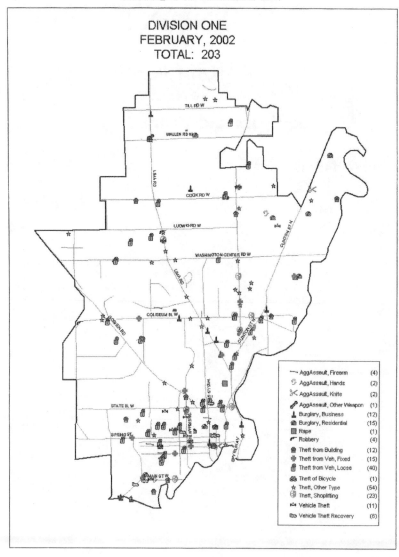

DIVISION ONE
FEBRUARY, 2002
TOTAL: 203

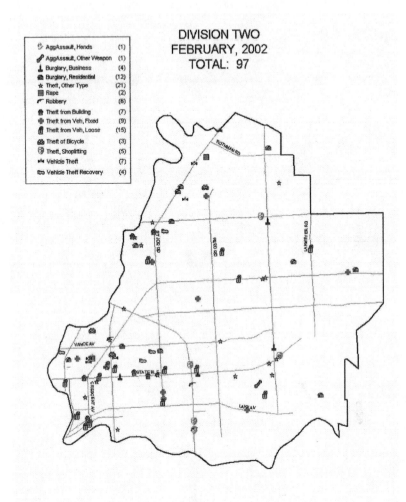

DIVISION TWO
FEBRUARY, 2002
TOTAL: 97

AggAssault, Hands	(1)
AggAssault, Other Weapon	(1)
Burglary, Business	(4)
Burglary, Residential	(12)
Theft, Other Type	(21)
Rape	(2)
Robbery	(6)
Theft from Building	(7)
Theft from Veh, Fixed	(9)
Theft from Veh, Loose	(15)
Theft of Bicycle	(3)
Theft, Shoplifting	(5)
Vehicle Theft	(7)
Vehicle Theft Recovery	(4)

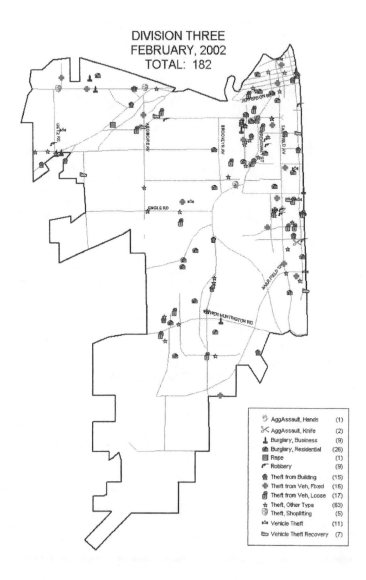

DIVISION THREE
FEBRUARY, 2002
TOTAL: 182

AggAssault, Hands	(1)
AggAssault, Knife	(2)
Burglary, Business	(9)
Burglary, Residential	(26)
Rape	(1)
Robbery	(9)
Theft from Building	(15)
Theft from Veh, Fixed	(16)
Theft from Veh, Loose	(17)
Theft, Other Type	(63)
Theft, Shoplifting	(5)
Vehicle Theft	(11)
Vehicle Theft Recovery	(7)

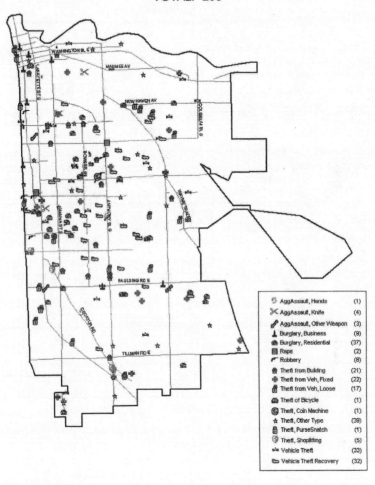

DIVISION FOUR
FEBRUARY, 2002
TOTAL: 236

AggAssault, Hands	(1)
AggAssault, Knife	(4)
AggAssault, Other Weapon	(3)
Burglary, Business	(9)
Burglary, Residential	(37)
Rape	(2)
Robbery	(8)
Theft from Building	(21)
Theft from Veh, Fixed	(22)
Theft from Veh, Loose	(17)
Theft of Bicycle	(1)
Theft, Coin Machine	(1)
Theft, Other Type	(39)
Theft, PurseSnatch	(1)
Theft, Shoplifting	(5)
Vehicle Theft	(33)
Vehicle Theft Recovery	(32)

ABOUT THE AUTHOR

Robert J. Girod, Sr. is a career law enforcement officer, an adjunct professor, an author, and a former military officer.

Dr. Girod earned a double Doctor of Philosophy (Ph.D.) in Criminology and Public Administration from The Union Institute and University and a post-doctoral certificate in Leadership from Harvard University. He earned a Master of Science (M.S.) in Criminal Justice Management at Central Missouri State University. He also received a Bachelor of Arts (B.A.) in Sociology from Huntington College, a Bachelor of General Studies (B.G.S.) in Social and Behavioral Science and an Associate of Science (A.S.) in Criminal Justice, both from Indiana University. He also earned a technical diploma in Forensic Science from the Institute of Applied Science.

Girod has attended more than sixty advanced police training schools and more than twenty military schools. He is also a graduate of the U.S. Air Force Squadron Officer's School, the U.S. Marine Corps Command and Staff College, the U.S. Naval War College (graduate-level professional military education programs), and the National Police Institute Command and Staff College.

Girod is the supervisor for the Robbery-Homicide Section of the Investigative Support Division's Detective Bureau with the Fort Wayne Police Department. He is also a member of the FBI's Fort Wayne Resident Agency's Federal Bank Robbery Task Force and a part-time "special deputy" for the U.S. Marshal's Service.

He has been a police officer with the Indianapolis Police Department and the Indiana University Police Department, a special agent with the Ohio Bureau of Criminal Investigations, and an investigator for the Indiana Department of Insurance and the Wells County Prosecutor's Office (IN).

Major Girod served in the U.S. Army Reserve from 1979-1996 and was a captain assigned to the U.S. Army Criminal Investigations Command. He served as major in the Indiana Guard Reserve from 1996-2000.

Professor Girod is an adjunct professor and associate faculty member at seven universities. He teaches criminal justice at Indiana University in the School of Public and Environmental Affairs, at Concordia University of Wisconsin's Fort Wayne campus, and at Taylor University's Fort Wayne campus. He also teaches management courses at Huntington College. At Indiana Wesleyan University he instructs both undergraduate and graduate courses in management, history, political science, and sociology. He teaches graduate and doctoral courses in criminal justice and public administration for Northcentral University and is a facilitator-consultant for Boston University and the Embanet Corporation in the graduate on-line criminal justice program.

Dr. Girod has authored several articles, which have been published in *FBI Law Enforcement Bulletin*, *The Police Marksman*, *Security Management*, *Musubi*, etc. He has served on several boards and commissions and as a member or officer of several professional, civic, church, political, and fraternal organizations.

0-595-33277-3